Psychotherapy
supervision

SUPERVISION IN CONTEXT

Series editors:
Dr Peter Hawkins, Bath Consultancy Group
Robin Shohet, Centre for Staff Team Development, London and Scotland

Staff in all the helping professions are working under increasing amounts of pressure. They are having to balance growing levels of distress, disease and disturbance, while at the same time managing an increasing speed of change in the financing and organizational structures of their employing organizations. Staff will only stay effective at their important work if they are supported and well supervised. Often their supervisors move straight from being a skilled practitioner into a management and supervisory position, with no training in the skills that staff supervision requires.

This series is aimed at the increasing number of people who act as trainers, tutors, mentors and supervisors in the helping professions. It is also designed for those who are studying to become a trainer or supervisor and for supervisees, who can use the books to reflect on the many complex issues in their work.

The series is designed to follow on from the success of the bestselling title *Supervision in the Helping Professions* by Peter Hawkins and Robin Shohet. Each book explores the key issues, models and skills for trainers and supervisors in the main areas of the helping professions: social work and community care, the medical and nursing professions, psychotherapy, counselling and mentoring for managers.

Current and forthcoming titles:

Meg Bond and Stevie Holland: *Skills of Clinical Supervision for Nurses*
Allan Brown and Iain Bourne: *The Social Work Supervisor*
Maria Gilbert and Kenneth Evans: *Psychotherapy Supervision*
Peter Hawkins and Robin Shohet: *Supervision in the Helping Professions (2nd edition)*

Psychotherapy supervision

An integrative relational approach
to psychotherapy supervision

**Maria C. Gilbert and
Kenneth Evans**

Open University Press
Buckingham · Philadelphia

Open University Press
Celtic Court
22 Ballmoor
Buckingham
MK18 1XW

email: enquiries@openup.co.uk
world wide web: www.openup.co.uk

and
325 Chestnut Street
Philadelphia, PA 19106, USA

First Published 2000

A catalogue record of this book is available from the British Library

ISBN   0 335 20138 5 (pb)   0 335 20139 3 (hb)

Library of Congress Cataloging-in-Publication Data
Gilbert, Maria.
    Psychotherapy supervision : an integrative rational approach to psychotherapy supervision / Maria C. Gilbert and Kenneth Evans.
        p.   cm.
    Includes bibliographical references and index.
    ISBN 0-335-20138-5 (PB) – ISBN 0-335-20139-3 (HB)
    1. Psychotherapists–Supervision of.   2. Psychotherapy–Study and teaching–Supervision.   I. Evans, Kenneth (Kenneth Roy), 1947–   II. Title.
    RC480.5.G495 2000
    616.89′14–dc21   00–035623

Typeset by Graphicraft Limited, Hong Kong
Printed in Great Britain by Biddles Ltd, Guildford and King's Lynn

Contents

List of figures

Series editors' preface

It is a great pleasure to welcome this book and to introduce you as the reader to it. This book provides a new integrated model of psychotherapy supervision which we believe will set a new landmark for the profession. The first landmark in the field of psychotherapy supervision was laid down by Ekstein and Wallerstein's in their creation of their classic model in *The Teaching and Learning of Psychotherapy* in 1972. Our own process model of supervision in *Supervision in the Helping Professions* (1989; second edition 2000), provided a new way of thinking about the various areas of focus in supervision and provided the first integration of humanistic and psychoanalytic processes in supervision. However, our book while being used extensively to train psychotherapy supervisors, grew out of work across all the helping professions, and was not specific to psychotherapy. Thus although there has been a real growth in the field of supervision books and articles in the last ten years, most of it has been from the fields of counselling or counselling psychology, with only a limited contribution from the field of psychotherapy. In this same period the field of psychotherapy has also greatly changed and developed and in our view the time was ripe for a major new theoretical approach specifically from the field of psychotherapy supervision.

If we take the period of time since Ekstein and Wallerstein wrote their book in 1972 we can see how much has changed in the field of psychotherapy in all parts of the world. The field has grown enormously, with many more people entering the profession and many new training institutes being established. The variety of people entering the profession has also expanded, with more people coming from fields beyond psychiatry and psychology, greater numbers from different cultures and many more women.

In 1972 the field of psychotherapy was still dominated by the psychoanalytic institutes in both Europe and the United States. In the 1970s and 1980s there was a proliferation of different psychotherapeutic approaches. Over the last ten years there has been more of a move to find integration across the different approaches. This movement has been nurtured by many psychotherapists who, having qualified in one approach go on to have psychotherapy and/ or supervision from a psychotherapist from a different orientation. This in turn has led many psychotherapy supervisors to consider how to develop approaches to supervision that are fundamentally integrative and can be used for supervising psychotherapists from different orientations.

Also in the last ten years there has been a great deal happening in the politics and organization of the profession. In many countries new umbrella organizations have been established and they in turn have set up processes for evaluation and accreditation of both training organizations and individual practitioners. These organizations have also been at the forefront of developing the codes of ethics and practice for the profession and the complaints and grievance procedures for maintaining good practice.

The two authors of this book were specifically chosen as they have both been at the forefront of not only developing integrative approaches to psychotherapy and supervision, in their work training both psychotherapists and psychotherapy supervisors; but have also been active in the wider development of the psychotherapy profession, both in the UK, across Europe, the USA, South Africa and other parts of the world. They bring to the book a breadth of knowledge of the current state of the profession, with a depth of interest in developing new understanding of what happens in the psychotherapeutic and supervisory relationships.

We often forget how young the psychotherapy profession is, with its origins just over 100 years old. For the first half century the emphasis was very much on the psychotherapist objectively understanding the patient's inner world and finding ways of intervening in it. Only in the 1950s with writers like Searles and Winnicot, was more emphasis put on understanding ones own reactions as being key to understanding the patient or client.

In the last ten years there have been two parallel developments that have taken this trend even further. In the USA, some of the selfpsychologists that followed the work of Kohut, developed the approach of intersubjective psychotherapy (Stolorow *et al.* 1987, 1992, 1994). At the same time some of the Gestalt psychotherapists (Hycner 1991, 1995 and Yontef 1993) were developing 'dialogical psychotherapy' which also emphasized the attention to the space between the psychotherapist and the client which both parties co-create and which forms the medium through which they relate and understand each other.

This book is the first to explore in depth how an intersubjective approach can be used in supervision, where there is an interplay between the intersubjective relationship of psychotherapist and client; and the intersubjective relationship between psychotherapist and supervisor.

Gilbert and Evans also provide very practical guidance in the areas of professional development such as evaluation, assessment, ethics and equal opportunities. We believe that this book will not only prove invaluable to the psychotherapy supervisor but also to all those who teach or manage psychotherapy, counselling psychology or counselling trainings.

Preface

In our training of supervisors we have drawn heavily on many of the interesting texts on supervision that have been written in recent years. To mention only a few, we have been indebted to the excellent work of the following authors: Michael Carroll, Elizabeth Holloway, Peter Hawkins and Robin Shohet, Stephen Page and Valerie Woskett, Patrick Casement, Rudolf Ekstein and Robert Wallerstein, and Gaie Houston.

In this process of training and supervising supervisors we have increasingly felt the need for a book on psychotherapy supervision from a humanistic integrative perspective that would honour the revolution in thinking, which has come with the focus on an intersubjective perspective on the psychotherapeutic relationship. This change in thinking has had a far-reaching impact on both our clinical practice and our work as supervisors. We remain rooted within the value base of humanistic integrative psychotherapy, which has been substantially enriched by contributions from dialogical psychotherapy, from psychoanalysis, and in particular from intersubjectivity theory and self psychology.

For the sake of simplicity we have used the pronoun 'she' for the supervisor and 'he' for the psychotherapist or client throughout the book where this pronoun could refer to either a man or a woman. Where the gender is clearly indicated from the text we have used the relevant form of the pronoun, particularly in the chapter on the model in action where Kenneth Evans is the supervisor and the gender of the supervisees is clearly indicated.

Except where specifically indicated, the examples of supervision given in this book are synthesized examples from our work with many supervisees over the years and are not drawn from any one particular case. Rather, we have used generic examples of the kind of issue that comes up regularly in supervision in slightly different forms in order to illustrate the points that we are making.

Acknowledgements

We wish to acknowledge the support we have received from our families in this demanding process. A special thanks to Matthew Gilbert to whose expertise in computer graphics we are indebted for the diagrams. We wish to express our gratitude to Mairi Evans whose article on developmental stages linked to the work of Daniel Stern has served as a source of inspiration in the development of our model of supervision.

Much of the material in this book has evolved from our training and supervisory work at The Institute of Transactional Analysis Metanoia Institute, Sherwood Psychotherapy Training Institute and the Gestalt Psychotherapy Training Institute. We wish to thank all our supervisees and our colleagues who have contributed directly and indirectly to this book. In particular we wish to thank Michael Carroll for his unfailing readiness to help out with references, copies of articles and sundry other requests for help.

We are grateful to those people in our supervision practices who have allowed us to reproduce samples of their work; the transcripts in Chapter 3 and the examples of supervised supervision in Chapter 8 are in this category. We also wish to honour all the people we have supervised over the years; these people have inspired us in our work as supervisors and have contributed substantially to our resolve to write this book.

Finally, we wish to thank Peter Hawkins for his help and feedback as series editor and also Geoff Heath for his detailed and exhaustive feedback.

Introduction

What is supervision?

What is supervision? When a psychotherapist or a supervisor consults with a more 'seasoned' and experienced practitioner in the field in order to draw on their wisdom and expertise to enhance his practice, then we would call this process of engagement *supervision*.

There exist many definitions of supervision that stress different aspects of supervision, *inter alia*: the importance of the supervisory alliance, the educational or instructional goals of supervision, the primary focus of the supervisory process as the welfare of the client, a central focus on the professional development of the supervisee and the idea that supervision can be seen as a form of 'metatherapy' (Ekstein and Wallerstein 1972; Hess 1980; Holloway 1995; Carroll 1996; Martindale *et al.* 1997; Holloway and Carroll 1999; Hawkins and Shohet 2000).

Generally there is agreement that supervision is a learning process in which a psychotherapist engages with a more experienced practitioner in order to enhance his skills in the process of his ongoing professional development. This, in turn, promotes and safeguards the well-being of his clients. Supervision is a branch of knowledge with associated skills in its own right, derived from research, closely linked to clinical work and based in the supervisory practice of many experts. Supervision as a discipline possesses a growing body of literature and recent years have seen the development of sophisticated models of supervision differing from those of the psychotherapies. These models provide conceptual frameworks for supervision, a discussion of developmental stages in supervision as well as a focus on the tasks and functions of supervision. The discourse of supervision is not simply psychotherapy transposed to a different domain; it is a discipline in its own right!

It is important at the outset to distinguish between personal psychotherapy and supervision; they are two separate activities with differing aims and goals. In our view, the purposes and objectives of psychotherapy are as follows: to understand, change, resolve or alleviate conditions of suffering in the client and to promote self-knowledge and experience of self in the wider context of the person's life. Psychotherapy aims at enabling a person to make better use of his potential in his interactions with individuals and groups. The psychotherapist's role will include the ethical objective of promoting the existential potential of the individual as well as of the society/ culture, and so to foster a dynamic balance between self-determination and adaptability. Supervision of the psychotherapist has as its primary goal the promotion of the welfare of the clients in his care; this is achieved through thoughtful reflection on and a critical exploration of the therapeutic relationship between them.

Supervision includes specific learning goals for the supervisee; the supervisor's role is to stimulate the integration of personal development, knowledge and skills in the process of evaluating the interaction between the supervisee and the client. In this respect, the welfare and development of the supervisee becomes as important as that of the client since the supervisee's growing expertise will benefit that person's client base. The central importance of the working alliance is common to both these processes: psychotherapy and supervision.

The intention informing this book

This book aims to provide the reader with a model for accessing supervision through focusing on the dynamics of the relationship in both psychotherapy and supervision. For this reason, we provide an integrative relational framework, which is as relevant to psychotherapy as it is to supervision. Whereas we do not believe that one should conflate the two processes, we do consider them as inextricably linked with both their similarities and their differences. To fully appreciate supervision in its context, an understanding of the nature of psychotherapy is indispensable. While psychotherapy and supervision have separate and distinct objectives as outlined above, some of the issues that are relevant to the supervisor will be equally applicable to the psychotherapist, in particular the importance of the working alliance in the interests of the welfare of the client.

Supervision: a space to reflect

Providing a reflective space for the supervisee is one of the primary responsibilities of the supervisor so as to enable the clinician to review his caseload and his own reactions to his work with clients in a supportive atmosphere. In this sense, we regard receiving regular supervision as an important aspect of the supervisee's self-care. In the supervisory process the supervisee is enabled to gain a meta-perspective on his psychotherapeutic work so that he can reflect on it and consider ways forward with a client. The supervisor will encourage links between theory and practice: aspects of theory will be drawn in to highlight certain client dynamics or the nature of the therapeutic relationship itself so as to enhance practice. At other times, aspects of the therapeutic encounter that lead the clinician to 'feel stuck' will be minutely analysed in order to be understood in the context of the psychotherapeutic relationship that has been co-created by these two people. Such a micro-analysis of the therapeutic dialogue can reveal particular points in the inter-action that are problematic for the psychotherapist. This in turn may lead to a focus on a characteristic style of interaction for either the therapist or the client that leads to a non-productive outcome.

These problem points in the therapeutic dialogue have been variously referred to as 'empathic failures' (Kohut 1984) or 'therapeutic alliance rup-tures' (Safran 1993). An exploration of such miscommunications or discord lie at the heart of our approach to the supervision of psychotherapy. We see that it is only through attending carefully to the times when we reach another person and the occasions on which we 'miss' that person in the course of our interactions that we can truly communicate effectively. In that sense, I can only learn to communicate effectively with you by the mistakes I make and by learning from you how to redress these! This process of gradually learning to match one another's communication styles is as relev-ant to the supervisory alliance as to the therapeutic relationship. Careful attention to communication at this microscopic level will lay the foundations for a firmly based relationship that is able to tolerate conflicts and disagree-ments and provide a container for growth and change.

Training and consultative supervision

We recognize a distinction between training supervision and consultative supervision as is now beginning to be more widely honoured in the field of supervision (Carroll 1996). The term 'training supervision' is used to describe the process of supervision of psychotherapists during training. The term 'consultative supervision' is used to refer to the process whereby an experi-enced and qualified practitioner seeks consultation with a peer or with a more experienced psychotherapist concerning client work. The responsibil-ities of the supervisor will differ considerably between these two endeavours. The training supervisor will be required to report regularly to the training course about the development of the trainee and to play an active role in the assessment process. Consultative supervision involves much more a dis-cussion between peers about aspects of the psychotherapy practice of the consultee. The difference between these two types of supervision is very dependent on the needs of the supervisee. In our experience of training super-vision, supervisees need regular guidance, teaching, support, discussion of ethical practice and an ongoing overt assessment of their development as psychotherapists.

In training supervision there is also frequently the need for supervisors to be orientation-specific, unless of course they are involved with super-visees from an eclectic or integrative training. Even in the latter case, it is important for the supervisor to be well apprised of the particular approach to integration on which the course is based. In consultative supervision, experienced psychotherapists are more often looking for an extension to their existing knowledge base, for the integration of new perspectives to their current orientation to client work – both theoretically and in terms of techniques/therapeutic strategies. Of course, even in this type of supervision engagement, the role of the supervisor as the monitor of ethical practice will remain a duty of the supervisor. However, in our experience, consultative supervision takes more the form of a dialogue between peers, an opportunity to refine and extend clinical practice. We believe that an integrative relational model of supervision can be used to equal effect by training and consultative supervisors since it provides a generic model for viewing the supervisory process.

Possible applications of the model

Our integrative relational model of supervision can be integrated into the specific orientation to psychotherapy that is being practised since it is based in the primacy of the psychotherapeutic relationship as a vehicle for change. For integrative psychotherapy training courses, our model based in the mutuality of relationship has particular relevance because most of these courses have a primary focus on the therapeutic relationship, which forms the core of our model of supervision. We believe that the goal of all psychotherapy supervision is the attainment of a meta-perspective on psychotherapy practice, as this is embedded in its particular context.

Likewise in consultative supervision where cross-orientation supervision is often being sought, a model based in the centrality of the therapeutic relationship provides a common point of departure.

Frequently supervisors in National Health Service settings, or in voluntary or other organizations that provide client services to the public, are 'assigned' supervisees with orientations to psychotherapy different from their own. These supervisors are inevitably, therefore, required to supervise across theoretical orientation. Since such supervisors have the primary task of assuring the welfare of the supervisees' clients, and not specifically the brief to remain orientation-pure, considerable flexibility is called for on the part of the supervisor. After much experience of this process in the course of supervising and training supervisors, we could see the need for an approach to supervision based in the commonalities between psychotherapy orientations rather than on the specific differences.

In such supervision practice the first emphasis is on 'What is effective psychotherapy?' and only secondarily on 'Is this pure person-centred, or psychodynamic, or gestalt, or cognitive-behavioural psychotherapy?' We believe that these demands from the workplace have influenced many supervisors to adopt a more eclectic approach to 'what works' in psychotherapy practice rather than focusing on the 'pure' elements of approaches. We are offering these supervisors a coherent approach to supervision drawing on integrative relational theory, which spans orientations and provides a model that can be readily shared with supervisees.

Overview of contents

In Chapter 2 we present an integrative relational model of supervision grounded in intersubjectivity theory, developmental research and dialogical psychotherapy. This model is grounded in constructivism, phenomenology and field theory. Chapter 3 demonstrates the model in action giving four vignettes accompanied by a commentary and discussion linked to Chapter 2. The chapter concludes with the identification of four phases in the educational development of the 'internal supervisor'. Chapter 4 deals with the challenge of creating an effective learning environment for the supervisee. This chapter highlights the significance of the supervisory alliance, countering the effects of a shame-based educational experience, the need to develop critical reflective thinking and the importance of fostering a 'research mind set' in the psychotherapist to facilitate effective outcomes in the work with the client. In Chapter 5 we discuss clear contracting as a basis for effective supervision through establishing clear boundaries, which support the supervisory alliance. We emphasize the centrality of the contractual process for effective relating in any context. In the course of this chapter we overview two major traditions that have influenced the development of supervision as a discipline. Chapter 6 provides a critical review of contemporary theoretical and research foundations for our model of supervision. Here, too, we discuss the contribution of field theory and constructivism to our model. Chapter 7 focuses on the assessment, accreditation and evaluation of supervision practice. Chapter 8 looks at the evolution of the supervisor's personal style with a particular focus on the role of countertransference as a valuable source of information regarding the psychotherapeutic process. In this chapter we address the interface between psychotherapy and supervision. Chapter 9 grapples with the complexity of ethical decision making and gives examples of the process of dealing with ethical dilemmas. The chapter raises questions about the principles on which complaints are investigated. Chapter 10 builds on the preceding chapter on ethics by exploring the perpetuation of anti-oppressive practice in both psychotherapy and supervision. It highlights the need for reform in psychotherapy training organizations if a multicultural perspective is to be embraced fully. An example is given of an organization that reviews and implements changes in its anti-oppressive practice. In Chapter 11 we review supervision in the wider context. Finally we provide some examples of resources for the supervisor who seeks further training.

2

An integrative relational model of supervision

In this chapter we present our integrative relational model of supervision elucidating its roots in developmental theory. We describe the intersubjective aspects of the model, which focus on the co-creation of relationship and the importance of 'healing through meeting' in both psychotherapy and supervision. The supervisor and supervisee together create a new narrative that is aimed at facilitating the work with clients; this narrative can be deconstructed and reconstructed in the ongoing process of supervision. We show the importance of Buber's concept of inclusion to our model of supervision, namely the capacity to hold your own perspective, whilst appreciating the perspective of the other person and simultaneously holding the relationship between these. We conclude with a discussion of power in supervision, of the importance of developing a reliable internal supervisor and of transference and countertransference.

A relationally-based model of supervision in context

Our approach to the supervisory relationship is based on an intersubjective perspective (Atwood and Stolorow 1984; Stolorow and Atwood 1992), which focuses on the interactional field created by two people. Both participants are viewed as contributing to the construction of the relationship, the psychotherapist and the client alike. The intersubjective theorists challenge the myth of the isolated mind in which paradigm the analyst/therapist has tended to be seen as an impartial observer to the client's dynamics. In their perspective both parties to an encounter bring their own inner experience as this is embedded in their context 'in a continual flow of reciprocal mutual influence' (Stolorow and Atwood 1992). In such a model of human relationship it is assumed that personal reality is always co-determined by the context in which the relationship is embedded and by the unique meanings that each person brings to the meeting with the other. Even though it is claimed there are some four hundred plus different approaches to psychotherapy, we believe that the crucial division between the psychotherapies is not between 'schools' but between the positivist and the postpositivist/postmodern paradigms.

Therefore in our view supervision:

- is always interpersonal
- involves a systems perspective
- involves a process of enquiry rather than a search for 'truth'
- involves an immersion in the process and a standing back from it; the participant-observer dimension
- is the co-creation of a 'new' narrative by supervisor and supervisee that informs the work with the client, in other words the 'co-creation of meaning'
- fosters the development of 'inclusion' and a 'third person' perspective in all the participants in the process
- any meaning that emerges to create a framework for mutual understanding is always partial and open to deconstruction and reconstruction in the light of new experiences.

The following text explores an integrative theoretical framework for supervision from the perspective of the primacy of the psychotherapeutic and the supervisory relationship as the medium or container for change. We base our discussion for an integrative relational framework for supervision on a relational-developmental approach to psychotherapy, which is grounded in intersubjectivity theory, recent trends in developmental research and in dialogical therapy. Intersubjectivity theory has been described by its authors as a 'new paradigm', which embraces 'interacting subjectivities' and focuses on 'reciprocal mutual influence' in the psychotherapeutic dyad (Stolorow *et al.* 1994). Dialogical therapy refers to developments within relational approaches to psychotherapy that have evolved from Buber's concept of the I–Thou encounter between two people (Buber 1996), spoken of as the 'healing through meeting' by Friedman (1992). Stern's developmental research provides a helpful framework for understanding the development of a secure 'sense of self' over time that provides an internally reliable source of support for the person.

Supervision from a meta-systems perspective

Viewed from a systems perspective, supervision is a complex process involving many different levels of relationship. Initially, at least, it is the supervisor who will need to hold an awareness of these multiple interlocking relationships.

Figure 2.1 represents an attempt to portray the complexity of the field of supervision showing the multiplicity of the relationships involved in the process. A systems approach to supervision involves the supervisor's capacity to retain a sensitivity to her own countertransference reactions in relation to their origins. In addition, the supervisor must, at the same time, enter into

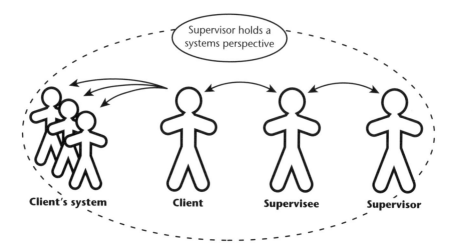

Figure 2.1 Supervision: A meta-systems perspective

the supervisee's world of experience in relation to interpersonal or intra-psychic events *and* achieve a view that takes into account the intersub-jective nature of the supervisory process. (The same process is relevant for the psychotherapist–client relationship.) At any point in supervision, any one of these elements may be the focus of the supervision intervention. These would include (1) the psychotherapist's reflection on and understanding of client dynamics or of his own countertransference, (2) the psychotherapist's empathic engagement with the client and (3) sharpening his awareness of the delicate dance between them. The supervisor faces a similar challenge: she needs to shift her focus from observing the psychotherapist's perform-ance, to assessing the client's dynamics, to an awareness of her own reactions to the psychotherapist/supervisee, which may impinge on the process, to an appreciation of the psychotherapist's possible countertransference reactions, to promoting the trust in the supervisory relationship. This inevitably involves a sharpened and sensitive awareness of the dance between them, which will then model for the supervisee the type of contact that is possible with clients.

An intersubjective perspective on the therapeutic process will demand of the supervisor the capacity to be aware of the many different angles from which this process can be viewed. Any particular perspective on the therapeutic relationship will be accorded as much validity as any other. This process is at the centre of an integrative relational approach to psychotherapy and super-vision; it does not elevate any one perspective over another but gives weight to the multiple factors operating in the psychotherapist's or client's fields at any given time. The client will contribute to the creation of meaning, as will the psychotherapist and the supervisor. It is the supervisor's role that is unusual here, since the supervisor will contribute to the making of meaning in a relationship in which she never (or only very rarely) directly participates.

Supervision involves the co-creation and negotiation of meaning between supervisor and psychotherapist in order to facilitate a similar process between psychotherapist and client. It aims to enable the client to be aware of the reciprocal mutual influence in all human relationships (even where his part in this process is denied by the other participant/s). We are well aware of the particular responsibility and challenge that the supervisor faces in that she is always involved with a system of interlocking relationships, which it is her task to 'oversee'; she rarely meets these people except for the psychotherapist on whom she is reliant for information about others in the system. The supervisor needs to attend very carefully to both the conscious and unconscious communication from the psychotherapist and the client in order to inform her meta-perspective on the psychotherapeutic alliance and the context in which it is located. Such a task can seem formidable, especially to the inexperienced supervisor who will be challenged to broaden her perspective to include a wide-ranging interconnection of relational possibilities in every supervision session.

Participant-observation as a core concept

In elaborating on the relational process that underpins both the psychotherapeutic and supervisory endeavours, we have been influenced by the concept of the participant-observer proposed by Harry Stack Sullivan in his writing on interpersonal psychiatry. Sullivan described psychiatry as 'an expanding science concerned with the kinds of events or processes in which the psychiatrist participates while being an observant psychiatrist' (Sullivan 1953: 13). He was making the point that psychiatry is a science in which the observer is an indivisible part of the work in which he is engaged and an inescapable element in the process. This concept is in line with the phenomenological method of enquiry, which in place of attempting to understand a person only from the outside tries to enter into the nature of the person's own subjective experience, whilst still being an observer of that experience. We can apply the phenomenological method to the observation of our internal process, to our exploration of our process with the other as well as to an enquiry into the internal world of the other person in the

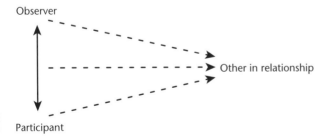

Figure 2.2 The participant-observer in psychotherapy and supervision

therapeutic or supervisory dyad. Both psychotherapy and supervision are 'participative processes' in which both the participating and the observing functions are an indivisible part of the interaction. Awareness of and careful attention to both of these dimensions is therefore essential and vital for effective supervision.

The centrality of Martin Buber's concept of 'inclusion'

The core process goal of the supervisory process is best expressed in Buber's elaboration of the concept of 'inclusion' (Buber 1996). This concept has been taken up and expanded on by dialogical and contemporary Gestalt psychotherapy as the heart of effective dialogue. Hycner (1991) explains that 'inclusion is the back and forth movement of being able to go over to the other side and yet remain centred in my own experience' (Hycner 1991: 20). Inclusion does not exclude the need for distance between self and other. Both Hycner (1991) and Yontef (1993) insist that inclusion is different from empathy in that the therapist maintains a sense of his own separate self when practising inclusion. This capacity to enter into the world of another and at the same time retain a sense of one's own separateness and difference distinguishes a truly mutual relationship from one in which all the emphasis is on self and self-interest or one which is focused exclusively on the other with little attention to the impact on oneself and to one's own responses. To this process we would add the vital importance of holding a meta-perspective on the relationship, *viewing self in relation to the other in context* – a standing above the field, whilst also being within it. We consider this a meta-systems perspective on the relational process.

Such a multiperspectival view of the relationship will usually be held for a short time only, because of the tension of holding both these polarities in awareness at once. However, it is this capacity for inclusion that enables the supervisor (as also the psychotherapist) to appreciate the many-faceted nature of the relationship and not sacrifice one aspect to another. We think that this process can easily be connected to the participant-observer dimensions, since inclusion involves holding both these poles simultaneously in relation to the client or the supervisee. This may result in considerable tension since as human beings we tend naturally to move into one or the other and may remain fixed there. The challenge in supervision is to facilitate in the supervisee a flow between these polarities whilst at other times encouraging a view from above of the interaction between them. This truly is supervision!

We believe that one of the main aims of 'relationship psychotherapy' is to facilitate for the client the capacity for inclusion, which marks the goal of the psychotherapeutic process. In this we are in agreement with Buber (1923). However, as Yontef points out, people who already exercise this capacity may sometimes come to psychotherapy so that they can explore their own experience of a situation while the psychotherapist practises inclusion and 'holds' the broader perspective for them. We consider that supervision serves a similar purpose (especially for experienced psychotherapists seeking consultative

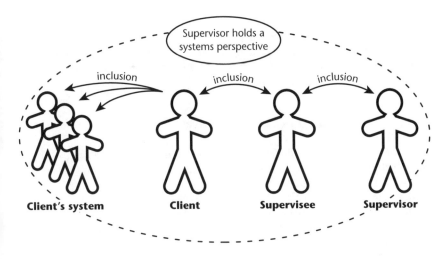

Figure 2.3 An integrative relational model of supervision: a meta-systems perspective

supervision). The supervisee is offered the safe space in which to feel his feelings unedited and for that period not to hold the client's perspective. The supervisor holds the inclusive stance for the period of exploration and at the point of completion brings the psychotherapist back once again to view the relationship with the client in its totality. This exploration of the supervisee's countertransference in a safe place frees the person up subsequently to resume a relational stance with the client that holds the possibility of 'inclusion'. Similarly, an opportunity to explore the intrapsychic dynamics of a client or to explore dimensions of diagnosis freely in an atmosphere of inclusion allows the supervisee to take relevant insights back into the relational work with the client.

For the inexperienced supervisee, achieving a position where he can practise inclusion successfully may be more a process over time and form one of the ongoing supervisory goals. Initially the goal is to assist the psychotherapist/ supervisee to develop the practice of inclusion in relation to clients and then to continue to provide a safe space where multiple perspectives on the psychotherapeutic relationship can be explored whilst the supervisor 'holds' the overall process. The capacity to practise inclusion to good effect in reflecting on and exploring the therapeutic relationship (and also where appropriate the supervisory alliance) is at the heart of effective integrative psychotherapy supervision. In fact, this is one of the main process goals of our integrative relational approach. Inclusion, understood in this way, is integral to a relational view of psychotherapy and of supervision; it can also be seen as a primary goal for the client in a relationship-focused therapy. Absence of true mutuality in the client's everyday relationships may well be related to difficulty in establishing and maintaining satisfying relationships. Therefore, the relational goal for the client in his daily encounters is similar to the therapeutic goal between psychotherapist and client, which in turn is reflected in the supervisory goal between psychotherapist and supervisor. What works effectively in one context will work in another. This is a process view of relationships whatever the focus of the particular relational 'contract' between two people.

The 'third person perspective'

In his interesting book on development, *Vision and Separation*, Kenneth Wright (1991) discusses the move in the child's development from a two-person to a third-person perspective; that is, from the dyadic to the triadic perspective on human relationships. At first the child is dependent on the mother (primary caretaker) who reflects back to him what she sees: 'The baby looks in the mother's face and sees a reflection of himself' (Wright 1991: 12). At this stage the child is totally dependent for his view of himself on this reflection back from the primary other. This may be positive, affirming and attuned to the child's needs or it may not be responsive to the child at all, and so misattuned. If the other's look is rejecting and hostile, the child will experience this as alienating or in more extreme cases as annihilating. The child at this stage is entirely dependent for feeling good or bad on one other person's perspective on himself which inevitably defines and shapes his own view of himself.

What is introduced by the father (or a second significant other) is the possibility of a further perspective, a view of the primary caretaking relationship from the outside, from a third-person perspective. This third-person perspective provides another view of what is happening, and another view of the 'self' of the child in relation to others and to the world. The child's experience of self with mother/primary carer is now part of a larger field in which the child is no longer the centre of attention, but part of a larger interdependent world of people and objects that affect one another reciprocally. From this position, too the absolute 'validity' of the mother's perspective can be challenged. The child is no longer dependent only on one other's view to mediate his attitude to himself and to the world, but can draw on the perspective of third 'persons' to help him develop a multi-perspectival view of reality.

Wright's discussion of this third-person perspective adds a helpful dimension to our view of the integrative supervisor's role: 'taking the view of the third person makes possible for the first time an appreciation of the subject's position within an interactive behavioural system' (Wright 1991: 234). To gain an objective sense of self we need to see ourselves through the eyes of another person; as we view ourselves from the outside, from the perspective of another we are able to see ourselves in relation to other people and objects. This capacity for a perspective from outside of ourselves assists us in the process of developing an understanding and an empathy for how others may perceive us and leads to an appreciation of the multiplicity of narratives that may arise simultaneously for different observers. This seems close to the description of the process of inclusion.

Depending on the nature of developmental process, the move to the position of the other will either remain dyadic and become fixed in that position or it will become triadic as described above. In shame-based systems, a person may never have the freedom to move to the triadic position because of the loss of self associated with being 'frozen out' in the original dyad when certain behaviours are unacceptable to the other. In that sense we 'become what the other sees'. In order to move to a third-person perspective, the child needs to feel securely contained and viewed lovingly by the primary caretaker. Where the primary carer repeatedly rejects and looks with hate at the child, the child may lose his ground and descend into a well of nothingness where the experience is of emptiness of the self and even of annihilation of the self. When the view of the other in the dyad is claimed by that person as the 'truth' of the situation, there is no room for negotiating another point of view, and in this way the authority of the primary carer adds weight to her judgement on and view of the child.

The child's vulnerability and dependence for survival on the significant other play a vital role in this process. Such a child may well take on the perspective of the other in the original dyad and not experience sufficient support to move out from that position to develop an alternative perspective on self. This process will be exacerbated if the 'father' or other significant carer(s) share the primary carer's perspective on the child as 'mad' or 'bad' or 'worthless'; or if the father is significantly absent and there is little exposure for the child to the perspectives of significant others, such as extended family, friends or teachers. Without relational support for self-development, the child may sink into an abyss of shameful worthlessness.

This is a phenomenon that we have encountered in supervision. Where a supervisee comes from a shame-based system (Kaufman 1992), such a person may, in response to any feedback that they construe as critical (whether from outside or from their own internal response to their work), descend into a place of shame and the annihilation of the self, that makes any further learning impossible until they can regain a more balanced 'third-person perspective'. Often it is the supervisor or trainer who supplies such a third-person perspective to supervisees and this helps them to evaluate and assess their own work more realistically in terms of current reality. This could well mark the beginning of the process of incorporating the 'internalized supervisor' (Casement 1985) into the supervisee's internal world. Wright considers the move to the third-person perspective as 'transforming' in that it enables us to enlarge our vision of ourselves by providing an additional (to the dyadic) perspective. He associates this third position with that of the father, though essentially he is stressing the addition of a perspective on self that transcends the child–mother dyad (the original caretaking relationship).

As Wright makes clear, enlarging our vision does not depend on 'widening the angle of our original view', rather on being able to move to a broader variety of positions to obtain new and different perspectives on ourselves. This is the process by which the person gradually achieves a multi-perspectival view of the world and develops an appreciation of difference, related to a systems competence. Wright elaborates on this third-person perspective by pointing out that it provides us with a view of ourselves that is outside our own immediately lived experience so that it becomes a 'means of scanning both the perceptual field and the inner field of the mind' (Wright op.cit.).

The third position can provide us with a perspective on the original dyadic relationship that transcends that relationship and places it in its relative importance in the world of others. We are enabled to view from the 'father's' perspective the nature of our relationship with the mother. This gives us more than one perspective on that process.

We consider that such a third-person perspective can also be supplied by the primary carer in the original dyad if that person models for the child this capacity to view their relationship from the outside. It makes good sense to us that a person able to take a multi-perspectival view of reality can transmit this capacity to another. This statement is not meant to undervalue the importance to the child of contributions from a second or several other carers.

We agree with Wright that if children are never encouraged or enabled to develop such multiple perspectives they will remain at the mercy of the dyadic perspective and have difficulty in viewing their relationships from the outside and appreciate their relative position to others in the world. This may seriously affect their capacity to estimate the impact that they have on others or appreciate the impact of their behaviour on those around them. The attainment of the 'third position' is essential we believe for the successful practice of inclusion, which involves a sensitive awareness of my own position, an empathic attunement to that of the other and the capacity to appreciate the interaction between these two processes at a meta-level. It is also intimately related to the concepts of 'participant-observation' (Sullivan 1953) and 'critical subjectivity' (Reason 1994).

A dimension we add to this process is a capacity to evaluate the impact of our behaviour on the other and to be sensitive to the impact that others have on us. This capacity is at the heart of a multi-perspectival view of the world. In some people this sensitivity to a 'feedback loop' seems almost entirely absent. It is as though they see no connection between what they say or do and how other people respond to them, as if these were all entirely arbitrary occurrences. This can be traced to the absence of effective early mirroring from the primary caretaker and/or if the child has been subjected to arbitrary child-rearing practices where there is little relation between what the child does or says and the response the child elicits from the parent. Children who have grown up with alcoholic parents often report that they were never sure whether they were going to be cuddled or beaten and that the actual response seemed to bear little or no relationship to their own behaviour. For both clients and for supervisees this can be an important part of a new learning process, where the emphasis is on evaluating the impact we have on others and in turn developing a sensitivity to the impact that others have on us. This process can provide useful feedback on both the psychotherapeutic and the supervisory relationship.

An integrative relational approach to supervision

Like psychotherapy, supervision holds the possibility for a 'healing through meeting' in the supportive and reparative dimensions of the supervisory relationship in the interests of both the supervisee and his clients. In our experience, many beginners come to supervision for the first time bearing the scars of educational wounds that have resulted from a system in which shame has been used in an attempt to force learning. We have found relevant here Daniel Stern's developmental perspective on the emergence of the sense of self in a relationship where affect attunement is provided by the primary carer (Stern 1985). For people who have missed effective mirroring and instead have become victims in a shame-based system, the importance of the supervisory relationship as a safe and contained framework for growth and healing cannot be overestimated. Without the support of this holding relationship, the essential work of focusing openly and honestly on clinical material in the interests of the welfare of clients may not prove possible.

The gradual growth of trust and openness in the supervisory relationship is often mirrored by the progressive decline of defensiveness on the part of the therapist in the relationship with the client. In the supervisory process the destructive effects of shame will need to be actively redressed. We regard this as a 'therapeutic' process within supervision in the service of the primary supervisory goal of ensuring the welfare of the client. A therapist disabled by shame, will not be in a position to open himself to learning, nor, in our experience, to be fully available to clients in the therapeutic relationship.

In an integrative relational model of supervision, the conceptualization of the process of psychotherapy is reflected in the conceptualization of the process of supervision. A contactful dyadic relationship that forms the basis of psychotherapy also forms the basis for effective supervision. The process is similar at every level and we see the goals of supervision, psychotherapy and living as the same. It is the task, the contract and the context that distinguishes the processes from one another. Mutuality in relationship is a goal shared by all these processes. The supervisor who models good contact in supervision is simultaneously providing a model for the psychotherapeutic relationship. Consequently, what happens in the supervisory context is a mirror for therapist–client relating.

In such a process the supervisor will be providing an ongoing modelling dimension in supervision that teaches the therapist how to be with the client in a contactful, respectful manner. We regard this process as the core of both psychotherapy and supervision. Without an effective supervisory alliance, the teaching of specific skills or the imparting of relevant theoretical information often prove to be empty charades to which the supervisee may submit herself in the interests of a 'good report' or to 'save face' and avoid dealing with the issues that really trouble him in his work with clients. In our experience of supervising, a supervisee may arrive for supervision very well prepared with clear contracts and goals thought out in advance and proceed to 'conduct' the supervision session in a very organized manner so controlling the process in order to ensure that he faces nothing unexpected from the supervisor that may uncover his vulnerabilities. Such carefully orchestrated supervision on the part of the supervisee ensures that the supervisor does not come close to any of a person's real weaknesses, fears or deficits. We fear that in these cases the supervisor may never get close to the actual process of therapy because she receives a carefully laundered version of the therapy sessions.

The co-creation of relationship and the co-construction of meaning

We view the supervisor as an indivisible part of the context in which she is operating, as both a participant and an observer in the supervision process and in this way co-creating the experience. Our philosophical base is in phenomenology, constructivism and field theory. We take the position that the meaning of events can only be understood from the perspective of the experiencing subject relative to the context. Nietzsche (1968) believed that truth is always the product of human construction and this position forms a central component of our approach. Traditional science whilst being a systematic and methodical attempt to search for 'essential' truth does not, however, acknowledge the human capacity for constructing meaning in the ongoing ever changing ebb and flow of experience.

Reason (1994) claims that in traditional research, method is given priority and the subjects of the research are subordinated to the research goal. In this process science and life are viewed as separate 'and the researcher as subject in a world of separate objects' (Reason 1994). Reason, clearly influenced by phenomenology, maintains that there has been an over-emphasis in research on intellectual experiencing at the cost of our physical inner processes or knowing through sensation. He believes that 'we can only do research with persons if we engage with them as person, as co-subjects and thus as co-researchers' (Reason 1994). He describes this balancing of participation and observation as 'critical subjectivity' (Reason 1988). Moustakas (1994), also writing from a postpositivist paradigm, maintains that science has 'failed to take into account the experiencing person and the connections between human consciousness and the objects that exist in the material world'. We very much ally ourselves with this emphasis on immediate experiencing as indivisible from the experiencing person in relation to the particular and unique context in which we operate.

Supervision is a similar process in which two people are 'co-subjects' and 'co-researchers' in the service of the client's best interests. Indeed, psychotherapy could also be described in this manner, as a process in which two people co-construct the relationship in a particular intersubjective context to meet the client's goals. Whilst Reason is referring to the research endeavour in the material quoted above, we believe that the following statement applies equally to the psychotherapeutic and supervisory processes: 'a deep engagement, participation and commitment to the moment; and simultaneous reflection, standing back, self-awareness' (Reason 1994: 50). This complements Sullivan's work some 40 years ago on the understanding of participant-observation in the psychotherapeutic relationship. Our view of both psychotherapy and supervision are grounded in the centrality of Reason's concept of 'critical subjectivity' (Reason 1994) and Sullivan's concept of 'participant-observation' (Sullivan 1953) within a relational framework.

Along with the writers mentioned here we have moved to a position that human beings exercise choice and construct their own meaning from life experiences. In our view both psychotherapy and supervision are processes of co-constructing meaning in an ever moving and ever changing field of experience. The recognition of the contribution of both participants to the process is an inescapable consequence of this position. Safran (1998) reviewed different stances that psychotherapists can take in relation to reality. He outlined three possibilities, where a privileged view of reality is held by: (1) the therapist, as in classical psychoanalysis; (2) the client, as in person-centred therapy; and (3) neither, as in relational therapies based on inter-subjectivity theory. In the third instance, therapist and client are perceived as co-creating meaning and in that sense building between them a new narrative related to their shared experience. Safran himself prefers a view that sees the two people in (3) negotiating between two different subjectivities rather than co-constructing an agreed meaning. We incline to this view of relationship as the ongoing negotiation between two different subjectivities where there may be some shared meanings, and several other areas of difference. The respect for difference forms an integral part of the negotiating process between two people in any communication.

In both psychotherapy and supervision, these three stances need not be mutually exclusive. In supervision, for example, there may be occasions when it is relevant for the supervisor to share her expertise and experience of a particular client group with the supervisee and so assume an authoritative position. At other times, for example when dealing with the supervisee's countertransference experience, it may be more appropriate for the supervisor to support and empathize with the supervisee's feelings and responses and give these a central place until some understanding has been reached that frees up the supervisee to attend again to the client. Also, there will be times when the supervisor and supervisee will be co-creating meaning between them, for example when they discuss the most suitable way forward with a particular client with whom the supervisee is struggling. But throughout supervision, there is the underlying process of two people, with two very different subjective experiences of the world, sharing their different perspectives and negotiating agreed meanings whilst respecting differing frames of reference, differences of culture, individual life experience or gender, to mention only a few possibilities. As supervisors we can at best gain only an approximate knowledge of the experience of the supervisee with the client from which vantage point to assist the supervisee in assessing ways forward in the work of therapy based on psychotherapeutic principles. For effective relating, complete agreement about the meaning or definition of the particular relationship is neither necessary nor, we believe, possible!

Existentialist philosophers like Nietzsche, Heidegger and Sartre tended towards an individual authentication of life, putting their primary emphasis on the individual perspective. However, Martin Buber, also an existentialist philosopher, criticized this over-emphasis on individual existence believing that this was at the expense of human inter-existence. 'He was primarily concerned with an inter-subjective existentialism, or what he preferred to call the inter-human dimension of existence' (Hycner and Jacobs 1995: 116). Following Buber, we espouse an interhuman focus, which observes a move between the two polarities of 'participant' and 'observer' in the processes of both psychotherapy and supervision. The interhuman focus incorporates both the I–Thou and the I–It dimensions of experience. When I am in an I–Thou encounter (or in full contact) with the client I will be at the 'participant' end of the spectrum; when I sit back and reflect on the process between us even momentarily, I have moved to the observer end. This I may do at certain points in the session, or when I subsequently reflect on the therapeutic hour. In this sense the emotional and psychological distance/closeness between therapist and client will regularly be shifting along the participant-observer continuum in the process of therapy.

Relating this to Buber's concepts of the I–Thou and I–It relationship stances, then at the participant end of the spectrum I am more likely to be in an I–Thou stance with the client; at the observer end of the spectrum I will be taking an I–It stance towards the client's 'material'. Both the close involvement with the client, the 'real meeting', and the more objective reflective stance are crucial components of effective psychotherapy from our perspective. It is with careful attention to both these polarities that the effectiveness of psychotherapy is enhanced; the careful reflective meditative stance being as crucial to the process as the psychotherapist's capacity for empathy and contactful engagement with the client. This paradigm is equally relevant to the supervisory process, which also fluctuates between the I–Thou and I–It modalities as different aspects of the task come into the foreground, or in turn recede into the background. However, we believe that a good and holding supervisory alliance will always have as its basis an I–Thou relational attitude on the part of the supervisor.

Relationship stances and psychological distance/closeness

We also recognize other relationship stances between psychotherapist and client, supervisor and supervisee, which may involve less psychological distance than that of the observer and yet not be as close as those rare moments of intimacy of the I–Thou encounter. These intermediate stances form as much a part of the relationship between psychotherapist and client/supervisor and supervisee as in any other human relationship. For example, when the supervisor and psychotherapist are engaged in consultation regarding a client, they may be sharing ideas, feelings and responses in a meaningful and mutually enjoyable way. This process may not perhaps be called an I–Thou moment of encounter, yet it may tend towards the I–Thou end of the continuum in terms of closeness and contact. When they are both focusing on analysing diagnostic features of a particular client presentation, they may well be tending more to the I–It end of the continuum in relation to the client. When the supervisor is evaluating the work of the supervisee in a formal report, she will be closer to the observer end of the spectrum in this evaluation process.

The question of personal distance has been linked by Holloway (1995) to the issues of power and engagement/involvement in supervision. In any supervisory relationship, Holloway sees a balance between power (whether it be 'power over' or 'power with') and affiliation or intimacy in the extent to which people mutually confirm one another. Holloway uses a classification of different types of power proposed by French and Raven (1960, quoted in Holloway 1995). French and Raven outline five different types of power that operate in relationships. *Reward power* refers to our perception that the other person has the power to reward us; whereas *coercive power* is attributed to a person we perceive as able to punish us. *Expert power* derives from a person's knowledge and skills in a specialized area. *Referent power* comes from inter-personal attractiveness, whereas *legitimate power* is that inherent in a professional role that is socially sanctioned. Holloway discusses how the exercise of power varies according to the particular function or task that is undertaken in supervision (French and Raven 1960, quoted in Holloway 1995).

She lists five functions or tasks of supervision (monitoring/evaluating, instructing, modelling, consulting and supporting/sharing) and shows how different types of power will differentially affect these different functions. For example, in the instructing or advising function, when the supervisor provides information and makes suggestions based on her own experience, she exercises expert and legitimate power. In our terms, this may place the supervisor in the middle of the participant-observer continuum; neither at one polarity nor the other, but balancing the two in relation to the supervisee. By contrast, when the supervisor is engaged in the monitoring or evaluating function, Holloway sees her as exercising reward and coercive power and sees the communication as 'largely controlled by the supervisor' (Holloway 1995: 34). We hypothesize that in this instance the interpersonal distance will be greater between supervisor and supervisee than in the previous example and that the supervisor will be close to the observer end of our continuum. In the supporting task, Holloway considers that referent power is the most relevant and in our view this is one of the areas where the I–Thou meeting is most likely to occur. In these examples, we believe that the distance between the supervisor and supervisee varies in accordance with what power is exercised and particularly by the way in which power is handled by the supervisor.

If the supervisor can maintain an I–Thou relational attitude towards the supervisee throughout, then the supervisory relationship will be robust enough to contain the challenges of monitoring and evaluation, and the psychological distance although greater than in more intimate moments, will not divide the participants in an alienating manner. However, if the supervisor depersonalizes the supervisee and distances the person in a shameful manner, then there may well be a rupture in the supervisory alliance. In the latter instance, the supervisor will generally have moved out of an I–Thou stance to a position of devaluing and discounting the supervisee and will no longer be providing the containment essential to the supervisory alliance. Whatever the supervisory task, the basis in an I–Thou (Buber 1965) or an I'm OK – You're OK (Berne 1961) attitude to the other is, we believe, essential for effective supervision. If such an attitude of respect and valuing of the other is absent, then the exercise of power is experienced by the supervisee as undermining and destructive. In such an atmosphere, effective learning will not take place. This accords with Holloway's research findings about the importance of engagement in cementing the supervisory alliance (Holloway 1995).

Dimensions of relationship in psychotherapy and supervision

Hycner (1991) following Trub talks of a dual emphasis in psychotherapy: the 'dialogical-interpersonal' and the 'dialectical-intrapsychic'. These dimensions are also central to supervision. The 'dialogical-interpersonal' refers to the immediacy of relating, of meeting the other in genuine open encounter. The 'dialectical-intrapsychic' refers to the joint exploration of the client's internal world with a view to understanding and change in the internal mechanisms that support the client's world view. The relationship therapist's task is to help the client explore the intrapsychic components of personality, while maintaining an interpersonal focus. 'There is always this tension of looking at the dialectical-intrapsychic material and accepting and exploring these conflicts, yet always trying to elevate this aspect to a dialogical-interpersonal relatedness to others and the world in general' (Hycner 1991: 74).

This delicate balance between intrapsychic exploration and effective interpersonal relating forms the kernel of a relational approach to psychotherapy. We consider this process as central to effective supervision as well, whether the intrapsychic exploration be of the client's dynamics or of the supervisee's countertransferential responses. Equally the interpersonal dimension under exploration may be the intersubjective process between the psychotherapist and the client, or the immediate interaction between supervisor and supervisee or the interrelationship between these as explored in the concept of parallel process.

The tension between the 'dialogical–interpersonal' and the 'dialectic–intrapsychic' that Hycner names is reflected for both the psychotherapist (and for the supervisor) in the shuttling between the participant and observer ends of the relationship continuum described above. When both psychotherapist and client are analysing the client's intrapsychic process, they are more like 'observers', in the position of the audience of the internal drama. This may be seen as the working alliance in action. 'We are in this together and we are both on the same side' captures the essence of this position. When psychotherapist and client are in dialogue with one another, they are moving closer to the I–Thou of genuine encounter: a meeting of 'souls'. This is the essence of the I–Thou or the 'dialogic' relationship in psychotherapy and supervision. We consider that the aim for both the psychotherapist and for the supervisor is the same. The supervisor too needs to be able to stand back, observe and evaluate the supervisee's work, but this process will be effective only if it takes place within a trusting supervisory alliance. The dialogical-interpersonal dimension of the supervisory relationship is the supervisory alliance itself, which at times becomes the focus of the supervision session. This may occur in particular when a failure of communication has occurred between supervisor and supervisee, which requires attention before supervision can proceed.

The dialectic-intrapsychic dimension will come to the fore, for example, when the supervisee's countertransferential response becomes the focus for supervision. For the supervisor the challenge to maintain this delicate balance between an internal and a relational focus is greater in some respects than it is for the psychotherapist since the supervisor also has the task of assessing competence (and the limits of competence) and evaluating the supervisee's work, whilst maintaining the trust and respect of the other. If the supervisor emphasizes the intimacy of the relationship at the cost of the monitoring and evaluative functions, supervision may become a comfortable and 'pally' process, which does not leave space for confrontation or new learning; or it may turn into a psychotherapeutic rather than a supervisory process. If the supervisor focuses too heavily on the 'normative' aspects of supervision (Proctor 1986) and assumes an overly critical stance towards the supervisee, which may ignore the person's level of development as a clinician, supervision may well become a punitive process in which learning does not take place and the welfare of the clients is placed in jeopardy.

Reason (1994) discusses the risks involved in over-emphasizing 'participative identity' (among co-researchers) resulting in 'a loss of perspective' consequently becoming 'immersed in a seamless web'. On the other hand, over-emphasis on perspective leads to alienation from each other and from their immediate experience (Reason 1994). Alternatively he advocates the further possibility of movement between the two poles with the simultaneous articulation of both (Reason 1994: 31). Reason's 'critical subjectivity' like our approach of 'the co-creation or negotiation of meaning' describes the balancing of participation and reflection, unique to human beings. The supervisory relationship requires living with the paradox of being part of the process and reflecting on it. Like Reason we believe that this paradox 'encompasses both opposition and unity' (Reason 1994: 30) in the ever-changing dynamic of a relationship that is highly sensitive to contextual variables. This balance counteracts the tendency to polarization where the supervisor may merge with the supervisee by over-identification or where the supervisor may move into a position of judgemental isolation as in shame-inducing situations. Thus, inadvertently the supervisor may either relinquish his authority by merging unhelpfully with the supervisee or replicate earlier undermining educational experiences that the person may have had by an unhelpful authoritarianism.

Effective supervision involves a delicate balance of awareness and entails the capacity both to be in our own experience, appreciate that of the other and stand back in order to reflect on the interaction between the two, reflecting the capacity for 'critical subjectivity' and 'inclusion'. The more effectively supervisors and psychotherapists can practise inclusion and hence sharpen their self-supervision in a constant ongoing way, the more efficiently they will be able to aid the client's capacity for inclusion.

Developing a reliable 'internal supervisor'

For us the development of inclusion links with the concept of gradually developing a reliable 'internal supervisor' (Casement 1985: 32). At first a supervisee will tend to apply to his process of learning therapeutic skills his own internalized 'shoulds' (for example, 'you must get this right' or 'do it perfectly') from significant others in his early environment and educational context. Gradually the person will internalize the supervisor's attitudes and knowledge base in the process of discussing case material. Casement distinguishes between the 'internalized supervisor' and the 'internal supervisor' (Casement 1985: 32) in describing this process of development.

At first the supervisee will internalize the supervisor and rely on this internalized voice, working to the perceived formula, as it were. In Transactional Analysis terms, at this stage the supervisee will be introjecting the supervisor as a 'new' Parent and will tend to use the new Parent messages as though they are inviolate 'rules', the 'right way to do therapy'. Gradually supervisees will develop and integrate their own internal supervisor, which will incorporate their own independent thinking, spontaneity, autonomous judgement and result in the creation of their own internal map of the psychotherapeutic process. At this point, the clinician will, in our view, have developed the capacity for inclusion and draw on the sophistication that results from a multi-perspectival approach to the client.

A competent internal supervisor enables the supervisee to monitor both the transference and the countertransference dimensions and the dynamic interaction between these, keeping both in view. Educating the observer or the 'internal supervisor' in this way is consequently the primary objective of the supervision process. 'I believe that the process of supervision should develop into a dialogue between the external supervisor and the internal supervisor' (Casement 1985: 32).

Transference and countertransference: an intersubjective perspective

We view transference and countertransference from an intersubjective perspective. Intersubjectivity theory regards transference as an instance of the person's 'unconscious organising activity', which is shaped by archaic perceptions of self and other 'that unconsciously organize his subjective universe' (Stolorow *et al.* 1994: 10). Both the psychotherapist and the client bring to the relationship their own characteristic ways of organizing the field between them based on their particular pasts, which will tend to shape the way they perceive the present. The therapist is not 'immune' from this process. The therapist's organizing principles will be influenced by his own personal history and by his knowledge base in psychology and psychotherapy, which in turn will influence the material he chooses to attend to in the encounter with the client.

This concept of embedded organizing principles operating just outside the person's awareness resembles the notion of 'creative adjustment' in Gestalt therapy, which describes the child's survival choices as the best possible option available to him in the circumstances. The adult will bring to each new relationship the creative adjustments and 'best possible' options developed in childhood, which may be out of date and dysfunctional in the present. What Stolorow *et al.* stress is the inextricable relationship, the 'system of reciprocal mutual influence', existing between the client's transference and the therapist's countertransference (op.cit.). The one cannot be understood without an attention to the other in context. Such organizing influences will include factors such as race, culture, language, religion, the sociopolitical factors impinging on us, the part of the world in which we grew up and the present context in which the therapy is occurring.

Every therapeutic dyad is uniquely different and a client can never have the same experience with different therapists. Much psychotherapeutic literature is written from an assumption of the 'neutrality' of the person of the psychotherapist, as if psychotherapists are somehow all similar beings, and, in this process of 'neutralizing' the psychotherapist, individual differences are underplayed. This often loses sight of some of the crucial elements in the change process, namely what does this particular psychotherapist have to offer that uniquely suits the needs of this particular client. Likewise, what does this particular encounter provide for this client that is specially relevant to his growth and the development of new perspectives.

These same considerations apply to supervision. No two supervisory relationships are ever alike; each particular supervision constellation provides a uniquely different experience to both participants. For the supervisee this means that there are different skills to be learned from different supervisors; and uniquely differing styles of relating to be experienced. From the supervisee's perspective, a certain supervisory relationship may provide a reparative dimension in addition to the learning gained whereas another relationship may prove to be shame-inducing and undermining to the person's confidence. In the latter encounter the supervisee's selfobject needs would not be likely to be met and instead undermining and destructive experiences from the past will be replayed.

The intersubjective theorists consider that there are two dimensions of the transference, which they have termed the 'selfobject' and the 'repetitive' dimensions (Stolorow and Atwood 1992: 25) and which can be used to explain the difference between the two situations outlined above. As regards the 'selfobject' dimension of the transference, the supervisee will look to the supervisor to meet some of their selfobject needs to be confirmed and accurately mirrored in their ability and effectiveness as psychotherapists as they develop their skills in an ongoing way. Clients heal selfobject disruptions from childhood by internalizing the psychotherapist's sustained empathy. Early empathic failures are re-experienced and healed by the new relationship. When clients internalize the psychotherapist's empathy they develop a capacity to assume a reflective, understanding, accepting, comforting attitude towards their own emotions and needs. This process will also be occurring in supervision.

The 'repetitive' dimension refers to the person's fears and expectations that the current experience with the other will be a repetition of the developmental failures from the past (op.cit.). Such repetitive dimensions will be linked to the person's core interpersonal schema particularly as this is connected with unsatisfactory learning experiences from the past. These two aspects of the transference constantly oscillate so that at any given moment one may be in the foreground whilst the other takes the background in the interactional field. When the psychotherapist or supervisor is perceived as understanding the client or supervisee, the selfobject dimension will be in ascendance; when the person feels misattuned to and 'missed', the repetitive dimension becomes figural. In order to deal with misattunements, the supervisor (like the psychotherapist) will need to attend to the alliance rupture before supervision can proceed effectively. This may involve a careful and minute analysis of the interaction that has led to the rupture and an exploration of the assumptions that both people have brought to the relationship. This will inevitably mean some level of self-disclosure on the part of the supervisor whose process is as much part of the relational field as that of the supervisee.

In conclusion

The main aims of our model of supervision are focused on the development of the processes of inclusion and the attainment of a meta-perspective on the relationship that will provide the psychotherapist and the client with an overall view of the interactional field. Within the supervisory alliance, the supervisor and the supervisee engage in a process of mutual negotiation of meaning so that the supervisee can gain insight and awareness into his clinical work, which, in turn, will facilitate his work with the client. A 'meta-systems perspective' involves an awareness of self in relation to the other(s) in a social context, appreciating the many complex interrelationships involved in this network. The supervisor is both part of the system and will stand outside it in the role of participant-observer in order to promote in the supervisee a multi-perspectival view of reality, which, in our view, characterizes a mature internal supervisor.

Questions for further reflection

1 What are the consequences for the supervisory alliance of taking an intersubjective perspective in supervision?
2 What do you consider to be the most important process goals of psychotherapy supervision?
3 In what ways do you conceptualize the differences and similarities between psychotherapy and supervision?
4 How might you use Sullivan's concept of 'participant-observation' with supervisees?

The model in practice

3

Objectives of the model in practice

In this chapter we discuss written transcripts of work with four separate supervisees. These are used to demonstrate the theoretical model in practice and to illustrate the primary objective of supervision, namely to foster growth and development of the 'internal supervisor' (Casement 1985). In each transcript the supervisor is seen to critically monitor the transference both in the supervisee–client relationship and in how this is re-presented in the supervisory relationship. This enables the supervisor to elicit and understand the developmental issues being triggered in the supervisee by the client. In turn this 'critical subjectivity' (Reason 1994) on the part of the supervisor serves as a model to the supervisee in furthering his own ability to practise inclusion. Inclusion requires of the supervisee a capacity to delicately hold in balance an awareness of his own experience and that of the client, together with a capacity simultaneously to stand back and reflect on the dynamic interaction between the two. Keeping both in view, without neglecting the significance of either perspective, is essential to understanding the relationship with the client and is thus central to our model of supervision.

To understand the discussion that follows, it is important to remember that Stern's (1985) model of child development is a phase model not a stage model. (See Chapter 6 for a more detailed discussion of Stern's model of development and of Kohut's notions of selfobject needs/transferences). That is, Stern's verbal phase is not necessarily more advanced than any other; it is not a linear progression from the emergent through the core, to the intersubjective to the verbal to the narrative. Rather, maturity at the verbal phase of development includes the ability to access all other phases of development. The supervisee therefore reaches maturity when there is sufficient capacity to 'mediate' the various phases of development; that is, the person has the flexibility to move between phases in new situations or under stress (Evans 1998). In the various phases of development Stern indicates the conditions necessary for successful progression towards the next phase.

In each of these phases the various conditions could be subsumed within a particular theme; we suggest that in the emergent phase the major theme is *security*, in the core phase *identity*, in the intersubjective phase *contact*, in the verbal phase *communication*, and in the narrative phase *inclusion*.

In the emergent phase of development Stern's various conditions for progression seem to us to add up to a toleration for uncertainty. That is, that the child has sufficient security to be curious, to be allowed to explore his world, to be adventurous. This develops the ability to enter into new situations without necessarily having to know what to expect or to be able to predict everything that is going to happen. In the first transcript the emergent phase of development is figural and dominates the field. Historically, in this phase Graham was meant to 'know everything', to 'take responsibility for everyone' and to 'get it right'. This has affected his tolerance for uncertainty and proved a considerable burden throughout his life both personally and professionally. The supervisor works with the idealizing and mirroring selfobject transferences in order to support Graham through this phase and enable him to contact his internal support system.

In the core phase identity is the major theme. Here the child says this is me and while 'curious about you I am mostly concerned with myself'. Here the emphasis is on I. In the second transcript the core phase of development is figural and dominates the field. Christopher appears 'locked' into the core phase where others exist only to support his 'I'. He has not developed a sufficient sense of the other to be able to practise inclusion. In working with Christopher the supervisor focuses on the twinship selfobject transference 'let's you and me figure this out' and facilitates him to suspend his clinical practice and enter long-term therapy whilst continuing with his training.

In the intersubjective phase the major theme is contact; 'this is me and I am curious to explore who you are'. Contact requires the ability to tolerate difference; to be available for meeting without merging into the other or without erecting barriers between self and other. This requires the capacity to both meet the other and stay our separate selves. In the third transcript it emerges during the supervision session that Patricia has developed a core sense of self but without sufficient support to engage with vulnerability in relationships. Under sufficient stress the core phase becomes figural and dominates the field where Patricia may give the appearance of being in contact but the focus of contact is unilateral, one way only, and she operates as a compulsive caregiver. In working with Patricia the supervisor focuses on the mirroring and idealizing selfobject transferences.

In the verbal phase the major theme is communication. A person develops a capacity to reflect on their own experience and communicate this verbally or, in the written word, to others. In the final transcript Margaret appears to function at the verbal phase of development and this is reflected in the high regard in which she is held by colleagues and by the fact that they refer 'difficult' clients to her. However, under sufficient stress the emergent phase dominates the field such that she loses her confidence and her ability to think clearly becomes significantly impaired. In working with Margaret the supervisor focuses on the mirroring and adversarial selfobject transferences.

In the following four vignettes, the four supervisees were at different levels of professional experience and at different stages of sophistication in the evolution of a stable and mature internal supervisor. Inexperienced practitioners can in the course of a supervision session attain a degree of inclusion be it somewhat unstable; while experienced practitioners can sometimes lose their ground and need to be supported to regain their balanced perspective on client work. The goal of effective supervision is ideally where the supervisee gradually reaches a stage in the session where he is able to reflect on courses of action and to assess the impact of these on others; to evaluate possible interventions in terms of an inner map of the psychotherapy process; and to develop a narrative that describes the interrelational complexities and the course of therapy. The attainment of these goals represent the narrative phase marked by a developing capacity for inclusion. We are not advocating inclusion as a permanent invariable state since we believe this is both unattainable and undesirable. The ability to sustain vulnerability is an essential part of relating and a measure of personal and professional maturity. Being vulnerable opens the psychotherapist (and the supervisor) to resonating with the client's internal process more significantly where this is marked by chaos and fragmentation.

In each of the four transcripts the supervisor is guided by the theoretical model outlined above that identifies the developmental phase presented. This involves both the external observation of the supervisee's behaviour and the internal experience (countertransference) of the supervisor. The supervisor allows himself sufficient immersion in his own countertransference responses to the supervisee to speculate on the historical dynamics that are presenting as figural for the supervisee in the here and now. The supervisor detaches sufficiently from his internal responses to reflect on what early child-significant caretaker dynamic may be inviting a parallel process and thus clarifies what actual responses, in relation to the emerging selfobject transferences, may model a healthy developmental process. The assumption here is that transference phenomena primarily draw attention to unmet developmental needs rather than to resistance, displacement or regression (Stolorow *et al.* 1987). This requires of the supervisor the discipline of practising inclusion in relation to his own process.

It is possible to have developmental deficits in one or more of these phases of development. As a result a person may give the appearance of maturity that is actually adaptive and diminishes under stress. We believe it is important that professional therapists recognize that whatever their level of maturity as clinicians they remain vulnerable human beings. No one negotiates childhood without some degree of developmental deficit in one or more of the phases of development. This being so, even the more experienced practitioner can regress under stress. It is important that we recognize this and have the capacity and the ability to know when we need supervision for work with a particular client who may be pressing some 'script buttons'.

Supervision vignette 1 – security: emergent phase

Graham is in his mid-40s. He completed an integrative psychotherapy training course five years ago and has a small private practice including clinical supervision. He is a university lecturer in the social sciences. Graham
is a member of a supervision group with three other men. The supervisor
has been supervising this group for 18 months. On this occasion Graham
came uncharacteristically late for supervision and looked nervous and ex-
hausted. He presented as confused and appeared to be discussing two clients
simultaneously.

Graham: 'I have this client who is 35 years old and gay. In therapy last
week he focused on problems of sexual identity and informed me that he
considered harming himself. He said he was on the brink of suicide. My
response was to experience a deep fear, indeed I was really scared and have
remained so. I wonder whether I'm picking up his fear? He had been wanting to tell someone that he is gay but is terrified to do so. He seems to be
something of a loner although he has two friends. Recently he was wanting
to 'confess' to them that he was gay but he was worried that they would
think he was 'dirty' and 'wrong'. He seemed to work himself up into quite a
state in order to tell these two friends but then backed out. Apparently these
friends knew something was wrong. When he arrived for therapy last week
he was suffering with chronic irritable bowel syndrome and his whole body
was extremely tense, as it was when we first worked together some two years
ago. He watched a programme on Channel 4 about 'coming out'. Immediately after he felt driven to reveal everything and he has this extreme persecutor inside him; for example, if he goes into a shop he is convinced everyone
is looking at him and expecting him to buy a gay newspaper. He then thinks
everybody knows, that it's so obvious. He spent most of this past week
settling his bills and dealing with his affairs so his threat of suicide felt very
real and I have been very scared all week. I'm thinking if he kills himself I've
had it with therapy. Actually I feel very deskilled. I even thought I won't go
to supervision today!

All this is juxtaposed with a female client who dumped on me and dis-
appeared in an emotional maelstrom two weeks ago. She is a client I have
brought to supervision before, a client who has gynaecological problems.
Recently she has said she feels too weak to come to therapy. Some three
sessions ago she forgot her cheque book. The next session she missed and
then telephoned me. For some reason I found myself listening to her for
almost 45 minutes on the telephone! I was aware of feeling really resentful
but continued to listen. She telephoned a few days later wanting more time
on the phone and I challenged her to make an appointment for therapy.
When she turned up for therapy she was complaining about her boyfriend,
complaining about the team leader at her place of work and complaining
about everyone else who works in her office. I challenged her to explore
what responsibility she might have in these situations and then she began to
complain to me. She again said she did not have her cheque book. Later she
telephoned to say that she might be stopping her therapy and made all kinds
of verbal swipes at me . . . I felt very discounted by her.'

Commentary: The supervisor is aware that it is out of character for Graham to be seduced into providing therapy via the telephone. He usually presents as functioning at a competent level of personal and professional development. The supervisor gradually becomes aware of a feeling akin to being 'over-whelmed', which gives him some insight into what Graham was experiencing. There is clearly a considerable amount of information and the supervisor therefore decides to establish some boundaries and introduce a little order into the seeming chaos.

Supervisor: 'Okay Graham, clearly there's a lot going on with both these clients. I suggest we work with one at a time?'

Graham: 'Yeah . . . okay.'

Supervisor: 'Your female client sounds rather like a complaints department?'

Commentary: Clearly the supervisee is quite regressed and needs support but not rescue.

Graham: 'Yeah, she complains about everyone in her life. Except her father whom she idealized and he never set any boundaries around her, it seems to me.'

Supervisor: 'How did she react when you challenged her about her responsibilities?'

Commentary: Here the supervisor endeavours to encourage Graham to begin to stand back and observe the process and to engage his thinking.

Graham: 'I think she felt extremely angry but did not express this directly but through adding me to the list of people who have failed her. She has two sisters who are very successful and she complains that they always get more out of life than her.'

Supervisor: 'What do you understand is happening?'

Graham: [appears very confused] '. . . um . . . er . . .'

Commentary: Graham appears very hesitant and looks anxious again.

Supervisor: 'Do you have any idea what is going on?'

Graham: 'She wants a fairytale world, my challenge dared her to bring more reality to bear on her life.'

Supervisor: 'What personality orientation do you imagine your client to be?'

Commentary: The supervisor realizes that his 'rapidly fired' questions are taking Graham too much into his anxiety and he is losing the ability to think clearly. He is aware that Graham has studied the personality disorders contained in the DSM IV (APA 1994) and has a background in psychiatry from earlier in his career. The supervisor's goal here was to be more specific and establish a higher level of confidence in Graham's own abilities.

Graham: 'Oh God, I'm sure to get this wrong . . . um . . .'

Commentary: Clearly the experience of both these clients is raising considerable anxiety in Graham. He seems to be driven by a need to get things right and/or not get things wrong. The supervisor decides to support Graham in his thinking by providing information that characterizes a particular personality orientation without actually providing him with the answer.

Supervisor: 'She complains and blames a great deal and you seem to think that she is very angry.'

Graham: 'Yeah.'

Supervisor: 'And what are your countertransference reactions to this client? How do you feel towards her?'

Commentary: Graham is also familiar with the work of Frances Allen who has specified certain characteristic countertransferential responses to each of the personality disorders contained in the DSM IV (APA 1994). Again the supervisor's goal is to support Graham without rescuing him since he suspects that the female client is looking for rescue rather than support for her own thinking.

Graham: 'I feel deskilled, guilty . . . I'm not getting it right . . . I think she's passive aggressive.'

Supervisor: 'Do you have any other feelings towards her?'

Commentary: The supervisor is aware that a typical countertransferential response is anger towards a passive aggressive client and he endeavours to support Graham to contact his anger in order to move beyond his anxiety, which is impeding him.

Graham: 'I don't think so.'

Supervisor: 'So, this client adds you to the list of people she complains about, she keeps you on the telephone for 45 minutes, she forgets her cheque book on two occasions and is thinking of stopping therapy?'

Graham: 'Okay I feel bloody angry . . . there is no way I'm getting it right for her . . . mmm I'm beginning to feel a little relieved . . . (deep sigh) . . . I've been seduced into working far too hard with this client and I'd like to figure out why.'

Commentary: By contacting his feelings of anger Graham has moved sufficiently beyond his anxiety to engage his thinking. That is, he is now more grounded. At this point the supervisor decides to switch the focus to the other client. His thinking here is primarily governed by the threat of suicide and his responsibility as a supervisor to attend to this. The supervisor intends to return to the female client later in the supervision. Furthermore, the female client appears to be taking up the other client's space, that is Graham began by talking about the client who was threatening suicide but then the female client cut across this. By returning to look at the client who was first presented the supervisor is modelling the maintenance of boundaries.

Supervisor: 'Okay, before we explore this particular client any further I would suggest that we first spend some time with your other client.'

Graham: 'Yes okay . . . this is more immediately urgent and . . . mmm . . . I'm feeling much lighter now . . . beginning to see my process with Linda . . .'

Supervisor: 'Graham, I know you have a background as a professional in the psychiatric services and will have had considerable experience with patients who self-harm. Is there any link between this client and your past experience?'

Commentary: Given his quite extensive background as a professional in the psychiatric services the supervisor is curious as to why Graham should become so uncharacteristically anxious about this particular client and appear so deskilled.

Graham: 'What immediately comes to mind is an occasion when one of the hospital's secretaries was murdered by a patient.'
Supervisor: 'What was your reaction at the time?'
Graham: 'Shock . . . horror . . . I felt very alone and began to doubt whether I wanted to do this work.'

Commentary: The supervisor noticed a possible connection with a previous comment questioning whether he wanted to be a therapist or not.

Supervisor: 'Any other historical connections come to mind?'

Commentary: Given Graham's background in psychiatry the supervisor imagines that there may be other historical reasons why this particular client is creating such anxiety.

Graham: 'My mother was often psychotic when I was a child but I don't think there is a connection. I was kept mostly in the dark by my father about what was happening. My client . . . is working on feeling lonely and suicidal . . .'

Commentary: The information that Graham's mother experienced periods of psychosis when he was a child is clearly significant as is his apparent resistance to the idea that this has any connection with his client.

Supervisor: 'Is he touching your loneliness in some way?'
Graham: 'What I'm thinking now is that as we approach the end of term at the university I'd arranged for a social night with a disco to facilitate contact between staff and students. Several weeks ago all the staff agreed that this was a good idea but as the date comes nearer people are backing off and I'm left doing all the organizing and having to sell the tickets in order to pay for the disco and the hire of the hall. I'm taking a lot of responsibility and feeling unsupported. I had a similar experience when working in psychiatry.'

Commentary: The supervisor intuits that this reference to the social evening has deeper connections with Graham's history.

Supervisor: 'Are there any connections with your family?'
Graham: 'Yeah . . . I couldn't speak with my father about what was happening with my mother . . . he never spoke about . . . I learnt very early to become Mr nice guy, Mr funny, Mr caring person . . . holding up the whole world. And now I'm in my mid-40s and re-evaluating my life and what's important and my client is re-evaluating his life also . . . I don't actually think he will kill himself . . . he telephoned me two days ago and did seem in a much better place . . .'

Commentary: The supervisor speculates as to why Graham has not told him until now that he does not actually believe the client will kill himself? He did not offer this information at the beginning of supervision. Perhaps he is inducing the supervisor to carry the burden of responsibility.

Supervisor: 'I am impacted by you taking responsibility for the whole world as a child?'

Graham: 'Yeah . . . I know in my head that there is little I could do to stop this client if he really was determined to kill himself but . . . on an emotional level . . . a part of me thinks . . . I will be to blame if he does . . . society will point a finger at me.'

Commentary: In sharing his fear with the supervisor he may be seeking the kind of support that his father apparently did not provide?

Supervisor: 'So how does this relate to your past?'

Graham: 'Well . . . what's different is I'm talking this through here with you . . . I cannot be Mr nice guy . . . and I'm not withdrawing . . . I'm acknowledging my fear. I did wonder whether to come to supervision . . . which was my old script . . . to withdraw . . . because it's all too much.'

Commentary: The supervisor begins to see a possible connection between these two clients. As a child when Graham's mother was experiencing periods of psychosis his father provided no support. With a lack of support it is possible that Graham's only alternative as a child was to withdraw and appear to be coping? He acknowledges in the above response that his old script would have been to withdraw and not attend for supervision. Clearly he has overcome his script sufficiently to come and seek support. At the same time he cannot get it right for this female client who is quite heavily passive aggressive. So, Graham is left with two clients who in unison seem to be conveying the idea that 'I have to take responsibility and I'm not going to get it right'.

Supervisor: 'Yes I acknowledge that you are not withdrawing and that you are sharing your concerns with us.'

Graham: 'Yes and I feel a lot better for it.'

Supervisor: 'Let us then recap Graham. You said that as a child you took responsibility for the "whole world". You also said that you realize you're working too hard with your female client and feeling very responsible and scared around your suicidal client. So what do you think is happening to you?'

Graham: '. . . um . . . well I'm working too hard with one client and feeling very frightened with another . . . so I guess these two clients are tapping into my old script of . . . I must get it right . . . I must take responsibility for the whole world . . . or it will fall apart . . . both . . . I'm beginning to feel much clearer now, thanks.'

Commentary: Graham appears to have resurrected sufficient observing ego to stand back and begin to understand the process.

Supervisor: 'Now that you are feeling much clearer do you think you need to think through how you're going to respond to these two clients?'
Graham: 'No . . . I can think this through on my own . . . later . . . oh shit! I'm doing it again . . . yes I would like to explore with you the way ahead.'

Commentary: Graham's response above demonstrates just how seductive script is but on this occasion Graham recognizes that his tendency to autonomy and self-sufficiency is actually adaptive. This raises the interesting challenge to the theory and practice of psychotherapy in the West, which is heavily influenced by the idea of maturity equating with independence and autonomy. A more postmodern attitude towards maturity recognizes the importance of autonomy and independence but also the capacity to seek support when necessary.

Supervisor: 'Graham I acknowledge you are perfectly capable of thinking this through on your own but I appreciate you taking support here.'

Commentary: Here the supervisor is simply supporting Graham in his move out of his adaptive presentation.

Graham: 'Do we ever get rid of our life scripts?'
Supervisor: 'No, I don't believe so.'

Commentary: Graham and the other members of the group look surprised and interested. There follows a period of some 15 minutes while the group discuss this question. The general conclusion is that life scripts (Berne 1961) cannot be cured but may be brought into awareness and healed sufficiently. Overall, the consensus was that there would always be occasions when situations arise that may result in an earlier phase of development becoming figural with the potential to overwhelm us. How we handle these situations will generally improve but we will always be susceptible to them. This discussion provided support to further disempower the internal critic in all members of the group. Subsequently Graham was able to think through, in a mature and professional manner, how he might respond to each of his clients.

Concluding comments: Graham has an adaptive front, which can give a false impression of a mature verbal self able to access all other phases of development as appropriate. However, this is based on a script decision that demands taking responsibility and getting things right. Underneath this the above transcript illustrates that Graham's emergent self gets lost when 'the other' impinges on or threatens his boundaries. With reference to Kohut's selfobject transferences his need for an idealized other to provide support was lacking with his father. In coming to supervision he was probably projecting this selfobject need onto the supervisor. It was of course important that the supervisor did not become overwhelmed with anxiety about a potential suicide nor neglect to focus on this safety issue. Furthermore it was important that the supervisor did not try and 'get it right' for this female client and thereby parallel Graham's process.

The transcript and commentary demonstrate that Graham was blocked in the emergent phase of development (Stern 1985). Through the idealizing and mirroring selfobject transference the supervisor supported Graham to proceed into the core phase where he could understand 'this is my past, this is who I am and this is how my history affects me today'. Towards the end of the supervision session Graham appeared to be at the verbal phase while recognizing that this was adaptive. With support, he was then able to use information about himself with an objective-observing ego rather than through an adaptation. When Graham loses the support of his adaptation (creative adjustment) he then withdraws in interpersonal relationships (intersubjective phase) but can give the appearance of being present. He can then lose contact with what he thinks and what he feels, that is with his core self. The development of a core self depends on a supportive relationship with a primary caregiver in the emergent phase of development. Graham was able to work with the supervisor from his emergent self and gradually come through to a more objective perspective.

Supervision vignette 2 – identity: core phase

Chris (Christopher) is in his mid-30s; he is a sales manager for a large marketing company. He frequently changes his jobs but all within the same area of work. He has a successful track record and earns a high salary. He has a history of several short-term relationships and he appears to have had a considerable number of short-term voluntary engagements with voluntary agencies in the advice, basic counselling arena. He has attended numerous personal growth workshops over the past 10 years. He has attempted also to establish a training workshop himself but it did not recruit. He is in the first year of a counselling training, which normally requires weekly personal therapy. He has persuaded the trainer to exempt him from personal therapy unless 'something comes up'. He has had two clients in the first few months of the training year and each one has left and then subsequently written giving what appear to be superficial excuses. Chris is of the opinion that counselling is probably too challenging for them.

In listening to Chris the supervisor is immediately impacted by his egotism, by his lack of experience or understanding of the nature of the counselling process. He appears unaware of his level of ignorance. In the countertransference the supervisor experiences being part of an audience as he holds forth and feels tempted to be sarcastic and humiliate him, to 'cut him down to size'. The supervisor also has a serious concern about his potential for unwittingly harming clients and bringing the profession into disrepute. He does not listen, he gives advice and he appears to have no understanding of the client's need for self-determination. He appears genuinely puzzled as to why his clients have not continued in counselling with him and basically responds with 'some people just can't hack it'. The supervisor has a strong sense that if he confronts Chris directly with his concerns Chris will defend against his humiliation by in some way making the supervisor wrong and leaving supervision. He would then be let loose on clients without professional support. The supervisor decides to find a way of modelling the process of counselling by trying to help Chris gain sufficient insight to discover for himself his lack of experience and knowledge together with his need for personal counselling.

Supervisor: 'I appreciate you acknowledging your puzzlement as to why your clients have left therapy after such a short time.'

Chris: 'Yeah ... I guess counselling is too challenging for them both, they just couldn't hack it.'

Supervisor: 'In your professional life you need to take decisions and exercise considerable responsibility.'

Chris: 'Oh yes (Chris goes into a long narrative about his responsibilities at work and the important decisions he has to make).'

Supervisor: 'Let me share something important with you [appealing to his egotism]. In your professional life you clearly need to make common-sense, quick decisions; decisive action is paramount and you clearly are very good at working under pressure within this kind of culture.'

Chris: 'Yes, you're absolutely right.'

Supervisor: 'It must be frustrating that your two counselling clients don't appear to function well using this approach that works so well for you in your work context.'

Chris: 'Yes, bloody frustrating ...'

Supervisor: 'I think the problem may be that what works in one context in your workplace is not working well in the counselling context.'

Chris: [looks interested but also quizzical]

Commentary: The supervisor realizes that he could lose the supervisee here as he senses an edginess in him, the beginnings of defensiveness and argumentation.

Supervisor: 'Perhaps a different approach is needed [appealing to his problem-solving perspective]. As I said, you're clearly good at problem solving and I imagine that you size up situations in the workplace very quickly and think through things that need to be done and get on with it.'

Chris: 'Oh yes.'

Supervisor: 'Well, you're probably going too fast for your counselling clients.'

Chris: 'Yes, now I come to think of it I probably am. Maybe I need to slow down and recognize that they're not as experienced as me.'

Supervisor: 'Mm.'

Commentary: The supervisor experiences a powerful countertransferential reaction wanting to cut the supervisee down to size.

Supervisor: 'Perhaps then it's not the experience of the workplace that they need.'

Chris: 'Mm [looks thoughtful].'

Supervisor: 'You see, no wonder you're frustrated, you're transferring what works well in one culture to a different culture, which requires a different approach.'

Chris: 'Say some more . . .'
Supervisor: 'Well, you're working within a humanistic counselling framework?'
Chris: 'Yes, one which emphasizes "taking responsibility" [said with a note of defiance].'
Supervisor: 'Yes, but you're probably going too fast for your clients. Moving from A to Z involves a process whereby the clients will grow, often slowly, to understand themselves through all the letters from B to Y. You see, if a client begins to understand for themselves how they operate in the world and why, then it's possible that they can transfer learning from one problem to other problem areas in their lives, rather than to keep returning to the counsellor for advice over the same issues all the time. This perhaps is the road to self-determination?'
Chris: 'Mmmm.'
Supervisor: 'Now you've attended an impressive number of growth workshops over the past few years.'
Chris: 'Yes, over the past 10 years actually.'
Supervisor: 'What's missing?'

Commentary: Here the supervisor decides to issue a challenge.

Chris: 'What do you mean?'
Supervisor: 'Well, I say again, what's missing from all these growth workshops?'
Chris: 'Well [looks puzzled], they've been about self-awareness and personal developing, taking action, being proactive.'
Supervisor: 'Sounds a lonely activity?'
Chris: 'No one can do it for you [said with a loud and assertive voice].'

Commentary: The supervisor imagines that there is a whole history in the simple statement, 'no one can do it for you'. This probably sums up Chris's early life history. What little knowledge the supervisor has of the supervisee's background suggests that his parents were very ambitious for him and pushed him beyond his capabilities.

Supervisor: 'Precisely, well done, and in giving advice you are doing it for your clients, you're not helping them to do it for themselves.'
Chris: 'Right (looks surprised and the supervisor senses that he is trying to determine whether he is being criticized or not). Well, how do I get them to do it for themselves then?'
Supervisor: 'Aah now you're on the right track.'
Chris: [looks pleased with himself]
Supervisor: 'How about we start with you?'
Chris: 'Me? . . . what do you mean?'
Supervisor: 'Well, you see the paradox often is that in order to "do things for ourselves" we need the support of other people. Fundamental to therapeutic counselling is the therapeutic relationship as the vehicle for change and the necessity of ongoing personal work, preferably one-to-one on a weekly basis.'
Chris: 'Mmm.'

Supervisor: 'In this way you begin to appreciate the nature of the counselling relationship from the inside.'
Chris: 'So you're saying I need counselling?'
Supervisor: 'One-to-one counselling.'
Chris: 'To achieve a greater understanding of counselling methods?'
Supervisor: 'In part, yes. Look you clearly have a demanding job and you appear to wish to transfer to a counselling career. Well I suggest that you support your training and equip yourself better for the counselling role by doing your own one-to-one counselling. By experiencing long-term counselling from the inside.'
Chris: 'Mmm [looks interested], how long?'
Supervisor: 'Well most counselling courses insist on ongoing therapy for the duration of the counselling training.'
Chris: 'Mmm.'
Supervisor: 'In this way you will learn from the inside, from being a recipient of counselling, what it's like to be in the long-term therapeutic relationship.'
Chris: 'Yeah, erm Pete, you know, one of your colleagues at King Street, we were talking socially one evening and he said something like, erm, "you can't take people where you've not been yourself".'
Supervisor: 'Well why not take the initiative and talk to your trainer and suggest that you go into one-to-one counselling.'
Chris: 'And learn the ropes from the inside.'
Supervisor: 'Yes.'
Chris: 'Good idea.'

Commentary: The supervisee seems to be engaged in the process now and more open. Clearly, stroking his ego whilst challenging him has given him enough self-support to be responsive to the supervisor's suggestion. The supervisor therefore decides to push the boat out a little further and attend to another professional issue, which has been of concern to him.

Supervisor: 'I understand your training course advises against seeing clients in the first year of training.'
Chris: 'Yes but my trainer said it was okay because of all my experiences in the growth workshops.'

Commentary: Clearly this supervisee has seduced his trainer.

Supervisor: 'Mm, well yes you've got a lot of experience of workshops Chris but . . .'
Chris: '. . . but a different culture, yep I get the point. So maybe I'll take the rest of the year off from seeing clients and just concentrate on my own therapy. Yes I'll do that. What do you think?'

Commentary: The supervisor is somewhat astonished at the way in which Chris seems to have turned this whole thing round so that it is his idea but nevertheless the supervisor decides not to pursue this.

Supervisor: 'This sounds like a sensible and mature decision.'

Concluding comments: Chris is clearly blocked at the core phase of development. In the development of his identity others seem to exist only insofar as they maintain his 'I'. His curiosity about others extends only that far. He would probably keep a dependent personality in therapy for many years feeding his ego but once they begin to grow and the idealization is confronted there would be serious problems. Chris does not have sufficient empathy, that is a sense of the other, to connect with the other, in order to practise inclusion. There is a developmental deficit here. It is likely that his parents' investment of their ambitions in his success has resulted in a kind of pseudo-competency (Clarkson 1994). In working with Chris the supervisor deduced that the selfobject twinship transference was prevalent, 'let's you and me figure this out'. There was probably some idealization also in that the supervisor was modelling the situation 'you do not have to do this on your own', which was an alternative way of relating to that experienced by Chris in his childhood. We believe that Chris's ability to develop into a counsellor will be directly related to his ability to grow in personal therapy. It is with people who have this narcissistic orientation that the Kohutian approach of empathic attunement might, in the long term, prove fruitful (Kohut 1984).

Supervision vignette 3 – contact: intersubjective phase

Patricia is in her mid-50s and has recently completed four years of training in Gestalt psychotherapy. Prior to this she trained as a counsellor and has an established private practice and experience of supervising counsellors. When Patricia arrived for supervision she appeared somewhat distant and preoccupied.

Patricia: 'This is a client I have not brought to supervision before. He is a university lecturer in his mid-30s. He presents as quite avoidant and has difficulty connecting with his feelings and is reluctant to express them. He has a history of unsatisfactory endings. He broke up with his most recent girlfriend just a few months ago. As you know . . . I've got a new job in the south of England and intend to take six months' holiday prior to taking up my post in September . . . I decided to inform all my clients early . . . told Peter about four weeks ago (mid-January) . . . I want him to experience a good ending to his therapy.'

Supervisor: 'What do you want to focus on in your supervision?'

Patricia: 'Well . . . when I told him I was going to be taking up a new job and moving out of the area and that I was going to have six months' leave he took it too well to begin with . . . that is . . . he seemed to . . . over the past few weeks he has occasionally shown signs of . . . he continually deflects away to other subjects. I've tried a whole range of techniques but got nowhere so I feel pretty certain that there is something going on in the process between us which I would like to understand.'

Commentary: While the supervisor is aware that Patricia is able to identify a general contract, that is a focus on process issues, nevertheless he becomes aware of feeling mildly frustrated with her apparent deflection. He speculates that this may be a parallel process with him experiencing the frustration that she is feeling toward her client (Doehrman 1976).

Supervisor: 'It appears that you want to explore transferential issues?'
Patricia: 'Yes.'
Supervisor: 'How do you feel towards your client?'

Commentary: The supervisor focuses on Patricia's emotional response to the client in order to facilitate the exploration of her countertransferential reactions.

Patricia: 'I feel he is not connected and avoiding facing the termination of the therapy.'

Commentary: Patricia is deflecting to her client's experience.

Supervisor: 'What do you feel about this?'
Patricia: 'I feel it will be difficult for him to face up to the ending. He has a history of difficult endings, which seem . . .'

Commentary: Again she deflects to her client's experience.

Supervisor: 'And how do you feel towards your client?'
Patricia: 'What I'm saying is . . . his mother and father had a very difficult and stormy relationship and she kept leaving and returning to the marital home . . . erm, before leaving forever . . . when he was 7 years old and . . .'

Commentary: Again Patricia is deflecting to her client's experience and the supervisor is aware of becoming increasingly frustrated in the countertransference. He self-discloses his frustration in order to 'model' being present rather than continue to parallel the supervisee's process.

Supervisor: 'Patricia, I am experiencing considerable frustration at this moment. I am attempting to explore how you feel towards your client and you keep sharing your thinking, and I notice that you keep deflecting to your client's experience.'
Patricia: 'I feel . . . phew . . . frustrated [laughs], irritated and I think . . . how long will this go on and . . . I'm wondering . . . whether he might prematurely terminate therapy because I am going away.'

Commentary: Patricia begins to contact her feeling. The supervisor suggests 'a Gestalt experiment' both because she is familiar with this theoretical approach and the particular experiment is designed to enhance immediacy (Zinker 1977).

Supervisor: 'I suggest we draw on your Gestalt background and I invite you to imagine your client is on this chair. You might step out of your therapist's role now and speak directly to him in the first person present tense and say freely what you think and feel towards him at this moment. Are you willing to do this?'

Patricia: 'Yes and I feel a little nervous . . . but . . . yes I'm used to this kind of work.' [Patricia remains seated but turns to face the chair, some three feet away to her right and my left] 'Yeah well Peter . . . I would like you to connect with yourself (speaks in a monotonous tone) . . . share what you feel about my terminating therapy. I would not like you to experience another unsatisfactory ending . . . when you might leave prematurely now . . . or simply continue in this closed down kind of way.' [Patricia looks at the supervisor and appears perplexed.]
Supervisor: 'You look perplexed?'
Patricia: 'Yes, there is something missing, I . . .'
Supervisor: 'You appear flat and unaffected as you speak to Peter.'

Commentary: Patricia again is paralleling the process of her client who appears unaffected by his therapist's premature termination of therapy.

Patricia: 'I feel sad . . . I think . . . mmm . . . I'm now thinking . . . that . . . he is flat and monotonous . . . so I'm paralleling the process.'

Commentary: Patricia now has some insight into her own process, which provides her with sufficient support to enter more fully into the experiment.

Supervisor: 'So, how about you step out of the role of therapist and express yourself more fully in order to connect with . . .'

Commentary: This experiment provides an opportunity for the therapist to temporarily suspend responsibility for the client, which is taken on by the supervisor.

Patricia: 'Okay . . . well . . . I feel sad that you're denying yourself . . . that you are not . . . I feel frustrated (voice raised) . . . I want you to be here (sounds angry) Oh . . . um . . . I . . . I feel a bit dizzy . . . am I doing the right thing? . . . oh be quiet . . . [voice raised and Patricia appears to be speaking to herself . . . the supervisor imagines she is talking to a familiar internal critic] . . . yes I want contact with you [voice stronger and clearer] . . . I'm going to miss you . . . I am missing you [sounds angry] . . . where are you?' [sounds very angry] . . . [long pause for some two minutes].

Commentary: By the supervisor's temporarily taking responsibility for the client Patricia gives herself permission to experience how strongly she is feeling towards him and encounters her internal critic in the process.

Supervisor: 'What are you thinking Patricia?'
Patricia: 'I'm putting all the responsibility on my client aren't I . . . I'm wanting him to do all the work.'

Commentary: It is now quite apparent that the therapeutic relationship is rather one sided. The client needs the support of his therapist being present if he too is going to be able to be present.

Supervisor: 'Yes, perhaps you might say hello before you say goodbye!'
Patricia: [looking very interested] 'What do you mean?'

Supervisor: 'It appears to me that this work may be about contact first before saying goodbye.'

Patricia: 'Yes that's it . . . I'm not in contact with me . . . I'm wanting him to feel for both of us . . . no wonder he's not able to be present. I've not been connected . . . not in contact with myself . . . oh dear . . . I'm going a little blank . . . no . . . [the internal critic appears to have returned] no . . . [Patricia continues to protest to the internal critic] . . . this is OK . . . [sounding more confident] . . . I can accept that I am in my process and yes I can be curious about what's happening and I don't have to beat myself up but learn from this.'

Commentary: Patricia's internal supervisor is able to overcome the internal critic, reflect on the process and not get overwhelmed.

Supervisor: 'Do you have any idea why you've not been connected?'

Patricia: 'Yes, I'm very excited about my new job and the six-month vacation but I also feel guilty . . . it's a real treat for me and a real challenge to my life script. I was brought up to be the family caretaker, so for me to take six months out to have a vacation . . . and also I feel anxious . . . scared . . . and I've not been letting myself know this either.'

Supervisor: 'So how has this affected your work with Peter?'

Patricia: 'It's becoming a lot clearer now . . . I have been projecting my needs onto him, expecting him to feel and be present in order that I do not have to be present and feel my own feelings. I think my expectation of him is also influenced by my own history.'

Commentary: Patricia appears to recognize the parallel process and understand her countertransferential reactions (Rycroft 1979). The supervisor recalls that Patricia began the supervision by alluding to having 'tried a whole range of techniques but got nowhere'. He inserts a paradoxical intervention to test the efficacy of Patricia's insights.

Supervisor: 'So what new technique will you be exploring with Peter?'

Patricia: [looks at the supervisor quizzically and laughs] 'No, my experience of working through process issues in supervision is that this usually frees something that is stuck in the therapy without my having to necessarily *do anything*.'

Supervisor: 'Patricia, we have explored what you're bringing to the therapy that has been affecting the process, the proactive countertransference (Clarkson 1992). What do you think is going on for Peter? What may he be inducing in you?'

Commentary: The supervisor now switches the focus to explore the therapist's reactive countertransference (Clarkson 1992).

Patricia: 'Um . . . well . . . yeah . . . I must be repeating his history. My going away is like his mother going away I guess . . . [pauses, looks thoughtful] . . . I have gone away . . . I've not been present when I've been with him . . . that's just what his mother did. When she was around she took little or no interest in him!'

Supervisor: 'So, in a way you have left the relationship prematurely and yet you began by being concerned that Peter may leave prematurely?'
Patricia: 'Yes that was my projection . . . from my own history and I think I have been induced by Peter into a projective identification.'

Commentary: Projective identification is likely to occur when the client's hypnotic induction, for the therapist to respond in a particular way, locks into the therapist's own history (Cashdan 1988).

Concluding comments: Patricia has not yet reached full maturity in the development of her internal supervisor. With this particular client she has gone into script and presents as a compulsive caregiver; she is able to care but not share. She is blocked at Stern's core phase and is not able to access the intersubjective phase in this instance without the support of the supervisor. The supervisor hypothesizes that the client has touched abandonment issues, which have brought the supervisee's script into focus. In terms of Kohut's (1971, 1984) selfobject transferences, the supervisor provided both mirroring and idealizing responses, and thereby validated the supervisee's abilities and offered protection and support against the stress of script enactment.

Supervision vignette 4 – communication: verbal phase

Margaret is in her 40s and was a school teacher for 18 years, which included work with a range of special needs children and adolescents. She is in the second year of training as a psychotherapist and is currently working with three clients. She is in her own personal therapy and a member of a supervision group of four, two men and two women. This group has met on two previous occasions each for four hours. All Margaret's clients were referred to her by teaching colleagues who appear to have considerable respect for her personal and professional capabilities.

Margaret presents as intelligent and joins in thoughtfully and constructively when other members of the supervision group are working through issues. However, the supervisor has noticed that when the focus is on her own work she presents as hesitant, confused and bordering on tears. This conflicts with her normal, sociable, outgoing personality. He has also noticed difficulty in establishing a supervision contract on each of the two previous supervision sessions.

Margaret seems to have great difficulty in sharing her thinking and this becomes increasingly apparent during this session. It becomes clear that Margaret had two highly narcissistically oriented parents who gave her little or no space to express her own needs and thoughts. Instead her role in the family was to caretake her parents. Her mother appears weak and somewhat ineffectual and her father appears dominant and bombastic. Margaret seems able to tune into others' thoughts and feelings but becomes confused and frightened when the focus is on her own needs. She appears to have a classic 'don't exist' script injunction (Goulding and Goulding 1979).

In the countertransference the supervisor notices that following two previous meetings he has left feeling frustrated and he has also noticed that increasingly he has given advice. While Margaret seems appreciative of his input he recognizes that he is doing too much of the work, taking up space and is left not really knowing where she is or what she wants. Is there a parallel process with her presenting as her mother and the supervisor being pulled into the role of dominant father? He decides to work slowly with Margaret to elicit her thoughts and feelings and to confirm them. Also to use specific enquiry rather than general enquiry as the latter is more likely to promote anxiety.

Supervisor: 'Margaret, which client are you presenting today?'
Margaret: 'Claire, she's a young girl of 15 years. There's a safety concern . . .'
Supervisor: 'What do you mean?'
Margaret: 'She er sleeps around and . . . drinks heavily . . . I wonder if she might be taking drugs . . . [pause several seconds, begins to look troubled].'
Supervisor: 'How long have you been seeing Claire?'
Margaret: 'I've seen her for three sessions . . . [silence].'
Supervisor: 'What's happened in the sessions so far, what stands out for you?'
Margaret: 'She . . . recounts what she's doing in the week. She told me she slept with two men . . . and has been drinking a lot. She hates her parents, they continually "nag her". She doesn't want to hurt herself and that's why she's come . . . she's scared that she will harm herself. She self-referred, she asked an old friend of the family who is a former colleague of mine [the name of a counsellor] . . . [silence].'
Supervisor: 'What do you want from supervision Margaret?'
Margaret: 'I'm concerned that she'll . . . hurt herself . . . [silence].'
Supervisor: 'So what is it you want from me?'
Margaret: 'I'm not sure . . . she's a lovely girl . . . I think she's rebelling and she's the only one that's getting hurt [Margaret begins to look agitated].'

Commentary: As Margaret begins to share her thinking so the supervisor notices that her agitation begins to grow.

Supervisor: 'Why do you think she's rebelling in this way?'

Commentary: The supervisor seeks to confirm Margaret's thinking and asks for more specific information. He is also aware that he is beginning to work too hard.

Margaret: '. . . erm . . . her father is restricting and controlling . . . her mother is weak and unable to stand up to him. I think she's like her father, she has little respect for her mother and doesn't want to grow up to be like her.'
Supervisor: 'So why do you think her rebellion is taking this particular form of sleeping around, etc?'
Margaret: 'To punish her father [silence].'
Supervisor: 'Say some more.'
Margaret: 'It's her way of hurting him.'
Supervisor: 'Say some more.'

Commentary: In the countertransference the supervisor is feeling frustrated and working too hard. Margaret's responses are interesting and insightful but very economical. The supervisor considers two possibilities: either respectfully to challenge her by sharing his countertransferential responses: 'I'm working too hard, feeling frustrated and am wondering what's happening in the supervisory relationship.' Or the alternative is simply to recapitulate on what she has told him thus far, seek clarification, confirm her assessment and continue to enquire what she wants from supervision. The supervisor chooses to take the latter course of action being concerned that through disclosing his countertransference he would take up the space and thereby parallel the process of her parents. He also estimated that she would hear self-disclosure as criticism, that she was getting it wrong. Later the supervisor realizes that this was an error of judgement on his part, that he had been induced into 'rescuing her ineffectual mother'. This touched on his own proactive need to 'take care'.

Supervisor: Here the supervisor simply repeats and clarifies what Margaret has said so far and asks her what she requires from supervision.

Margaret: 'What I'd really like is for you to tell me what to do [deflective laughter] but I know you won't. I do need some direction I think but what stands out for me most at the moment is my fear that she'll seriously harm herself.'

Supervisor: 'I understand her behaviour is worrying you. Is that your chief concern at the moment?'

Commentary: The supervisor suspects that Margaret is somewhere in the emergent phase of development where clear boundaries are significant.

Margaret: 'Yes I'm scared for her [looks tearful]. I think she's depressed . . . [looking agitated].'

Commentary: The supervisor notices a sharp intake of breath when Margaret expresses the view that her client was depressed, confirming his notion that Margaret finds it extremely difficult to share her thinking.

Supervisor: 'I can see this is an issue of safety for your client. What have you learnt about safety issues from your training?'

Margaret: 'To up front issues of safety with the client, to assess . . . erm . . . erm [silence].'

Commentary: As Margaret is getting more in contact with her own feelings she is becoming increasingly hesitant in her responses and the supervisor is beginning to experience a repeat of the strong frustration in the countertransference. He experiences the urge to want to push her, even perhaps bully her as she becomes more hesitant. He becomes aware that in asking the supervisee to provide information without sharing his feelings in the process that he is paralleling her process of hiding and rescuing her ineffectual mother. Furthermore, Margaret is mildly paranoid in her fear and finely tuned to any perceived criticisms. Somewhere she is probably aware that the supervisor is feeling frustrated and will be interpreting this as criticism. He decides to focus on the supervisory alliance as a necessary prerequisite for any further work either in this session or in subsequent sessions. He therefore decides to disclose his countertransference response.

Supervisor: 'Margaret, as you are engaging with your feelings and beginning to share more of your thinking about your client I'm also noticing you're becoming increasingly hesitant and I am experiencing increasing frustration. I'm experiencing the urge to hurry you up. I'm also aware of a reluctance in me to share this information with you as you may experience this as me pushing you. Is your history being repeated in some way?'

Margaret: 'That's not what I really want . . . for you to hold back . . . I mean [silence].'

Supervisor: 'Is this connected with your history?'

Margaret: 'When you ask me what's going on I'm afraid you're asking me in order to criticize me.'

Supervisor: 'So what has this got to do with your history?'

Margaret: 'I was criticized a lot when I was a child, whenever I shared any need, whenever I shared my thoughts about anything. I learnt to keep quiet [Margaret is now looking tearful]. I've just begun to work on this in my therapy.'

Supervisor: 'Who criticized you Margaret?'

Margaret: 'Well sometimes my mother, most of the time she was very needy but would sometimes get exasperated and lash out at me physically, but mostly it was my father. He rarely hit me but was always intimidating. He shouted at me very loudly and humiliated me. I think my mother took her frustration with him out on me. He ruled the roost. It was necessary for me to be quiet.'

Supervisor: 'Margaret, I find it frustrating when you keep quiet, not when you're speaking. So you don't have to keep quiet with me. That's what I want from you if we are going to work effectively together.'

Margaret: [tears rolling down her cheeks, big sigh] 'That's such a relief . . .'

Supervisor: 'I guess you've always done things on your own or for other people.'

Margaret: [tears flowing down her cheeks] 'Yes, absolutely!'

Supervisor: 'I now understand more of where you're coming from. We can do it differently together?'

Margaret: 'I'd really appreciate that. This is my current work in therapy and I know that I often put my father's face on the world. Indeed I seem to permanently put my father's face on the world. Whenever I feel I'm under the microscope. I would like you to let me know when you experience me hiding from you.'

Supervisor: 'Okay Margaret I will do that, not as criticism but as information and to alert us to the possibility that one or both of your parents may be around and impeding the supervisory alliance.'

Margaret: 'Yes, that would be very helpful.'

Commentary: Margaret has now recognized her transference reactions sufficiently to see the supervisor as benign rather than malevolent and he experiences a strengthening of their working alliance. Up to this point, the focus has been on decontaminating the supervisory alliance and raising awareness of the supervisee's transferring of her critical parents onto him. The supervisor identifies important boundary issues to do with the safety of the client. It is therefore necessary now to change the focus to the client in order to model potency.

Supervisor: 'Margaret I think we now need to talk about the safety issues in what time we have left.'

Margaret: 'Yes please.'

Supervisor: 'What have you learned in the past year of your training with regard to client safety?'

Margaret: 'It's important to up front the issue, to share my concern with the client and ask clearly where she stands with regard to self-harm and harming others and to watch for congruence in her answers.'

Supervisor: 'And if you suspect your client is in danger?'

Margaret: 'Then I would contract with my client to keep herself safe between appointments, establish a support system including her commitment to her therapy. I also think she should see her GP and get medical advice and protection around her sexual activity.'

Supervisor: 'I appreciate your clarity of thinking and I would suggest that you bring this client to supervision next time.'

Commentary: The supervisor is confirming Margaret's thinking and encouraging her to continue with collaboration to counter her strong tendency to self-sufficiency.

Supervisor: 'Do you have any medical backup?'

Margaret: 'Yes I have access to a consultant psychiatrist who is very supportive of psychotherapy.'

Supervisor: 'Do you have an initial contract with the client that covers confidentiality and when breaches of confidentiality might occur?'

Margaret: 'Yes, I give all my clients a written contract which they sign and agree and this includes instances when I might breach confidentiality, particularly with regard to client safety.'

Supervisor: 'Margaret, we've got a few minutes left. I suggest that we spend them with you sharing in general terms how you intend to work with this young woman.'

Commentary: Here the supervisor is 'pushing the boat out' a little and testing the efficacy of the newly established working alliance.

Margaret: [taking a deep breath] 'Well first I want to facilitate Claire to acknowledge and possibly express in time her anger with her father in the therapy room rather than punishing him at her own expense. Second, I'd want to help her to facilitate her anger with her mother and overall I wish to support her to individuate, to separate out more from her parents and to try and discover what she wants. In all this I think I need to be more reactive. I suspect that I have been too proactive to date and have been doing too much of the work [Margaret grins somewhat sheepishly]. Perhaps as I've been getting you to do all the work with me? One of the things I need to do is to establish clear contracts with Claire. She really is a girl with a lot of potential.'

Supervisor: [pushing the boat out further] 'Is there any projection here?'

Margaret: [sheepish grin] 'Possibly.'

Supervisor: 'Margaret I think we have the beginnings of an effective supervisory alliance.'

Margaret: 'Yes, I think so too. Thank you.'

Concluding comments: In her professional life Margaret functions from a verbal phase of development as suggested by the high regard in which she is held by colleagues, which is in turn evidenced by the fact that they make referrals to her with considerable confidence. However, when under threat, for example as evoked by the new supervision group, the emergent phase of development dominates the field and she repeats the family pattern with such messages as 'don't bother to think', 'I'll do the thinking for you'. In the transference she induces frustration and advice giving and in the parallel process with her, the supervisor can get into giving advice followed by wanting to push or even bully Margaret. Her adaptation is compliance with the weak and ineffectual mother. Her quiet resistance borders on 'you can't make me' and suggests a passive resistance designed to defeat all attempts to push her around. This appears healthier than compliance but ends up with her inviting frustration and anger from others as from her father. In this way she ends up getting hurt. There's a potential parallel process with the supervisee's client, who also is attempting to get back at her father in ways that result in self-harm. The basic issue for Margaret is security, her identity is clearly with the caregiver and she loses her core self when under threat. In terms of selfobject needs the supervisor believes that there was an emerging idealizing transference.

   At the social level Margaret knows that the supervisor is honest enough to acknowledge his own reaction, that 'I'm big enough to take this', unlike her ineffectual mother. At the same time his honesty is not persecutory in contrast to her bullying father. At the psychological level the supervisor is exposing the process and confronting the repetition and thereby inviting the supervisee to 'work with him, not against him'. This is the adversarial selfobject transference, that is, giving the supervisee something to push against but with the clear message that she will not be 'beaten up' for doing so. There is also a mirroring selfobject transference with the supervisor affirming the supervisee's potential, inviting her to collaborate as an equal and modelling potency through focusing on the issue of self-harm. By the end of the supervision session the supervisee has regained a considerable amount of adult standing and is able to verbalize clearly a general treatment plan.

Educating the internal supervisor

As an integral part of our model of supervision, we believe that it is essential for the supervisor to model the educational process through their way of being, through maintaining an I'm OK – You're OK attitude to people. A collaborative approach to learning which honours the contribution of the supervisee and extends that contribution is an antidote to shame and a direct challenge to the traditional competitive and power-based educational systems. A supervisor who is willing to share of herself, willing to open herself to reciprocal communication and sustain a level of vulnerability is practising transparency and showing the model in action.

We can identify four phases in the education of the internal supervisor: (1) learning to be inclusive without losing oneself in the client; (2) learning to be fully present without losing sight of the other; (3) holding both polarities albeit tentatively and sporadically (an intermediate stage); and (4) being able to move more smoothly and consistently between self and other while simultaneously reflecting on self in relation to other and the process between. Fundamental to this development is an appreciation and understanding of the significance of the transference phenomenon. Following a theme developed earlier, we would like to decontaminate the transference; for us this means replacing a negative judgement of this process with an attitude of curiosity and excitement in what we consider a natural human dynamic. In order to live we need to breathe, to eat and drink, and to 'transfer'!

One of the biggest challenges for the supervisor is to support inexperienced supervisees to deal with their fear of getting caught up in the transference. It is an inevitable and a necessary part of relationship; a way in which the wisdom of the unconscious of the client provides an opportunity for a healing moment in the present. The supervisor will encourage supervisees to appreciate their emotional responses to the client as a treasury of information; we think of this as promoting the psychotherapist as an 'emotional barometer', which teaches the supervisee to value and respect their countertransferential reactions. This in turn sharpens their awareness and heightens their appreciation of the validity of their own responses and those of the other in the immediacy of the relationship. We facilitate in this way the supervisee's capacity for reflexive practice, based in 'critical subjectivity' (Reason 1994).

We have found that some basic education on the nature and significance of transference is essential for inexperienced supervisees and for supervisees for whom this has not been a component of their school of psychotherapy. For this purpose we have found the drama triangle (Karpman 1968) to be a helpful tool because the concepts of rescuer, persecutor and victim are easily accessible, jargon-free and people readily identify their own customary positions. This is a good platform for starting an understanding of a complex process.

Questions for further reflection

1 For the effective supervision of any relationally based psychotherapy are knowledge of both transference and countertransference indispensable?

2 Do you agree or disagree with the following statement? The supervisee learns more from the modelling of the supervisor than through any formal or informal teaching/learning activity of the supervisor.
3 Discuss the following statement. Critical subjectivity requires of the supervisor a developed capacity to practise inclusion, which in turn requires the supervisor to be emotionally literate.
4 Can you identify your growing edge as a supervisor and how you might further your professional development?

4 Creating an effective learning environment

In this chapter we consider those elements that help create an effective learning environment for the supervisee. We focus first on the importance of 'thinking therapy' and fostering a 'research mind set' in the process of acquiring the skills of the profession; in this context we look at the concept of 'change moments' in psychotherapy and in supervision. We follow this with a discussion of the detrimental effects on supervisees who have previously been submitted to a shame-based educational system. We also review different ways of considering the individual learning needs of supervisees in order to achieve optimal learning outcomes in supervision. We conclude with a section on meeting the 'selfobject' needs of supervisees at different stages in the process of their training and development.

The importance of the supervisory alliance

The creation of an optimal learning environment to enable each person to attain his goals creates a solid basis for the supervisory process. An effective supervisory alliance needs to be based in an I–Thou relational attitude (Buber 1996), described in Transactional Analysis as an I'm OK – You're OK basic life position (Berne 1966). Research quoted in Chapter 6 suggests that the essential components of an effective supervision relationship are qualities such as empathy, acceptance, flexibility, openness with confrontation, a sense of humour and appropriate self-disclosure. Clear and direct feedback that points to specific areas for improvement is valued by supervisees. Receiving only positive input or being overly exposed to criticism and negativism both appear to undermine an effective learning process. Supervisees appear to trust the supervisor who is prepared to give both the good and the bad news!

The supervision relationship is unique in that two people spend time reflecting and considering the well-being of a third person(s) whom the supervisor generally never meets directly. Although supervision involves the discussion of treatment strategies, diagnostic considerations, specific interventions, transference and countertransference responses, amongst other possible foci, supervision remains a discussion of the principles of psychotherapy as these may apply to a particular client. It is not for the supervisor to say or claim to know that a particular intervention is the 'right' one for a particular client; the discussion is about possible options, about the preferred choice of direction given the diagnostic picture or about certain theoretical considerations as these may apply to a client. Many supervisees initially have the attitude that supervision will provide them with a blueprint of how to do therapy, with a handy catalogue of 'right' and 'wrong' interventions. We encourage mistakes to be explored as potential 'miss-takes'. It appears to us that as often as not mistakes are necessary prerequisites to moving the work forward and we surmise that mistakes are born in the cradle of the unconscious waiting to grow and develop into core therapeutic themes.

It is only gradually that supervisees realize that the purpose of supervision is more to explore the general principles of good practice and reflect on how these may be applied to a particular client than about rules of right and wrong, with the consequent negative judgement that thwarts curiosity and inhibits creativity. A client's response will differ depending on the style of the therapist, the stage of therapy, his own needs and goals, to mention only a few possible considerations.

'Thinking therapy' is at the heart of good practice

The supervision relationship involves the creation of a 'play space' or a 'transitional space' in the Winnicottian sense (Winnicott 1971). In this transitional space the supervisee is able to reflect, discuss, explore and hypothesize about his client work to enable him to gain an awareness of his own and the client's process and the therapeutic interaction between them. The aim of the supervision process is to help the supervisee to 'think therapy', to apply principles to practice and in turn to let practice inform her own theoretical framework. Indeed, we believe that a supervision process, in which the supervisor takes on the role of the 'one who knows all the answers' and consequently feeds these to the supervisee, creates the kind of dependency in supervision from which the supervisee may never develop autonomous thinking and learn to trust his own judgement in a well-developed internal supervisor.

Apart from this, such an approach to therapy and supervision suggests that there is one and only one 'right' intervention into a particular client's process and ignores the multiplicity of options that may result in an effective outcome. We do not deny that there are certain interventions that may be ill-timed or downright dangerous to a particular client at a particular time; it is crucial that the psychotherapist learn to grade interventions so that the client is able to assimilate and use these in the service of growth. A sensitivity to a particular client's needs in the context of the client's history and the client's current life conditions also needs to inform the choice of intervention on the part of the psychotherapist. It is precisely the refining of judgement in these crucial instances that forms the heart of effective psychotherapy supervision.

The 'research mind set' fosters a focus on effective outcomes

We favour, both in supervision and in training, what we have termed the 'research mind set', which evaluates the effectiveness of an intervention in terms of its outcome in relation to the original intention that informed it. In this framework of thinking there are no given 'right' interventions that invariably apply to a specific set of predetermined circumstances. There are rather 'effective' interventions, 'well-timed' interventions, 'safe' or 'risky' interventions, 'creative' interventions, or some combination of these possibilities. Such an approach focuses on the outcome of the communication between two people, so the relevant questions become: Did I manage to communicate with the other person in the way that I intended to in terms of this setting? Did my intervention achieve the desired outcome or did I miss the client in some significant way? We have found that certain questions are particularly helpful in guiding the supervisee's thinking and helping her focus on the minutiae of a session to assess the effectiveness or otherwise of her interventions.

Examples of such questions follow; these can be used retrospectively in reflecting on audio or video-taped material or on a process recording of a session with the aim of tuning the supervisee's sensitivity to the outcomes of his or her choices:

- Choose an intervention you considered effective and discuss this in terms of its outcome (the client's response).
- Choose an intervention where you consider that you 'missed' the client. How do you assess this? What did you do/could you do to repair this empathic failure (Kohut 1984: 66)?
- As you reflect on this section of work, are you aware of any particular choice points?
  - Focus on one of these choice points and share your thinking at that point. What other options were you considering?
  - What led you to make this particular choice (for example, client considerations, contextual factors, diagnostic considerations, because you 'felt' it was best)?
  - Do you consider that your choice led to an effective outcome? If so, why? If not, why?
  - How does your choice of a particular intervention relate to your own theoretical orientation?

These questions are meant to guide the person's thinking and to provide a framework for reflection. We do not expect immediate answers to all of these questions! They are meant as an aid to the reflective process. Their purpose is more to assist the supervisee in developing a 'research mind set', a curiosity about his work and its possible effectiveness or non-effectiveness that will in time lead to a refining of technique and to a keener awareness of the assumptions underlying the theoretical orientation to which he adheres. What we have found in practice is that if supervisees begin to reflect on their practice in this way, they gradually sharpen their awareness of the reasons informing the choices that they make, become aware of random choices based on no clear rationale that do not further the work at all and so become more intimately tuned into their communication with clients. 'I said that because intuitively I felt that it was the right thing to do' becomes a statement worthy of analysis and reflection, rather than being accepted on some semi-mystical basis as 'it is right because I feel that it is right'!

Attunements and misattunements become clearer in this micro-analysis of the process so that supervisees become sensitized to when they are 'meeting' the other and when they are subtly or not so subtly 'missing' the other. We believe that it is important for clinicians to develop a 'research mind set' that focuses both minutely and more globally on the effectiveness of their work with clients. With regard to misattunements and 'therapeutic alliance ruptures' we draw on the research of Safran and his associates (described in Chapter 6), which has indicated that alliance ruptures fall into several distinct categories, all of which are of interest to the practising clinician.

Supervisees may be referred in the course of supervision to the kinds of interventions that experienced clinicians have found to be effective with particular clients and in particular contexts, for example 'empathic immersion' (Kohut 1984) with narcissistic personality styles, or 'communicative matching' (Masterson 1985) with borderline patterns. However, these are guidelines not rules. There is a wealth of clinical expertise that forms the wisdom of the profession and supervisees are encouraged to draw on this in the spirit of enquiry so that they can learn from the successes and failures of other clinicians. Supervisees can also draw on the wisdom and experience of the supervisor to gain insight into and develop ways of working with particular client groups. Video recordings of demonstration sessions or detailed transcripts of sessions with clients can prove invaluable as a learning resource. But such material is not to be regarded as a 'cookbook' that gives recipes to be followed without deviation! At best this 'wisdom' provides guidelines not rules.

Each client is unique and will call for an unique combination of strategies and interventions based on the mutual co-creation of that unique therapeutic relationship. We stress that communication in a particular therapeutic dyad will comply with some general principles but always is a uniquely created delicate dance between two particular individuals, who bring their own history and their own particular ways of constellating their experience (schemata) to bear on the encounter. In this sense no two therapeutic relationships are ever the same. Similar considerations apply to the supervisory relationship.

'Change moments' in psychotherapy and supervision

In our consideration of both effective psychotherapy and effective supervision we have been influenced by the research on 'change moments' and 'change events' in psychotherapy (Rice and Greenberg 1984). This body of research focuses on those sequences in therapy where both client and therapist register and agree that a change in the client's process is occurring, a deepening of awareness, an emotional and cognitive realization that leads to insight and change. Such moments are marked by changes in voice tone and inflection, by a change in speech rhythms and are reported by the client as a point of deepening realization.

At a point of internal reflection and exploration, the vocal quality of the client changes from a more externalizing quality to being more focused, which the researchers describe as a process of 'being engaged in a real exploration, a turning inward of attentional energy' (Rice and Saperia 1984: 62, cited in Rice and Greenberg 1984). This research has produced challenges for both the therapist and the supervisor in identifying what therapeutic operations actually facilitate a process of change in clients. Both this and subsequent research suggests that therapeutic change is associated with the clients' exploring their existing constructs both through emotional re-experiencing and cognitive reflection to uncover the idiosyncratic implications of their own assumptions and behaviour, from which process new options naturally flow (Safran and Greenberg 1991).

Supervision, in our experience, is likewise marked by change moments when the supervisee's frame of reference undergoes a shift that enables him to become aware of facets of the psychotherapeutic relationship in a new and enlightening manner. We are not aware of any research into the supervision process from this perspective but can see that this would be a fertile ground for further exploration. In the course of our own supervisory practice, we have begun to explore with our supervisees the moments within supervision where they experience a shift in awareness with an accompanying emotional tone. We find likewise that these moments of increased awareness and change in perception of events is accompanied by an emotional and cognitive re-examination of previously held assumptions and beliefs. These assumptions may be related to the theoretical basis of the supervisee's work or to more personal assumptions about the nature of life and reality that inform the supervisee's vision of the world. One of the tasks of the supervisor is to gently pull the supervisee beyond their current optimal level of self-support 'to enable them to boldly go where they have not gone before'. The supervisor needs to challenge with discernment so that the discomfort inevitable in change does not result in undue resistance and result in incapacitation and shame. It is important that the supervisor maintains an I–Thou attitude to the supervisee as a person and does not unwittingly objectify him by the indiscriminate use of technique.

An example from a supervision session relates to a particular intervention in which the client was saying how difficult his life was at the time and how he was struggling with several issues, to which the supervisee replied: 'Yes, life is difficult and struggles are an inevitable and unavoidable part of being human'. The suggestion that life was a difficult business may on the surface seem obviously 'true', however, the implication that this was always unavoidable militated against the possibility that the client could impact on his own circumstances in any way! When this was explored in supervision, the supervisee uncovered the origins of this belief in his own life and began to see how he did not consider alternative possibilities for himself when he experienced difficulties. He, therefore, was not alert to different choices for the client in times of crisis when these might offer themselves and did not even entertain the possibility of a change in their mutual attitudes to 'difficult' circumstances. The exploration of the supervisee's own countertransference involvement in this issue led to an opening up of possibilities both for him and for the client – a 'change moment'!

Becoming alert to change moments in supervision will support the supervisor in determining what makes for effective supervision with a particular supervisee. Enquiry into what has proved helpful will often bring to the surface such moments, for which a good supervisory alliance provides the fertile ground. Unless the supervisee is open to learning in a safe and containing environment, such realizations involving a radical shift in the frame of reference are unlikely to occur.

The core conditions that make for an effective psychotherapeutic relationship very much apply to the supervisory relationship. However, we agree with Lambert (1974, quoted in Carifio and Hess 1987) who suggests that the supervisory relationship contains less empathy and concreteness than the therapist–client relationship. We have already commented on the issue of concreteness above where we point out that supervision is an exploration of the principles of psychotherapeutic practice rather than the prescription of particular concrete interventions. We cannot see how the manualized programmes now emerging from psychotherapy outcome research can be routinely applied without damaging the integrity of the psychotherapeutic alliance.

Counteracting the effects of shame

The power base of supervision is different in several ways from the therapeutic endeavour. A supervision relationship begins with a clear imbalance of power and although this may change over time as supervisees develop their expertise and become colleagues, there remains the monitoring task in supervision, which obliges the supervisor to act as the gatekeeper of the profession. We note also the difference in the power balance between 'training supervision', where the supervisor has an assessing function in relation to the person's training and accreditation, and 'consultative supervision', where one qualified clinician is consulting with another whom he regards as more experienced, in order to enhance his work with clients. In the latter instance, there will be much more of a sense of equality than when assessment is an ongoing dimension of the relationship. The abuse of power in the supervisory relationship can lead to supervisees feeling undermined and the supervisor remaining unassailable and placing herself 'beyond criticism'.

Unfortunately, such instances are not uncommon in the field and we are therefore committed to training supervisors in becoming aware of the many nuances of the power base from which they operate and to becoming sensitive to issues of shame in their supervisees. We consider that power issues in supervision are best explored openly with supervisees and their fears and expectations brought to the surface so that they can be realistically addressed. An abuse of power in supervision can lead to shaming and undermining the confidence of supervisees in their learning.

Many of the people we have supervised have been subjected to shame-based educational situations where the focus has been on mistakes, on attaining 'perfection' and on the shame of 'not getting it right'. They have often been publicly shamed and humiliated, called 'stupid' or 'lazy' or other such epithets, which have led them to lose a belief in their own natural ability, creativity, intelligence or intuition, and in their very selves as viable human beings. This is frequently complicated by the unidentified presence of forms of dyslexia or other special learning problems, which has fed into the person's negative belief about his capacity to learn. This is the situation that may challenge the supervisor who is faced with the adult learner who has gone through years of a shame-based educational process. Such people will be hypersensitive to criticism or any comment perceived as such, so feedback will be fraught with pitfalls since the element of trust, essential to effective supervision, may not be there.

Kaufman in his exploration of shame (1992) writes of the mutuality of response that is essential to our feeling secure in a real relationship with another. 'The bond which ties two individuals together forms an *interpersonal bridge* between them' (Kaufman 1992: 13). In this process of mutuality we permit ourselves to both need and receive caring, respect and valuing from another. The interpersonal bridge is built on certain expectations of a relationship, which will be influenced by our past experience of rewarding relationships in general and of our interactions with a specific person in the present. If a significant other ridicules us and our needs, the interpersonal bridge will be broken by this rupture in the relationship. If there is sufficient trust vested in the relationship, such ruptures can be discussed and repaired. Where there is not, the shamed person may end up believing in her intrinsic 'badness', and may experience the shame as a deep injury to his sense of self especially if such experiences are repeated over time, as has happened at school and at home to many of our supervisees regarding their seeming inability to learn. A previous shaming learning experience of this kind will stand in the way of the supervisee's development in the process of supervision.

The supervisor is frequently faced with the task of helping the adult learner from a shame-based system to develop his learning in the supervisory relationship. This will require that the supervisor provide a reparative learning experience for the supervisee in the process of attending to the well-being of the clients brought for discussion. In this process the supervisor will bring to supervision a therapeutic dimension in the course of the teaching/learning process. Kaufman (1992) speaks of the importance of repairing the interpersonal bridge between the shamed person and others. What we have found important in supervision in this regard is affirmation of the person's thinking, of the person's previous training and life experience, of their contributions to the discussion regarding clients brought to supervision by other group members and an appreciation of the aspiring psychotherapist as a person. Of particular importance has been our stance that we are not looking at what is 'right' or 'wrong' in psychotherapy, in other words providing a blueprint that must be adhered to unthinkingly, but at what does or does not lead to an effective outcome.

Supervisees flourish once they are liberated from the 'right/wrong' model of learning therapy and realize that there are usually a number of possible interventions, which may all lead to effective outcomes and which are embedded in the particular client–therapist relationship and in the supervisee's orientation to therapy. Each therapist has a range of skills and abilities, different in constellation from those of his colleagues, combined with the richness of his own orientation to therapy and his special qualities as a person, which delineate him as the psychotherapist he is. We support the individual therapist to own his uniqueness and build on what he brings to the therapeutic relationship. It is the support for individual psychotherapeutic style that is one of the hallmarks of effective psychotherapy supervision and training.

Individual learning needs in supervision

We have discussed above some of the general considerations in providing an optimal learning environment in supervision; now we look at the individual learning needs that each person brings to supervision. For the supervisor a central question in this regard is this: 'What does this particular person need from me in order for me to help him or her learn?' Drawing on material discussed by Ekstein and Wallerstein (1972) on the differing ways in which people approach supervision and adding to this our own experience, we have identified several characteristic ways in which supervisees first approach the supervisor based on previous learning experiences and the manner in which they have learnt to cope with these.

We consider that people develop an image of self as learner, which is influenced by parents, teachers and others in authority and that this image will either facilitate or impede the person's subsequent learning. If learning has resulted in shame or if there has been significant educational deficit the person may learn to defend themselves against being shown up as wanting in a learning context and will approach supervision in a characteristic self-protective manner. These different styles of relating in supervision all in some way distance the supervisor since they were originally developed as a means for protecting vulnerability in shaming situations. For the supervisor, they constitute a challenge because she will need to find a way of attuning to the person and gradually winning trust to enable the openness that we consider essential to really effective supervision.

Below we describe some characteristic approaches to learning and to educational settings that we have encountered as trainers and supervisors, inspired too by the work of Ekstein and Wallerstein (1972) and Kolb *et al.* (1971) on different learning styles.

1 The prepackaging approach to supervision: 'I've got it all sewn up in advance and here is my supervision contract for today . . .'. This supervisee

comes to supervision extremely well-prepared with a very clear contract outlining his supervisory goals and his needs of the supervisor. Although on the face of it, this is a laudable approach to supervision, it may leave little or no room for the supervisor to move into new or challenging areas. Such an approach may also protect the supervisee from the ambivalence and uncertainty that goes with tolerating 'not knowing' and allowing a space for new learnings to emerge.

2 The information-flooding approach to supervision: 'You won't understand unless I give you every detail about my client...'. This supervisee produces a wealth of detail about the client and about the sessions under discussion, giving so much information that it is very difficult for the supervisor to get a perspective on the problem. The supervisor may well feel as flooded as the supervisee by the outpouring, a parallel process which may well reflect on the client's experience. In our experience, there are certain supervisees who are readily given to this way of presentation, seeming to believe that unless the supervisor has available every detail of the situation that the supervisee knows about, then the supervisor will be unable to be helpful. Teaching such supervisees to be more economical and focused in their presentation becomes one of the tasks of supervision.

3 Energetic denial of any need in the face of input from supervision: 'That is not really new to me... I'm familiar with that already... Yes, I've already tried that approach...'. Supervisees in this category experience difficulty in accepting any new material or insight from another, or even a slight change in perspective, which may be equally glanced off. In such a case it may be well worth exploring what the supervisee's internal experience is at the moment of being presented with a possible new learning and how this may threaten his self-concept and sense of self-esteem. This process may sometimes result from a person's experience of always having been expected to know what to do without adequate teaching or support. The person who has been expected to grow up too soon and to prematurely possess skills and knowledge of how to do things without being taught, may grow into the adult who assumes that he should know all about the skills and theory of psychotherapy by some magical process of osmosis. For such a supervisee one of the most liberating processes may well be the supervisor's recognition of this early learning deficit and the supervisor's readiness to assist even in details that the supervisee may believe should be self-evident to him at his stage of development in the profession.

4 The self-flagellation approach to supervision (or magnifying one's own shortcomings): 'I know I've made a mess of this session... I'll just never get it right... whatever you tell me I seem to forget as soon as I sit in front of a client...'. The person who responds to any suggestion as if this is a personal criticism and uses any and all feedback against himself is a challenge to any supervisor. The problem here is that the supervisor may move into being over-protective and take up the role of rescuer by avoiding any comment that the supervisee may construe as critical, so perhaps seeming to endorse practices about which the supervisor may indeed have reservations. In such a case, we have found it best to discuss the relational

process openly with the supervisee and find a way forward that does not effectively disempower the supervisor and prevent the supervisee's learning.

5 The approach to supervision as a personal assault: 'I know that you will criticize what I have done here . . . I think the problem is really the difference in our orientations to clients . . . I feel terrified of coming to supervision because it always ends in an argument . . .'. This person more overtly regards supervision as an attack upon self and his work with clients. Again the supervisor is being cast into a role that corresponds with some critical and attacking figure in the supervisee's internal world rather than being seen as a person in her own right. An honest contactful approach will probably work best for this supervisee so that it becomes clear that the supervisor perceives her role as potentially facilitative rather than attacking. The supervisee is responding in such an approach to supervision to an internalized figure; here a very critical and attacking other. Again it will be important to explore this dynamic and approach the supervisee authentically in the here-and-now with what you have to offer in supervision.

6 The faultfinding or 'nitpicking' approach to supervision: 'You make a good point there but I'm not sure it would apply to this particular client . . . Your input about diagnosis seems helpful although I don't entirely see its relevance here . . . Are you saying now that self-disclosure is permissible when last time you criticized my use of my own experience with a client?'. This supervisee needs to be encouraged to share his own thoughts and thinking about the client and then be supported to ask specific questions of the supervisor in areas where he wishes to receive input. Honouring the supervisee's own perspective in this way will reinforce for him that the supervisor respects and values him and his point of view, and open the person up to consider different perspectives on his work. Unqualified appreciation has neither been part of this person's experience nor does he find it easy to accept fully any offerings from other people. Generosity of thought and of spirit is a process that can be modelled by the supervisor.

7 The displacing of the problem in supervision onto the supervisor, or whose problem is it anyway? 'I certainly do not have angry feelings towards this client; are you sure that you are not angry here? I feel confident of my work with this client, but clearly you do not so feel free to share your discomfort with me.' Here the supervisee regularly focuses on the supervisor and defines any feedback or perceived criticism as related to the supervisor's own personal unworked through issues. This may indeed be accurate at times and it is important that all supervisors remain open to this possibility! However, as a defensive style this approach may ensure that the supervisee does not get to explore his own process in the therapeutic or supervisory relationships. It is possible to hypothesize that this supervisee may well have been on the receiving end of a parental process in which everything that went wrong was always regarded as his fault and he reproduces this internal process in supervision, putting the supervisor in his position as a child!

People with these approaches to learning all share a fear of exposure and an uncertainty about whether learning can be a pleasant and rewarding experience. In fact, careful consideration of these common styles suggests that they all share one or more of Nathanson's four points on the 'compass of shame', which he describes as withdrawal, avoidance, attack self or attack other (Nathanson 1992: 312). They constitute challenges to the supervisor who will need to empathize with the supervisee's reluctance and develop an understanding of the educational trauma or deficit that may underlie these defensive (or protective) manoeuvres. Sometimes a brief exploration of the original shame-inducing educational experience may benefit the supervisee who is then able to see how the present situation may differ from those in the past.

An understanding of the supervisee's core interpersonal schema related to learning may also be of assistance here. The core interpersonal schema (Beitman 1992) comprises the experience of self in relation to significant others connected by a strong emotional component. In adverse learning environments this frequently develops as follows: 'I am stupid/inadequate, the other person knows it all' and this belief is accompanied by shame and distress. Such a core learning schema may well prevent the person from admitting to gaps in learning and experience and identifying accurate learning needs for fear of being shown up as wanting.

The best form of reparation for such a supervisee is to establish a learning contract with the supervisor 'to ask any questions that I want to even if I think that the question is too elementary or stupid or relates to something that I have covered in training and therefore should know...'. Such a contract can be extremely liberating especially as the questions asked often do not have very obvious answers: 'What did Berne really mean by an ego state?' or 'I still have difficulty in understanding the exact nature of unconscious processes?' or 'When is self-disclosure harmful?' or as one of the authors was once asked: 'Why does talking help?' The resulting discussion in a supervision group may reveal that these are questions which other participants are regarding with similar difficulty and uncertainty. They are often also the questions that still form the heart of professional discussions in conferences on psychotherapy and it can be extremely healing for the supervisee to realize that he is by no means alone in his struggle with these seminal issues. What he may have been regarding as 'stupid' may turn out to be a profoundly challenging debate in the area of psychotherapy about which there is no certainty, only points of view from different theoretical perspectives.

The core learning schema will shape the person's expectations of subsequent events and lead him to protect himself in characteristic ways, as illustrated in the above examples. Where shame is the connecting emotion the person has often concluded that he is basically flawed or wrong as a person, a situation for which there appears no redress except to hide. Other people are usually perceived as critical, perfect in what they do, having prior knowledge that gives them an advantage and an ability to solve any problem. In such a process the person will have no faith in his own capacities, intelligence, creativity or effectiveness.

In supervision (and in training) the task will be to help the person begin to honour what he already does well and does not account for, and also to identify his areas of growth and deficit so that he can set realistic goals for himself. A shame-based person will tend to exaggerate defects and minimize strengths. What is vital for the supervisor is to remain reality based; not to over-emphasize and overplay strengths nor to underplay weaknesses, so that the person ends up with a realistic assessment of his points for development. This is a challenge for any supervisor because there is always the temptation to 'shore' up the person's weak self-concept by an over-emphasis on what is well done to the detriment of giving a well-balanced assessment of the work. The writers have experience of supervisees emerging from such falsely posit-ive supervision relationships feeling good about themselves and believing that they are expert at what they do with little objective evidence for this position and not actually having learnt much from the process of psycho-therapy supervision that would benefit their clients.

Kolb et al. *provide another perspective on styles of optimal learning*

Much has been written on individual differences in learning styles that can be of benefit to the supervisory process. A respect for each person's own individual approach to learning marks a central value underpinning our approach to supervision. In this regard we have found of great value the work of Kolb and his colleagues (1971) whose research into learning pro-cesses suggested that there was a characteristic learning cycle which was the hallmark of effective learning. This cycle moves from the concrete experi-ence of a new concept, to a stage of reflecting on and observing this process, which in turn leads to the construction of relevant abstract concepts from which hypotheses can be derived and put into practice (Kolb *et al.* 1971). In this way a person gains new experiences that can be integrated into his existing repertoire of behaviours.

If we apply this learning cycle to supervision, with regard to one of its main goals – the acquisition of new therapeutic skills by the supervisee, then we may see the following learning process. The supervisee may focus on a particular interaction with a client that led to a therapeutic impasse and in supervision try out a number of different options to test out their viability. His own knowledge of the client combined with feedback from the super-visor and other group members may facilitate the stage of reflective observa-tion. These observations may then be discussed and related to theory about psychotherapy, about development or about diagnosis to yield a new work-ing hypothesis for the supervisee to take back to the next session with his client. This hypothesis can be employed to generate a new range of options in the therapy room that may open up the work with the client in a more creative manner.

Here is an example from supervisory practice to illustrate this process. A supervisee whose training is in Gestalt therapy brought to supervision the problem that when he focused his observations on his client's body language in an attempt to increase his client's awareness of his body process, for example by saying 'I notice that you are making a fist with your right hand as you tell me of this incident', the client would either become silent and withdraw or apologize saying 'I'm sorry, I didn't mean to upset you', indicating that the remark was heard as critical not in the atmosphere of creative exploration that was intended by the therapist. When this problem was brought to supervision, the supervisee and the supervisor reflected on other responses to the clenched fist, from simply observing it and 'storing away the information' at this stage to perhaps asking a less directed question like: 'what are you experiencing as you recall this incident?' The supervisor, at the stage of reflective observation, wondered whether the client came from a place of deep shame so that being 'seen' by the supervisee was experienced as painful and the observation about the clenched fist could possibly carry the sense of 'being caught out in something that was not acceptable to a significant other'. His responses to the therapist's explorations of his body process seemed to evoke a defensive (protective) reaction. These observations led to the formulation of a hypothesis that the client probably came from a shame-based system and consequently that a gentler process of enquiry and empathic responsiveness would be more appropriate at this stage of therapy in preference to interventions that the client might possibly experience as 'exposing' and showing him up in front of the therapist. In employing this new approach to the client, the therapist reported that the client had relaxed and was gradually revealing how severely he had been shamed at home and subsequently teased and bullied at boarding school from an early age particularly as regards his appearance.

Kolb *et al.* (1971) found that different people tended to emphasize different aspects of the learning cycle in their own process of learning. This led to the discovery that not all effective learners learn in the same way! People combine these processes in different ways to produce several characteristic learning styles, which may all lead to effective outcomes. For the supervisor to identify the learning style of supervisees can therefore be of great assistance in the process of making supervision both more effective and more economical.

The researchers identify two main learning styles, which share opposite strengths. The 'convergent' learner relies mostly on abstract conceptualization and active experimentation. Such a person can move from conceptual hypotheses, from an overall appreciation at a theoretical level, straight into active experimentation. This person needs an intellectual map first, from which then to generate action. A supervisee who operates in this way, will be keen to engage in abstract discussion of relevant theory first and then from that basis derive a plan of action with a client. Such a supervisee will derive great benefit from literature in the field that describes a desired treatment direction for a particular category of client and will have no difficulty in moving from the general principle to the application of a procedure in the therapy with a particular client. Asking this supervisee to role-play or demonstrate their skills in vivo would not be helpful at a beginning stage of exploration. As the person gradually builds up confidence as a practitioner, he will be more ready to develop those aspects of the learning cycle that are underplayed in his style of learning.

The 'divergent' learner has the opposite strengths. Such a supervisee will be able to look at the actual work with the client, at his concrete experience with the person from many different perspectives and so reflect meaningfully on his observations. A supervisee who stresses concrete experience and reflective observation in this way, would benefit from an activity such as role-playing in supervision. From role-playing the client or the psychotherapist, the supervisee will gain a sense of different possible options which then provide the material for observation as to their differential impact on the client, leading to reflection on new possible interventions. A premature discussion of psychotherapeutic theory may prove quite unhelpful to such a supervisee. This will need to follow at a later stage as the person strengthens the opposite qualities in his learning pattern (Kolb *et al.* 1971). Identifying the individual learning style of the supervisee, whether by using the system described above or by employing other resources in this area, can open up supervision and create a more effective learning environment that takes into account individual differences.

Stages of development in the evolution of the supervisee

In the process of learning the art and craft of psychotherapy, we see the adult learner moving through three main stages of development. At first the person is very much tied into his past learning experiences, the introjected 'others' and the attitudes that have formed the dialogues of his internal world. The tendency will be to project onto the supervisor the internal critic from the supervisee's own intrapsychic world and then to respond to the supervisor as if she is one and the same. The novice supervisee and clinician will tend to assess their work from the vantage points of their own earlier introjected messages (you are no good unless your work is perfect; you will pay dearly for any mistakes you make; you must do this the right way; you are not working/trying hard enough for your client; you're too stupid to do this job). We have sometimes asked the supervisee whose voice they hear as they say a particular phrase to themselves, a typical response being: 'Ms K, my mathematics teacher in high school'. 'What knowledge did Ms K have about the process of therapy?' 'Well none really; she was against shrinks and all they stand for, which she told us more than once.' 'So why are you using her as an authority on your work as a psychotherapist?' 'Well that's a good point. Perhaps I need to look elsewhere for a good judge of my clinical work!'

As the trainee/supervisee gradually settles into supervision and into his work with clients and begins to develop more confidence, he moves into the second stage where he internalizes the supervisor and uses her voice to direct his internal dialogue concerning his client work. Casement speaks of the 'internalized supervisor' as a stage in the development towards autonomous thinking (Casement 1985). At this stage, the supervisee will give a great deal of weight to the words of the supervisor and sometimes introject these unedited and translate very literally what the supervisor states as a general principle. 'But last time you said that self-disclosure interferes with the transference relationship, and now you are suggesting it', or 'But you said never to do any two-chair work with a borderline client', and so on. Gradually the supervisee will learn to think in terms of psychotherapeutic principles and how to evaluate the interventions he makes in terms of the client, the problem, the context, the stage and quality of the therapeutic relationship and the particular dyadic relationship he has co-created with this client.

In the final stages of training and development, the supervisee will gradually develop his own 'internal supervisor' (Casement 1985), which in our thinking involves the capacity for inclusion and a multi-perspectival view of reality. Now supervisees will check out their thinking with the supervisor and engage in consultative supervision on a collaborative basis. A good internal supervisor is well informed about the practise and the principles guiding the practice of psychotherapy. Such an internal supervisor is also able to assess accurately the effectiveness or otherwise of interventions and of the course of therapy, and make appropriate adjustments in the process. The sign of a good internal supervisor is also marked by the capacity to acknowledge and review 'mistakes' and learn from ineffective practices or sloppy work in order to refine therapeutic style.

Selfobject needs manifest in supervision

As discussed above, people emerging from shame-based systems have experienced severe injuries to the sense of self, often experiencing the self as having been wiped out or annihilated. This 'wiping out of the self' is likely to be re-evoked by subsequent similar occurrences. However, even in the course of an ordinary 'good enough' childhood and a sound educational experience in a supportive environment, most of us will still have experienced some lack in confirmation of our needs for self-affirmation. Self-psychology, developed by Kohut and his followers, provides us with an interesting model for analysing selfobject needs, which we have also found of assistance in understanding the needs that surface in supervision. What is of relevance to the therapeutic relationship in terms of selfobject needs may be of equal relevance to the supervisory relationship particularly in a training context.

Kohut (1971, 1984), in dealing with narcissistic patients noticed that these people tended to treat him as if he were an extension of themselves, not as a person in his own right. An infant requires of the caregiver to attend to his needs and by the process of mirroring to attune to his psychological and emotional well-being. This provision of sensitive attunement by the caretaker is essential for the child's healthy development. The child gradually learns to perform these functions for himself through what Kohut referred to as 'transmuting internalization' (Kohut 1984). Where there is an early failure in empathic responsiveness to the child, we may later get an adult with a deficit in infantile selfobject needs, which manifests in current relationships.

Essentially the selfobject experience represents an internal experience for the child of being met and understood in significant areas of need. As a person develops a sense of self, the selfobject experiences provided by significant others assist the person in developing a healthy sense of self based in acceptance and affirmation. Kohut considered that the need for selfobject experiences continued into adulthood as mature selfobject needs; that we continue to need others to affirm and support our sense of self and to provide this function for us. Kohut identified different types of selfobject or relational needs: the mirroring need, the idealizing need and the need for twinship (Kohut 1971, 1984). These have subsequently been added to and extended, significantly by the addition of the adversarial selfobject need (Wolf 1988), which reflects the person's need to engage in confrontation with a benevolent and resilient other.

Tolpin (1997) says of the mirroring need: 'The child self actively seeks out and expects an alive, bright-eyed, engaged (mirroring) parent to whom he says "Look at me and admire and applaud me and what I can do".' This reflects the child's need for acceptance and appreciation and will manifest in the supervisee as a need for accurate appreciation and confirmation of both his skills and his very being. There is also a part of the child self that needs to look up to an admired (idealized) parent and to experience self as enhanced by the other: 'You're great, what you are and what you do is great; you belong to me, I belong to you, therefore I'm great too' (Tolpin op.cit.). This will manifest in supervision by a tendency to admire and sometimes idealize the supervisor for a period of time. The supervisor may need to learn to tolerate some part of this idealization in the process of gradually assisting the supervisee to learn and to develop his own competence. This we see as related to the mentoring role that the supervisor fills for the beginner or advanced supervisee who often uses the supervisor as a role model in the process of professional development.

Tolpin also describes a part of the child self that 'looks for and expects alikeness, belonging, and kindred spirit experiences – twinship/alterego experiences' so that the child is confirmed in a sense of being acceptable and like the other (Tolpin 1997). Supervisees will seek twinship experiences in supervision both from the supervisor and from other members of the group. Here the supervisee needs a sense that his experiences are not odd or bizarre, that he is like other human beings in his responses. This need is often supplied powerfully by his peers when they identify with his experience and share similar experiences of their own. The supervisee manifests selfobject needs in the process of developing skills in clinical practice, and it is often to the supervisor that he will look to serve these selfobject functions. In this sense, we consider that supervision may well serve a reparative function for the person as he gradually learns the art of the profession.

Where these needs to be enjoyed, admired and confirmed in our sense of who we are have been adequately met in childhood we develop in tandem a balance of the five senses of self described by Stern: the emergent self; the core self; the intersubjective self; the verbal self; and the narrative self. These five senses of self develop concurrently and serve as the foundation for the self-concept. We see the emergence of selfobject needs as they pertain to self-development as much in supervision as in psychotherapy.

Basch (1991) correlates the three different selfobject needs first defined by Kohut with the different stages of self-development identified by Stern (1985). He considers that these selfobject transferences follow a developmental sequence. During the emergent phase, he considers that the basis for kinship is laid down and leads to 'the later unspoken conviction that one belongs to humanity generally, and to one's particular subgroups specifically'

(Basch 1991). He considers that idealization is related to the development of the core self when the child internalizes and develops ways of accommodating to others around him. The child has the experience of being helped by an adult who has superior knowledge and power; this process lays the foundation for subsequent idealization of other significant people in the child's life. During the development of the subjective self, the process of mirroring is particularly in focus for the child at this stage is looking for the validation of his subjective experience (Basch 1991).

We can see the validity of what Basch is describing here, and how the attention to this hierarchy of development may be of relevance to the development of supervisees over time. Sharing this sequence with supervisees has at times liberated them to perceive these needs as 'normal' rather than pathological and so freed them up to use supervision fully to support their individual growth. However, any sequential model of this kind is usually limited in that many of these needs and phases may overlap in any particular person's experience and presentation, as has been our experience in supervision.

Given the nature of our lives, it seems inevitable that supervisees will have some deficit in the area of childhood selfobject needs and that these archaic needs will manifest in the supervisory relationship. If the deficit is not too great and the person does have a reasonably well-based sense of self, then it is possible for the supervisor to respond to and contain these needs within the supervisory brief. Where the person has an extremely fragmented sense of self, then it becomes an ethical question about whether such a person can take others into their care before he has been through a reparative process in psychotherapy.

Mature selfobject needs continue to find expression in supervision

Any normally well-functioning adult will continue to have selfobject needs into adulthood, which is currently argued by many authors in the field of self-psychology, so that the manifestation of these needs should not be equated with a developmental deficit but be regarded as part of normal adult functioning. Most would see as a hallmark of maturity a capacity to recognize the other as an independent person, yet simultaneously as a source for supporting the self-image of the person. In the process of development the child gradually learns to experience the other as a separate person, whilst also developing his own sense of subjectivity. We consider this to be at the heart of inclusion and the attaining of a third-person perspective, the capacity to be aware of oneself, of the other and of the relationship between the two. Kohut describes a gradual process for the person of moving from 'the self relying for its nutriment on archaic modes of contact' to an 'ability to be sustained most of the time by the empathic resonance that emanates from the selfobjects of adult life' (Kohut 1984: 70).

Hagman (1997) takes the position that mature selfobject experiences comprise a number of adult needs that are met in our relationships with others, whether in friendships, partnerships, work relationships, and, we would add, the teaching and learning relationship. These mature selfobject needs include: the experience of relationship; mature confidence; flexibility of function; personal agency; other recognition; the experience of reciprocity; the capacity to be empathic; self-transformation; and altruism (Hagman 1997). These dimensions could well be used to delineate an effective supervisory alliance.

We will look at each of these needs briefly in the context of the supervision process. The need for relationship underlines the importance of a good supervisory alliance, which will provide the framework for a person's development of confidence in himself as a practising clinician. Mature confidence in the self of the practitioner means that the person can tolerate uncertainty, can accept the feelings of a client without collapsing or losing ground, and can deal with the occasions when support and affirmation from others may not be immediately available. Flexibility of function in clinical practice means being able to use creatively the encouragement and positive strokes that are available to support the sense of self. The mature person is able to secure support in a range of ways and can depend on his own ability to obtain the recognition from others that is essential for his effective functioning. The capacity to recognize others as separate and different, with selfobject needs of their own is characteristic of mature relating; which will lead a person to reciprocate based on an understanding of the other's needs. The capacity to be empathic is a baseline for any successful relating and is one of the cornerstones of the process of inclusion. Becoming a psychotherapist involves a process of transformation, of developing in ways that are surprising and different. Altruism develops naturally from the process of inclusion and includes self and other interest: 'in instances of altruism, offering a selfobject experience to another functions as a selfobject experience for the self' (Hagman 1997: 96). These capacities all relate to an overall goal in supervision, which is to facilitate the supervisee's capacity for effective relating and for viewing his work with clients from a variety of perspectives so that he can make effective choices that take account of the multiplicity of factors operating in the interactional field.

Questions for further reflection

1 What do you consider may be some of the detrimental effects for the adult learner who has had prior experience of a shame-based educational environment?
2 How might you take individual learning needs of supervisees into account in the delivery of supervision?
3 What models have you found useful in considering the developmental stages that supervisees go through in the course of training?
4 Do you espouse the concept of 'mature selfobject needs'? How do you think psychotherapists in the profession can get these needs met in an ongoing way in order not to damage their clients?

5 ▷ The supervision frame: contracting and boundaries in supervision; styles and modes of psychotherapy supervision

In this chapter we discuss the contractual process as an essential component in effective supervision, stressing the importance of renegotiating and recontracting in the course of supervision. Three-cornered contracts affecting those who work in organizations are presented in relation to the concepts of psychological distance and power in such complex contexts. We follow this with an overview of the two different traditions that have influenced the development of supervisory practice in the United Kingdom. We refer briefly to different modes of supervision and to the importance of communicating to new supervisees the 'menu' for supervision. Finally we look at the supervisor's task of containing anxiety through the supervision process.

Good contracting forms a basis for effective supervision

Contracting is central to a relational model of supervision. We define contracting as an agreement between the supervisor and the supervisee about the goal(s) of supervision. In the contract the two participants focus on an agreed outcome for the supervision, which then gives a shape to the particular supervision session and defines the task for the supervisor. This is a process that stresses mutuality and is very much at the heart of a supervisory relationship that is co-constructed by the participants. Some people find the term contract too formal and prefer the concept of 'an agreed focus or goal' for the supervisory process. Supervision contracts can relate to one session of supervision or even to a part of a session or can be a longer-term contract for an agreed period of time.

In our practice we combine these two forms of contracting, so that sessional contracts are made in the context of an overall contract for supervision. We generally make longer-term contracts for a year at a time with agreed growth goals for that year. These are reviewed at the end of that time when it is also decided whether to renew the contract or not. We do not assume that people will automatically continue in a supervision relationship year after year. We believe that it is possible for a supervisory pair to settle into a comfortable and cosy place where most things are predictable so that little room for challenge remains. We regularly discuss with our supervisees how the supervision process is working for them and for us mutually to consider whether a change may not be important and aid growth.

It is also important to recognize that different supervisors have very different skills and areas of interest, which may suit a supervisee better at a particular point in his development. In training we encourage supervisees to consider a change of supervisor after the first two years so that they can experience a different approach to theoretical integration and to clinical thinking and a different style of being in the world. This is to provide supervisees with contrasts so that they can see that there is not only one way of being a psychotherapist or a supervisor. We have seen trainees benefit greatly from being in contact with different trainers and supervisors who provide them with a variety of models for practice. This variety both prevents them from assuming that there is only one way, for example, to be an integrative psychotherapist and also takes into account that different people will gel better with one another. It is simplistic to assume that all trainers and all supervisors will get on equally well with everyone!

In our model of integrative relational supervision, we consider the development and welfare of the supervisee as of equal importance to the welfare of his clients. We see as our responsibility the safety, growth and development of both partners in the psychotherapeutic relationship. Although we accept that the primary purpose of supervision may be stated as the welfare of clients, we cannot see how this goal can be achieved without an equal stress on the welfare of the psychotherapist, which will intimately affect his work with clients. The professional development of the supervisee therefore becomes an essential overarching goal of supervision alongside the concern for clients. We generally make clear to our supervisees that alongside client material and issues to do with their specific psychotherapeutic work, any matter that relates to or impinges on their professional life has a place in supervision. This opens up the supervisory space for the supervisee to bring concerns about his broader development as a psychotherapist.

As a result of this more open focus, we have known supervisees feel free to bring, for instance, their doubts about whether being a psychotherapist at all is the correct professional decision for them. We consider that this vital discussion is well placed in supervision and is important to clarify for the welfare of all concerned. If the space is there for a frank discussion then the supervisee and the supervisor will be able to sort out whether this is a temporary uncertainty due to a loss of confidence or whether it is a more deep-seated doubt about a professional choice. As one supervisee said, who subsequently moved into a different area of work: 'I can now see that I was attracted to therapy training because I really needed to sort out my own personal issue about compulsively caring for others in need. Now that I am clearer about an equal responsibility to myself, it seems as if much of the energy has gone out of my work as a therapist. I am now not sure any longer that this is how I want to spend my working life.'

We believe very strongly that people need the space to make these decisions in a supported place so that any changes that they make can be implemented in an ethical manner for the welfare of the clients and do not result from an importunate decision that rebounds on the clients in their care. In the above case, the closure of this supervisee's practice was carefully planned over a period of time during which he either finished appropriately with clients or carefully facilitated their transfer to another psychotherapist.

Renegotiation and recontracting

Although we very much favour the setting of a contract at the outset of supervision, we do not believe that this needs to be set in stone and agreed to no matter what emerges in the session or in the course of the year. Supervision contracts are subject to regular reviews and can be mutually renegotiated at any point in time when their relevance is thrown into question. A contract is not necessarily agreed on the moment the supervision session starts; it usually follows a period in which the supervisee outlines the problem and gives some of the relevant material about the client. A contract does not arrive fully formed but grows out of discussion and exploration, unless the supervisee has already done much of this work in a self-supervision process in advance of the session. In our experience, as supervisees become more experienced and are developing an effective and well-informed internal supervisor, they may generally come to supervision with a more clearly developed idea of what they wish to gain from the process. Such experienced supervisees have learnt what can be gained from supervision and know how to use the process. The more inexperienced supervisees may come with a more general or unformed request because they have not yet learnt how to make best use of supervision.

A contract needs to serve a containing function for the supervisory process so that the key issues in the supervision can be focused on and explored in a creative manner. If the contract becomes irrelevant or constricting, then the time has come for renegotiation. We consider that the supervisor has a responsibility to monitor this process. The primary purpose of the contract is to ensure that the supervision does not meander all over the place or become an interesting debate unrelated to clinical work or a comfortable chat about the vicissitudes of therapy, which does not subsequently relate back to the work with the client. The contract also helps to avoid supervision from developing into a psychological game (Berne 1964) in which the two protagonists engage in a discussion that has a covert agenda that undermines an effective process and prevents a satisfactory outcome.

A common example of a game in supervision revolves around the 'Why don't you, yes but...' dynamic so well described by Berne (op.cit). The supervisee brings a problem to supervision and asks for the supervisor's 'advice'. The supervisor makes suggestion after suggestion to which the supervisee replies 'I've tried that, but . . .' or 'That sounds like a good idea but I don't think it will work with this client because . . .' and so on and so on. The supervisor would be well advised to stop after the second suggestion has been blocked in this way and instead explore the relationship process between herself and the supervisee!

Process contracts support a healthy supervisory alliance

We have so far discussed contracts that are focused on the outcome desired by the supervisee in relation to the particular client material. However, we also consider it important that in a relational model of supervision where the emphasis is on the co-creation of the relationship, there is also a process contract that focuses on the maintenance of the supervisory alliance. For supervision to be effective, the alliance between the supervisor and the supervisee needs to be in good shape. The relational process contract involves an agreement to bring to the surface any issues that may be standing in the way of such an alliance. This may initially be a very general agreement to share any concerns, discomforts or fantasies that are impeding progress.

A contract of this type helps to create the trusting atmosphere that frees the supervisee to bring real concerns to supervision rather than concerns manufactured for the purpose of satisfying imagined requirements. Gradually this relational process contract may become more focused with each supervisee as the relationship unfolds and specific areas of difficulty are uncovered. For example, a supervisor and a supervisee may agree to stop and explore the process any time either of them begins to feel that it has become 'sticky' and that communication is not flowing smoothly. Such an agreement will have emerged from their experience together and will only work if the 'sticky' behaviours are clearly understood and recognized by both of them. Another process contract that we as supervisors have now had with several supervisees is an agreement that it is fine for the supervisee to ask any question no matter how simplistic it may seem to him, especially where the person has not experienced this freedom in a previous educational setting. The supervisor's side of this agreement is to answer the questions clearly and carefully without shaming the supervisee.

Relational contracts may also be initiated by the supervisor. For example, for us as supervisors it is important to clear the way to being open and frank about the work that is being brought to supervision without wounding the supervisee. We have found it best to articulate this dilemma very clearly to supervisees and agree a way to give feedback, especially the 'bad news' that is both open and compassionate and takes the individual's personality style into consideration. For supervisors one of the biggest challenges is to achieve a supervisory relationship characterized by an I–Thou attitude in which the supervisee feels free to bring real problems and concerns to supervision and in which we as supervisors feel free to be frank in our responses. We also make clear early on in our supervisory relationship that our monitoring role requires us to be alert to any areas of potential difficulty; that part of our task is to ensure safe practice. In sharing the challenges of our role with the supervisee in this way, we have generally found a steadily growing process of openness and frank sharing emerging in the course of supervision. Supervisees also in this process begin to learn what ensures effective and safe practice and how to take the necessary precautions to ensure their clients' safety and their own.

Kohlreiser in a workshop in 1984 stressed the importance of 'contact before contract', which very much picks up on our philosophy of the primacy of the supervisory relationship as the container for learning. What this phrase conveys to us is the crucial importance of establishing good contact with the supervisee before proceeding to focus on goals. We see this as important in every supervision session so that it is our common practice to have a 'check-in' period both in individual or in group supervision to renew contact with the supervisee(s) and establish the relational ground for supervision to progress. The premature establishment of a contract may foreclose on this free exchange and not allow the supervisory pair the space to 'settle into' the supervision session before getting down to the task before them. This principle also means to us that the relationship is primary and needs to be attended to first so that any work that is done can take place in an unimpeded zone. Here too we wish to mention our commitment to the contractual process as an important component of any relationship, and therefore as central to both psychotherapy and supervision.

The contractual process as a key to good relating

So far we have been discussing contracting as a point in time where a goal is agreed and then the supervisor proceeds to work with the supervisee on the completion of this goal. However, we also see the contractual process as the method through which these goals are achieved. This in effect means that the supervisor will make mini-contracts with the supervisee as the work unfolds to ensure that the process is meeting the supervisee's needs. Examples may be: 'Do you want to explore the problem formulation here?', or 'Do you want me to say more about Masterson's concept of communicative matching?', or 'Where are you now with an answer to your supervision question: are you satisfied or do you still have something that remains unanswered?', or 'What are you making of this piece of feedback on your intervention; do we need to take a pause for you to share your reflections and feelings with me?' In this manner the supervisor can determine in an ongoing way how the supervision is progressing and take stock regularly concerning the supervisee's responses and needs. The supervisee is also invited to enter into this contractual process in an ongoing way in the interests of keeping the process clear and ensuring that he does not receive material and input that is not useful to him. We consider a contractual process of this kind respectful and mutually enhancing of a co-created process. It is very much in the spirit of an I–Thou dialogue where both participants share responsibility for ensuring that the process between them is what they desire.

Such a contractual approach to relationship makes for a more equal sharing of power in any relationship and gives the supervisee, in this instance,
the power to change the direction of the supervision at any point in the
process. We believe that this goes some way towards alleviating certain
imbalances that are inevitable in an hierarchical relationship such as the
supervisor–supervisee relationship. It makes the process of supervision more
of a shared endeavour, and militates against a process where one person 'does
to' another at worst, or at least feeds another 'food' that they do not want
or need! We find that the contractual process as the basis of relationship
supports collaboration and mutuality of endeavour and is as relevant to
psychotherapy as to supervision. Indeed we believe that the contractual
process is central to any effective communication in supervision, in psychotherapy and in life outside!

The three-cornered contract: working in organizations

Contracting in an organizational context presents special challenges. We
have found the concept of the three-cornered contract (English 1975) to be
extremely useful. This applies to any supervisees who work in organizational
settings, whether in the National Health Service, voluntary services, psychotherapy departments, GP surgeries, student counselling services, or businesses
as workplace counsellors. Here there is always a three-cornered contract as described by English: an agreement between psychotherapist and client; between
psychotherapist and organization; and between client and organization.

In such a complicated picture there is much room for misunderstandings
and various unrealistic expectations that may have been raised in the client
by the contracting organization or sometimes by the psychotherapist delivering the service. The organization that is paying for the service may also
put pressure on the psychotherapist to produce results of a particular kind,
for example to assist the client 'in getting back to work as soon as possible'
even where this is clearly unrealistic. We alert supervisees in these contexts
to check carefully all three corners of the contract to ensure that they are
apprised of the various existing agreements that may potentially influence
the psychotherapeutic relationship. Clarity in this regard can act as a pre-
ventative measure.

Adding the concept of psychological distance and power

Micholt (1992) has expanded on English's original article in a fascinating
and eminently useful manner by adding the concept of perceived psychological distance/closeness to the equation. She demonstrates how the three-
cornered contract can become unbalanced and lead to conflict and to
psychological games that undermine the effectiveness of the psychotherapist's interventions. We reproduce here, with her permission, the four possibilities that she describes, starting from the psychologically healthy position
and proceeding to the three problematic and unbalanced situations. We shall

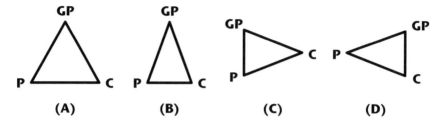

Figure 5.1 Psychological distance in the three-cornered contract.
GP = General practice; P = Psychotherapist; C = Client

comment briefly on each of these with examples. We wish to remind the reader here of Holloway's (1995) discussion of engagement and power in the supervisory relationship, since we see that what is operating here is an imbalance of power in the three 'unhealthy' examples, which can play straight into organizational conflict. We are relating our discussion to a general practice setting but it could equally apply to any organizational context.

In the first example (5.1 A), the distance between all parties is equal and 'the contracts and expectations are clear on all sides' (Micholt 1992). In this case the contracts have probably been very clearly specified and worked through in advance with input from all parties and to the satisfaction of all involved. In such a process of clarification, it is vitally important that any embedded fantasies, expectations and needs have been brought to the surface and explored in order to achieve contracts that are clear and behaviourally specified to all. In a GP practice, for example, the psychotherapist is encouraged to clarify his contract not only with the practice manager but also with all the GPs from whom he may receive referrals. Issues of confidentiality, of reporting, of supervision and of payment need to be clarified, *inter alia*. The therapist will then need to make a very clear contract with his clients concerning similar matters (confidentiality, reports, etc.) so that the client knows just where he stands in relation to him and to the practice that is paying for the service, and in relation to his referring GP. With trainee psychotherapists we are increasingly experiencing the advantage of the supervisor meeting briefly with the practice, particularly where this is an outside supervisor, in order to clarify her role in the process and to support the trainee in his placement. In such cases, of course, we are really dealing with a four-cornered contract; and indeed more corners than that may be added if we consider the role of the training organization in this process as well. We think that this example amply points to the complexity that can exist as soon as more than two people are involved in the contracting process.

In part (B) of Figure 5.1, the situation is complicated by the greater psychological distance between the therapeutic pair and the organization. Here the therapist and client may experience closeness and a sense of achievement but they may both feel some isolation from the organizational powers. From our supervisory experience, we note another example from work in a GP practice. In this instance, the psychotherapist was left 'to get on with his work' with very little consultation or support. He valued what he termed the 'lack of interference' at first, but gradually began to experience the lack of discussion as a problem, which also led him to feel undervalued as 'though once clients are passed on to me, they can forget about them'. This was not a productive relationship for any of the people involved and the supervisee was encouraged in supervision to request a meeting with the practice manager and the referring GPs to talk about his work, his position in the team and to give feedback from the audit he had done on his work over the past year. This intervention proved very productive and resulted in closer collaboration and consequently a more effective service delivery. The supervisee also began to experience a growth in confidence and self-worth as he became an increasingly valued member of the team.

In part (C), the therapist and the organizers may share a close affiliation but the client feels at a greater distance from both. In such a case it is unlikely that the client will easily trust the psychotherapist with his problems. This situation could arise in a workplace counselling context where managers refer people for counselling 'in order to improve your communication skills' or to 'deal with your depression'. The client may well experience the managers and the psychotherapist in a collusive alliance, with him being very much the victim of the situation. Where a person feels that all the powers are ranged against him, he is unlikely to feel open and trusting of therapy. The growing number of Employee Assistance Programmes that are external to organizations and provide a counselling service that is independent of management suggest that in-house counselling may be fraught with contractual difficulties unless the confidentiality of the process is scrupulously respected and people can freely choose to attend or not. Even then the perceived power base may still adversely affect the trust invested in the service.

In part (D), the psychotherapist may be out on a limb, whilst the 'organizer' and the client have a closer alliance. We have seen this happen as well in a GP practice setting where the prospective client is very close to her GP and only attends the therapy sessions in order to satisfy him. In this example, the client was split between the GP whom she saw as benevolent, warm and wise and the psychotherapist who was perceived as cold, withholding and ungenerous with advice: 'You just sit there waiting for me to talk . . .'. The therapist then put much effort into clarifying the contract with the client and dealing with the relational expectations and the nature of psychotherapy. For the longer-term success of his work in the practice, he approached the referring GPs for a meeting in which he clarified with them the type of client problems he was most likely to have success with, as well as requesting that patients be referred only if counselling was an option they desired or were at least willing 'to give a try'.

In all these cases, the clarification of all 'corners' of the contract was the most effective long-term intervention. Increasingly, we are aware that the assumption that a psychotherapist can work in isolation is a myth; we are all embedded in our contexts and everything we do impacts on the environment in which we live. McLeod (1999) suggests that the person approaching a counsellor comes because he is experiencing himself as an outsider in his social context; as not able to communicate his inner experience to the people around him. 'The task of the counsellor is to help the person to rejoin the human conversation' (McLeod 1999).

The supervisor contracts too . . .

Clear contracting is as important to the supervisor as it is to the super-visee. As we have gained experience as supervisors, we have also refined our needs as supervisors. The question we ask of ourselves is this: What do I as a supervisor require of my supervisees in order to do my job competently? We have focused on what we need to support ourselves in order to be effective in our task of overseeing the welfare of the supervisee and the supervisee's clients. We now regularly ask our supervisees to provide us with a compre-hensive list of their caseload (the caseload overview) that they will be bring-ing to us for supervision and then we ask for a regular review of progress with all these clients every couple of supervision sessions so that we are fully in the picture as regards the supervisee's clinical practice.

This process has proved a good discipline to both supervisor and supervisee. It keeps the supervisor well informed of the scope and developments in the practice and provides for the supervisee a regular reviewing arena for all his clients, including those that would be rarely brought to supervision because they are 'not presenting problems'. It can also lead to discussions about general themes or trends that emerge. For one person, for example, a review of this kind led him to conclude that he had taken on a number of clients with serious personality difficulties who were very demanding of his time and energy: 'No wonder I have been feeling so tired at the end of the working week. It is not the number of clients but the level of challenge that I have been dealing with that has tired me.' In this session he and the supervisor agreed to monitor his workload very carefully especially in relation to new clients that he may be taking on in relation to their presenting problems.

The other requirement that we make of supervisees is that we see them regularly and that cancelled appointments are rescheduled if possible so that we can maintain a sense of continuity with their work. These contractual requirements have grown out of certain experiences where we have not felt well enough informed to continue to render an effective service. We our-selves feel supported in our work by these arrangements. However, to some extent we would make a distinction here between training and consultative supervision. It is especially as regards trainees that we make these requests. However, where we do undertake regular consultative supervision, we have found a similar procedure remarkably helpful and often enlightening.

Two different traditions influence presentation in supervision

Clear and explicit contracting negotiated within an atmosphere of mutuality and grounded in a sound supervisory alliance provides the container for effective supervision. We now turn our attention to the format of supervision, to the styles and modes in which supervision may take place. Psychotherapy supervision in the United Kingdom is influenced by two major traditions in the world of counselling and psychotherapy teaching. From the psychoanalytic tradition with its origins in Europe, we have inherited an emphasis in supervision on the transference dynamics of the client as these manifest in the psychotherapeutic relationship. In this tradition, supervision has been focused on the transference manifestations, on the client's intrapsychic dynamics as enacted in the psychotherapeutic relationship and on an exploration of these in relation to the client's early experience. Traditionally, presentation in supervision has been in the form of 'case consultation' and the bringing of detailed handwritten case notes to support the discussion. In earlier years the psychotherapist's countertransference would have been considered solely in the light of its interference with the analytic process.

The more recent emphasis on the countertransference as a valuable source of information for the psychotherapist has meant that an exploration of this dimension is now regularly regarded as contributing to a direction for the psychotherapy and forms a central focus in supervision. The emphasis in this tradition has, therefore, been very much on the manifestation of the transference in the psychotherapeutic relationship as this reflects the internal dynamics of the client, and only more recently has a creative focus on the countertransference been added to the field of supervision. With the primary emphasis on these aspects, it makes sense that the psychotherapist's experience both of the transference and of the countertransference would become the main focus of supervision. This would focus very much on the psychotherapist's report of his experience of the therapy process.

The second major tradition that has influenced psychotherapy supervision in the United Kingdom comes from counsellor education, originally particularly from the pioneering work of Carl Rogers and now widely developed by many experts in both the United States and in the United Kingdom. Much of interest concerning counsellor education and supervision has emerged from research into the essential components of both counselling and supervision, particularly in the United States. With a strong basis in research, it is not surprising that we have gained from this tradition an emphasis on the directly observable elements of the psychotherapeutic relationship. In this tradition of counsellor education, the main emphasis has been on developing the counsellor's skills base, in teaching the counsellor the necessary skills to provide the core conditions for the counselling relationship and in refining skills of intervention, strategy and technique.

Supervision in counsellor education has focused heavily on the acquisition of the requisite skills base for effective counselling. In this tradition, supervision has been regarded as primarily educational in intent and has focused on skills development and refinement. For this reason, the supervisor has sought direct access to what is actually happening in the counselling session, either by the use of audio or video material, or by the use of one-way mirrors that give direct access to the counselling session. The assumption here is that the supervisor needs to know what actually transpired in the session without this being filtered through the memory of the psychotherapist who will inevitably add his own emphasis to what he recalls. By definition he is not going to be aware of his own 'blind spots' and will therefore not be able to render an 'accurate' account. By having access to the session material directly, the supervisor can listen for nuances of tone, possibly observe body language and with the supervisee assess the impact of interventions on the client.

This detailed process analysis allows for the teaching and refining of skills and the widening of the psychotherapist's repertoire. The focus on skills development relates to the view that the psychotherapist was learning the craft of therapy. This tradition carries a very different learning emphasis from the one outlined above, since it carries very little focus on the psychotherapist's internal process or on the client's transference manifestations. The influence of the work of Rogers can be very strongly felt here with his emphasis on those qualities that contribute to a good therapeutic relationship. Rogers *et al.* conducted some of the first research into therapeutic outcomes, and the development of measures such as the empathy scale demonstrate the observational base of their work (Rogers 1951, 1963; Truax and Carkhuff 1967).

The development of models of supervision in this tradition has very much focused on the elements of the process of supervision as these have emerged from relevant research in the field (Holloway 1987, 1995). The stress on research results and on the educational aims of supervision are two strands that we as supervisors in the United Kingdom have drawn on from this tradition. In this educational approach to supervision, it was customary for supervisors to have direct access to the material from sessions, by audio- or video-tape or by way of the one-way mirror. In some cases, where the trainee was an apprentice to an experienced therapist in a group therapy context, the 'supervisor' had direct access in person to the work of the psychotherapist.

Presentation in supervision was, therefore, very different in this tradition. Psychotherapists in training would expect to bring either video- or audio-tapes of their work to supervision for a micro-analysis of skills and for a macro-overview of the psychotherapeutic alliance. These would be supplemented by detailed information about the client and the client's history and presenting problem(s). The focus would be on learning the art and craft of psychotherapy. Role-playing might also be used as a way of practising and learning new skills; the therapist could take on either his own role or that of the client and 'try out' a range of different interventions and assess their impact on the other. The aim would be to teach a set of skills that relate to a particular theoretical base and/or client problem.

We see that both these traditions have had an influence not only on the goal-setting but also on the mode of presentation for supervision in this country where these two sets of expectations interface with one another and frequently clash. Supervisors from the first tradition would usually not countenance the use of audio-taping since they would consider this an interference in the holding capacity of the psychotherapeutic relationship, an intrusion into the therapeutic space. Supervisors more influenced by the second tradition would welcome direct access to the session by audio- or video-tape so that they could focus with the supervisee on the actual interactions between psychotherapist and client.

Interestingly, Kagan's Interpersonal Process Recall method of supervision, emerging from the educational field in the USA offers a possible interface between the two traditions (Kagan 1980). Kagan would ask supervisees to bring audio- or video-tapes of their work, which the supervisee would then 'take charge of' by stopping the tape where he wished to initiate a discussion. Kagan would then assist in an enquiry to help the supervisee recall and so explore what he was experiencing at that point in the session. Such a process recall is likely to bring to the surface the psychotherapist's countertransference feelings, his thoughts about the process, his rationale behind the choice of intervention and in this way facilitate the psychotherapist in extending his awareness of his own process and his choice points in the psychotherapy process. The advantage of this method of supervision is that it honours and respects the psychotherapist's right to focus where he feels the need, and this attitude of respect is combined with a detailed exploration of his internal process as a psychotherapist and his evaluation of the work with the client. We very much appreciate the richness of this method and have found its focus on critical choice points in psychotherapy a rich addition to our work as trainers and supervisors.

In our integrative relational approach to supervision, we seek to combine the richness from both these traditions, as we see others, like Hawkins and Shohet (2000), doing in their choice of the seven possible foci for supervision. A combining of the respective emphasis on the transference and countertransference dimensions with the emphasis on the importance of developing a skills base and acquiring the relational skills to establish a good therapeutic alliance leads almost inevitably to a focus on the intersubjective nature of the therapeutic relationship. Such an interactional focus can embrace the richness of both these traditions within a two-person perspective on psychotherapy.

A further consequence of this integration of traditions is that we would welcome a variety of presentations in supervision ranging from case notes to audio- and video-tapes to the supervisee seeking to explore a countertransference issue, since any aspect of the psychotherapeutic relationship or the skills and knowledge base of the supervisee could become the focus of supervision. This broadening of the range of possible foci in supervision is welcomed, since all these components contribute to effective psychotherapy. Effective supervision within this model can take place in several formats: individual, group or peer supervision.

Individual, group and peer supervision all have their place

Individual, group and peer supervision are all a regular part of our experience; and each of these has advantages and strengths. All three can provide an effective forum for an integrative relational approach to the supervision. Individual supervision provides a private and protected space for the supervisee to explore vulnerabilities and areas of sensitivity, which he may find difficult to raise in a group setting. There is also the advantage of being able to move at his own pace and to explore areas of clinical practice about which he has gaps or may experience fears because of his own particular background experience. For someone who has always had to share space and attention with others at home or in a learning environment, individual supervision may provide a reparative experience in the present when receiving the full attention of the 'teacher'. We have noticed how supervisees will gradually bring to individual supervision those issues about which they feel shame and fear inadequacy.

Group supervision, on the other hand, involves the creation of a mini learning community in which members can benefit from the accumulated wisdom of the group. Each supervision group develops its own culture and idiosyncratic ways of organizing the process, which will be shaped by the needs and the personalities of its members. We have noticed definite stages that supervision groups appear to move through, mirroring in some way the individual development of the 'internal supervisor' discussed in a previous chapter. In the beginning stage, there is a dependence on the supervisor's leadership and wisdom; the supervisor does the supervising and the group will listen and make some comments here and there or give feedback at the end of the process. At this stage, people will still be depending on what they believe is the 'right' thing to do and will be taking in the supervisor's words in this vein. The supervisor's task will be to facilitate and encourage contributions from the group members to engage their increased participation in the group. We have found it really helpful at this stage to honour the diversity of knowledge and experience that each member brings to the group and to encourage people to share this with others present. We make a point of welcoming these contributions and integrate them into the ongoing life of the group.

Gradually as each member starts internalizing the supervisor, they will begin to join in more but generally in the initial stages only mirroring the kinds of things that the supervisor himself may do or say with maybe the beginning of risking their own experience and insights. As the supervisor continues to support the contributions of group members and actively encourages them to share their own observations and intuitions, there is a shift in the process and the group members take a larger part in the proceedings. Group members are now at the stage where they are developing and refining their own internal map of psychotherapy and are willing to participate more fully and confidently in the supervision process. As this stage gains in strength, the supervisor is there more as a facilitator of the process, an almost equal participant much of the time, then able to take a back seat as the group functions as a vibrant and active learning community. At this stage, the participants may be taking a more active role in the professional community as a whole by presenting at conferences and bringing to supervision papers they are preparing for publication. The challenge for the supervisor throughout this development will be the task of providing a good holding environment and of modelling a supervisory stance that does not shirk confrontation, yet avoids demeaning and denigrating members.

Peer supervision provides a very different experience, supplying what has been referred to as the need for twinship (Kohut 1984). Peer supervision is an important adjunct to other forms of supervision and we actively encourage the setting up of peer pairings or groups as people begin to advance in their training and have gained sufficient knowledge of the process of psychotherapy to be in a position to contribute helpfully to others. A particular advantage of peer supervision is that there is no hierarchical structure and the power is more evenly distributed amongst the members (two or more). During training, the peer group offers an additional space for discussion of client material and of theoretical and clinical issues in a more general way. Support can be gained from this group through the sometimes taxing and always challenging training process. Participants will, of course, need to be alert to the possibility of collusion, but then this is equally a possibility in any supervision format. It may be helpful for a peer group to periodically employ an outside consultant to monitor the process and keep the group on task. After qualification, peer group supervision may also form an important part in a psychotherapist's support system. We have found that once people no longer have the support of an ongoing training group, gaining sufficient professional support becomes a challenge and a necessity. Peer supervision can provide some of this support, since a peer will be experiencing many similar stresses, joys and challenges. We have come to regard regular contact of this kind as essential to the well-being of a psychotherapist in the demanding professional climate in which we all operate.

What is on the supervision menu?

What is on the menu for supervision? Several writers in the field have given useful maps for this. Hawkins and Shohet's 'seven eyes of supervision' provide a series of foci ranging from the supervisor's countertransference to the client's presentation and the dynamics of the therapeutic relationship (Hawkins and Shohet 2000). Holloway (1995) provides a range of 'supervision tasks', which include case conceptualization, professional role and self-evaluation *inter alia*. Clarkson and Gilbert (1991) supply 'bands of supervision'; their list includes a focus on ethical issues, theoretical input and diagnostics.

In our integrative relational model of supervision, which embodies the concept of co-creation of relationship, any focus taken in supervision will be viewed from an intersubjective perspective in that the contributions of both participants will be taken into account in understanding the process between them. We are also acutely aware of the embeddedness of any psychotherapeutic or supervisory relationship in its context, which a supervisor needs to keep in focus to gain a comprehensive understanding of a problem. If a particular focus is taken in supervision it is possible through that emphasis to give the impression that this is the 'source' of the problem; hence the critical importance of retaining an intersubjective perspective on the process and a focus on multi-causality. Indeed, the supervisor's meta-perspective on the psychotherapeutic endeavour and the supervisor's capacity for inclusion will contribute vitally to the success of supervision. We could refer to this as a 'systems competence' on the part of the supervisor!

The containment of anxiety in supervision

In the complex process of supervision one of the primary overriding tasks of the supervisor will be the containment of anxiety; her own, that of the supervisee, that of the client and to some extent that of others in the wider context. The new supervisor is particularly prone to anxiety and tends to respond to her inner state by wishing to take immediate action, often without sufficient reflection, in a perceived crisis. This could be equally said of the newly qualified psychotherapist. This is where we see the role of the supervisor or the supervisor of supervision as critically important. In this position it is our task to listen carefully and assist the psychotherapist or the supervisor to assess the degree of 'danger' or the exact nature of the 'crisis' in order to take effective action. We make the point that breaking the psychotherapeutic frame needs to be a carefully considered action based on clear ethical thinking, and not simply undertaken as an immediate means of reducing anxiety.

We encourage and commend therapists and supervisors to seek supervisory support in cases of concern so that they are able to reflect alongside another who is outside of the situation on the parameters of their current crisis. We have become meticulously careful about any action that is based on vague information and paranoid fantasies, not borne out by the clinical or supervisory material at hand. From our clinical experience we know only too well how people can escalate their own anxiety through foreseeing imagined catastrophes that exacerbate and colour their perception of a situation.

The converse, however, also needs to be noted. Sometimes it is the supervisor who registers the appropriate anxiety and concern in a situation when the psychotherapist is not fully taking this into account. Where a psychotherapist is working in a context where many of his clients manifest a high level of acting out, of violent behaviour and of anti-social traits, the psychotherapist may begin to discount the significance of such signals and accept these as a 'normal' part of his everyday working life. In such a case, it will fall to the supervisor to account for the impact of the context on him and his work and insist that he take the necessary precautions to ensure his safety and that of his clients. This constitutes a serious responsibility for the supervisor whose judgement is involved in assessing risk and advising appropriate precautions.

Questions for further reflection

1 Do you consider that the contractual process promotes or inhibits the effectiveness of supervision?
2 Discuss any experiences that you have had with handling a three-cornered contract? Are there any steps you could have taken to support yourself better in this process?
3 What do you consider may be the advantages and disadvantages of group supervision?
4 Draw up a supervision 'menu' for prospective supervisees. What items on the menu do you consider may be most important for psychotherapists in training?

6 Theoretical and research foundations for an integrative relational approach to supervision

The integrative relational model of supervision meets the challenge of a multi-perspectival and cross-orientation approach to client problems. In this chapter we discuss the relevant theoretical and contemporary research foundations that underpin this essentially flexible approach to supervision. Particular emphasis is given to the research supporting the primacy of the relationship as a vehicle for psychotherapeutic change and the necessity of an effective supervisory alliance. Research findings in developmental theory further support our integrative model. The chapter concludes with a discussion of the importance of contextual factors and the contribution of field theory and constructivism to the model.

Why an integrative relationship-based model of supervision?

The integrative approach to supervision has gradually evolved from our interest in psychotherapy integration and from our study of the results of psychotherapy outcome research. In the wider field of psychotherapy there is a growing interest in combining approaches or elements of approaches that are compatible and mutually enriching. Clinicians are increasingly concerned with the challenge that was put by Beutler to the profession: 'What therapy activities are most appropriate for what type of problem, by which therapist, for what kind of client?' (Beutler 1983). We would add to this 'in what context', since we believe that contextual variables will intimately colour the therapeutic alliance and have a far-reaching influence on outcomes in psychotherapy.

Beutler's incisive challenge to psychotherapists remains at the heart of much of the integrative endeavour and covers one of the essential themes of the research related to integration. Many psychotherapists are moving away from applying one particular approach to all clients irrespective of presenting problems, but rather they are looking at what is most effective with a particular client group or with a particular client at a particular stage of therapy. This is probably one of the main challenges facing us as psychotherapists as we move into the new century: how can we best serve the interests of each individual client within the broader context of the psychotherapeutic relationship? This approach to client care calls for a flexible model of supervision that can deal with the challenge of a multi-perspective and cross-orientation approach to client problems.

With so many clinicians showing an interest in integration, it seems appropriate to look at supervision from an integrative perspective. Roth and Fonagy evaluated the particular approaches that are effective with certain symptom pictures and declared: 'Ultimately, theoretical orientations will have to be integrated, since they are all approximate models of the same phenomenon: the human mind in distress' (1996: 12). They do not consider this appropriate at present since they think such a process of integration would create confusion. They continue to say that their objection does not 'apply to the desirability of integration at the level of technique' (Roth and Fonagy 1996: 12). We consider otherwise. Processes of integration are occurring and have been growing in strength over the past 20 years.

First, there is a considerable body of outcome research into various approaches to integration as a process and into common factors that would appear to contribute to psychotherapeutic change. Researchers are identifying generic factors that appear to occur across different orientations to therapy (Lambert, cited in Norcross and Goldfried 1992). Second, there now exist many separate models of integration that involve a combination of one or more approaches, *inter alia* Cognitive-Analytic Therapy (Ryle 1990) and Dialectical-Behavior Therapy (Linehan 1993). Third, a growing number of practitioners currently define themselves as integrative as a result of a gradual process of assimilation from orientations other than their own in the course of their clinical practice. It would appear that as they gain in experience, many psychotherapists begin to range more widely into other orientations in order to find more effective models and tools for working with certain clients.

The Fiedler study in the 1950s first drew attention to the growing similarities between experienced practitioners from different orientations as they become immersed in their clinical practice. Fiedler showed that there are greater similarities between experienced clinicians from different orientations than between beginners and advanced clinicians of the same orientation (Fiedler 1950). This suggests that the practising clinician becomes more flexible in his approach as his experience increases and he turns to other approaches for assistance and insight. In a sense, this integration is born out of clinical necessity as the psychotherapist in his daily work looks for what will help his clients rather than for what is theoretically or technically 'pure'. This does not occur only at the level of technique or strategy but often involves a theoretical integration across modalities as well. An interesting example of such a theoretical (and strategic) integration is to be seen in the recent development in self-psychology in the United States. Self-psychology combines psychoanalytic and humanistic concepts and techniques derived from the evolution of empathy into a new system of psychotherapy that is particularly effective with clients who manifest narcissistic disorders of the self (Kohut 1984).

In our experience many supervisors will either be supervising psychotherapists who regard themselves as integrative (or eclectic), or will be called on to supervise across theoretical orientations, particularly in voluntary or in health care settings. In both of these cases, a model of supervision that focuses on commonalities between approaches and on an understanding of the essentials of the psychotherapeutic and supervisory processes shared by several orientations will serve as a support for supervisors. The integrative relational model stresses the relational context in which effective supervision can take place, as well as providing a way of conceptualizing the overall aims of supervision on a process level. Such an approach to supervision needs not negate the critical differences between different approaches; rather, with its emphasis on the essentials of the supervisory and psychotherapeutic relationships, it will provide a medium for dialogue across approaches.

Supervision as a process has commonalities that span different approaches to psychotherapy since it has now taken on its identity as a discipline in its own right. A relational approach based in outcome research can provide a model that is integrative in spirit and in practice. We align ourselves here with the initiative in outcome research that aims to find a common language for communication between clinicians. Some of this recent research into a common language for psychotherapy has proved of particular assistance in developing a way of communicating about client dynamics that picks up on central psychological insights and is not tied to any specific orientation to psychotherapy. For example, Goldfried (1995) has provided a 'common language' for formulating clinical problems that transcends any particular orientation to psychotherapy and uses simple language to describe client dynamics. Material of this kind can be readily assimilated into an integrative supervision process.

In Chapter 2 we presented an integrative approach to supervision which is based in psychotherapy outcome research that suggests that the therapeutic relationship is the primary vehicle for therapeutic change. In this chapter, we therefore survey different aspects of the outcome research in psychotherapy, research into supervision and into related fields (for example, developmental studies and memory research) that have supported us in the development of our model. Since our model is based on the premise of the primacy of the therapeutic relationship as the main underlying 'given' for effective outcomes in psychotherapy, we look first at this aspect. This is followed with a review of relevant research findings regarding supervision, the current research in developmental psychology and concludes with reference to relevant research into the nature of memory that supports our model of supervision. We then contextualize the model in field theory, intersubjectivity theory and constuctivism.

The relationship as a vehicle for therapeutic change

In a summary of outcome research Lambert points out that 30 per cent of improvement in psychotherapy patients can be attributed to common factors, which include 'a host of variables that are found in a variety of therapies regardless of the therapist's theoretical orientation such as empathy, warmth, acceptance, encouragement of risk taking etc.' (Lambert 1992, cited in Norcross and Goldfried 1992: 97). He maintains that these common factors produce a collaborative working alliance in which the client gradually builds up increased trust and a sense of safety, along with a diminishment of anxiety and threat. This leads to 'changes in conceptualizing his or her problems and ultimately in acting differently by refacing fears, taking risks, and working through problems in interpersonal relationships' (Lambert op.cit.: 104). Orlinsky, Grawe and Parks in an impressive summary of outcome research over the past two decades report in their survey of communicative contact between therapist and client that 'therapist empathic understanding' shows a significant positive association with outcome in 54 per cent of the research studies investigated and none of the findings are negative with regard to this variable (cited in Bergin and Garfield 1994: 326). Horvath and Greenberg, in evaluating psychotherapy outcome research over the past five decades, likewise point out that research results suggest 'that different therapies produce comparable outcomes despite differences in premises, different assumptions about the etiology of human dysfunction, and different techniques' (1994: 1). For this reason, they stress the crucial importance of an effective working alliance between client and therapist.

The importance of a good psychotherapeutic relationship as the basis for change has also been supported from research emanating from another rather unusual source. The US *Consumer Reports*, in November 1995, published the results of a survey into consumers' attitudes to therapy to which Professor Martin Seligman was the consultant. In an article entitled 'Mental health: Does therapy help?' they have the following to say about the therapeutic relationship: 'Once in treatment, those who formed a real partnership with their therapist – by being open, even with painful subjects, and by working on issues between sessions – were more likely to progress.' Their advice to potential consumers of therapy: 'When you look for a therapist, competence and personal chemistry should be your priorities' (*Consumer Reports* 1995: 739).

Since diverse treatments can produce effective results and no treatment can claim superiority over another except in a few circumscribed areas, interest has gradually shifted to the nature of the relationship between psychotherapist and client as the significant factor in the change process. Horvath and Greenberg point out that current findings suggest that the therapeutic alliance is 'a common factor to all forms of treatment' and 'that the quality of the working alliance in the initial stages of treatment is predictive of a significant portion of the final outcome variance' (1994: 2). In their discussion of the working alliance in psychotherapy they stress the crucial importance of collaboration. 'At the core of the current formulation of the alliance is the notion of *collaboration*' (op.cit.: 1, original italics). Horvath and Greenberg (1994) go on to discuss the quality of such an alliance in which the psychotherapist and client join together to confront their 'common foe' in the client's problems. In the process of building a working alliance, the psychotherapist can simultaneously attend to the establishment of the therapeutic alliance and focus on the client's relational issues and difficulties. 'A unique feature of the alliance concept is that it integrates the relational and technical aspects of treatment into an overarching model of the therapeutic working alliance . . . The emphasis on these two features – the *interactive* nature of the relationship and the *integration* of the technical and relational aspects – sets the alliance apart from other relationship constructs' (op.cit.: 2).

Our approach to supervision follows this definition of the working alliance. We consider that the supervisory alliance incorporates these same two dimensions, the relational and the technical; the first referring to the supervisor's relational skills, the latter to the tasks undertaken in the supervision process. We are the first to agree that sometimes these overlap, and that they always interact with one another in any supervisory process, for good or for ill. Some supervisory tasks such as the evaluative and monitoring tasks (Carroll 1996) could not, in our view, be effectively discharged without a pre-existing firm supervisory alliance.

Hans Strupp likewise considered the psychotherapeutic relationship as the basic framework for therapeutic change in all psychotherapeutic modalities. He emphasized four crucial dimensions: (1) that the therapist possess facilitative qualities like those of a good parent; (2) that the therapeutic relationship resemble a parent–child relationship in which the client will seek to gratify a powerful parent; (3) that this relationship will enable the normal developmental processes of learning to unfold; and (4) that the success of the new learning will depend on 'preexisting patient qualities that permit at least a beginning level of trust and openness' (Strupp, cited in Horvath and Greenberg 1994: 54). His analogy of the therapist–client relationship as similar in certain ways to the parent–child relationship we would accept as being one important dimension of both the psychotherapeutic and the supervisory relationships. We agree that both psychotherapeutic and supervisory relationships often include a reparative dimension that heals in the present the deficits of the past. However, this parent–child analogy may lead to an exclusive focus on the early developmental dimension, which can result in a simplistic and reductionistic view of both psychotherapy and supervision and lead to what has been referred to by Mitchell (1988) as the 'developmental tilt' in theory and practice. In such a view all relational needs may be characterized as infantile and 'their persistence in later life is often regarded as a residue of infantilism, rather than as an expression of basic relational needs' (Mitchell 1988: 134).

This view needs to be carefully counterbalanced by accounting for the significance of other contributing factors in the client's experience, past and present. Humanistic psychotherapies and self-psychology in particular have emphasized that relational needs span the lifetime; we do not outgrow the need for relationship. As mature adults we seek relationship to enhance our lives and continue to need feedback from others to support a healthy sense of self. This mature need for confirmation and engagement in relationship will form an essential dimension of any supervisory relationship, which provides not only technical support to the supervisee but also affirmation of that person's being in the world. In addition, the client may have been subjected to trauma or catastrophe, which has had a far-reaching effect on his life and in the treatment of which a developmental hypothesis may prove inadequate but will need to be supplemented by information from other fields such as the contemporary research into the neurological implications of trauma (van der Kolk *et al.* 1996).

Research into the supervisory alliance

We have summarized some aspects of the research into the importance of a good psychotherapeutic relationship pertaining to effective outcomes in therapy to underline the reasons behind our choice of an integrative relational approach to both psychotherapy and supervision. We now look at some of the research relating to the supervisory alliance.

There has been a proliferation of developmental models of supervision, which aim to relate effectiveness in supervision to responding appropriately to the developmental level of the supervisee. However, Holloway (1987), in a survey of developmental models of supervision, concludes that the quality of the supervisory relationship may well be the more crucial variable that contributes to changes in the trainee in supervision from the initial stages of their development to the point where they reach a stage of independence. Holloway and Allstetter Neufeldt (1995), reporting on research conducted into supervisor characteristics by Carey, Williams and Wells in 1988, point out that the researchers found that trustworthiness of the supervisor was significantly related to trainees' performance in their counselling. This is supported by Carifio and Hess in a survey of research into supervision where they draw the conclusion that research findings suggest that the ideal supervisor 'is a person who shows respect, empathy, genuineness, concreteness and self-disclosure in his or her dealings with supervisees' (Carifio and Hess 1987: 245). Leddick and Dye in their survey of research into trainee preferences regarding supervisors draw the following conclusions: 'trainees expect to be treated as individuals, with keen awareness by the supervisor of sex roles, cultural, educational, and professional backgrounds' (Leddick and Dye 1987: 149). They add that 'trainees seem to want their supervisors to be wonderful people but in highly idiosyncratic ways' (op.cit.: 130). Carroll's research suggests not only that the supervisory alliance is central to effective supervision but also that the supervisor needs to be flexible in the use of different roles in supervision. He states in summary 'effective supervision is characterized by flexibility across roles' (Carroll 1996: 56). In our view, these research findings, which emphasize the importance of the supervisory alliance, point the way to a relationally based model for supervision.

Lesser (1983) recommends a 'collaborative–coparticipant model' of supervision in which both the supervisor and supervisee are open to one another's observation. 'In being observed, the supervisor offers the supervisee the experience of the supervisor's willingness to be self-aware and genuinely responsive to the supervisee's observations, even in the face of potential anxieties. This may well encourage the supervisee to do the same' (Lesser 1983: 127). This challenging position involves the supervisor in a shared endeavour with the supervisee in which both people are open to learning from the other and supervision becomes a co-creation. This stance accords well with the theoretical model we are presenting in this book, which we describe as *'supervision as co-creation of relationship and the shared negotiation of meaning'*.

Research into negative supervision experiences suggests that people may be seeking (but not necessarily finding) a mutual relationship in which both parties are engaged in a collaborative endeavour. Rosenblatt and Mayer listed the following as unsatisfactory forms of supervision: constrictive supervision; amorphous supervision; unsupportive supervision; and therapeutic supervision (quoted in Albott 1984: 33). In the constrictive type there is limited autonomy, there are strictures on certain techniques and innovation is frowned upon; the amorphous type involves too little supervisory input, a *laissez faire* attitude to the supervisory process; unsupportive supervisors are aloof and distant and supervisees would not readily approach them with their difficulties; whereas therapeutic supervision turns the supervisee into a 'patient' and the supervisor takes on the role of the therapist often in an invasive and intrusive manner, which infantilizes the supervisee. Students found this style of supervision the most objectionable (Albott 1984).

These findings led us to envisage effective supervision as a warm collaborative supervisory alliance in which the supervisor provides expert guidance, whilst fostering the growth of the supervisee. Supervisees favour a style of supervision that fosters their autonomy and is challenging them to extend their skills and knowledge, yet is at the same time warmly supportive and interactive. The situation where the supervisor takes on the role of psychotherapist in a unilateral decision and defines the supervisee as the 'problem' to be analysed suggests an abuse of power that may well undermine the person's self-confidence and create an unhealthy dependence on the supervisor.

Conflict resolution in supervision: a central issue

In establishing and maintaining an effective supervisory 'working alliance' the question of conflict resolution is of paramount importance. Moskowitz and Rupert (1983) in a research project on this subject identified three major types of conflict that emerge in supervision: (1) conflicts primarily due to differences between supervisor and trainee in theoretical orientation; (2) conflicts related to the supervisor's style of supervision; and (3) conflicts related to a personality clash between supervisor and trainee. Their research with a trainee population indicated that in most cases these conflicts were discussed and resolved, which resulted in a more productive supervisory alliance. Trainees were quite clear that they preferred conflicts to be addressed directly in supervision though it was their preference that the discussion be initiated by the supervisor (Moskowitz and Rupert 1983). Of particular interest is one of their conclusions that interactions were ineffective when 'supervisors ascribed the problem solely to the trainee rather than considering their own contribution to the conflict' (Moskowitz and Rupert 1983). This underlines the importance of supervision as a co-operative endeavour in which differences can be mutually negotiated and resolved.

Related research into the working alliance in psychotherapeutic relationships is also of interest here. Jeremy Safran and his colleagues have done research into therapeutic alliance ruptures, which they consider a transtheoretical phenomenon. We agree with this position and see the value in their findings as these may also be relevant to ruptures in the supervisory alliance (Safran 1993; Safran *et al.* 1994). Safran (1993) suggests that there are other terms in the literature to describe a rupture for example 'therapeutic alliance breach, miscommunication, misunderstanding, misattunement, tear in the alliance, misencounter' (Safran 1993: 34); he also sees it as analogous with Kohut's term 'empathic failure'. In line with an intersubjective perspective, he stresses the interactional nature of the phenomenon in that both parties contribute to the rupture.

The research conducted by Safran and his collaborators focused on the characteristics of therapeutic alliance ruptures and explored the factors involved in the resolution and non-resolution of such ruptures. Safran (1993) describes three types of ruptures that were identified in the analysis of therapeutic dialogue. First, the client misperceives what the therapist says in line with the client's own way of construing events; that is, the person interprets the response to fit his own core interpersonal schema or basic mind set concerning relationships. For example, the person may experience as threatening an intervention, which by most other people would be experienced as facilitative. For example, in the supervision context the supervisee experiences as critical and devaluing a supervisor's enquiry about what aspects of theory informed the person's choice of a particular psychotherapeutic strategy.

Second, the therapist participates in a 'dysfunctional cognitive-interpersonal cycle' that is part of the client's characteristic way of operating in relationships. In this instance the therapist and the client are caught up in 'a vicious cycle' of miscommunication (Goldfried 1995) or in what would be termed a 'game' in transactional analysis (Berne 1961). Such a cycle of interaction has a self-perpetuating, repetitive quality about it and tends to reinforce the person's own negative evaluation of self. For example, in the supervision context the supervisor is 'hooked into' a pattern of constantly 'reassuring' a supervisee about the adequacy of his performance, but the supervisee is never satisfied, nor it appears is likely to be.

Third, the therapist refuses to participate in such a negative dysfunctional pattern and in effect refuses the 'invitation' to enter the game. The person may feel misunderstood because he is not receiving the usual 'expected' response that fits in with his core interpersonal schema. For example, in the supervision context the supervisor does not accept the invitation to yet again make one suggestion after the other, which is rejected by the supervisee with a 'yes, but . . .', as the supervisee finds fault with each succeeding idea. The supervisee may then experience the supervisor as 'unhelpful and withholding'.

For the supervisor then, all three possibilities are ever-present in the supervisory relationship. Being alert to the possibility of these alliance ruptures will help the supervisor identify and address them when they arise.

In the research quoted above, it was found that resolution of these ruptures resulted when the psychotherapist, on noticing the frustration or the emotional withdrawal of the client, immediately explored the person's experience of the rupture and then encouraged the person to be assertive, for example, in saying directly what he wanted of the psychotherapist at that point. If the person became avoidant and gave indication of a rupture in this manner, then an exploration of the 'block' in the communication also proved productive for repairing the alliance. The common factor in repairing ruptures appeared to be the psychotherapist's willingness to focus on the patient's immediate experience in the here-and-now of the therapeutic encounter (Safran *et al.* 1994).

The value of this material to the supervisor is immediately evident. From our own supervisory experience, we have met with 'ruptures' of each of these kinds in supervision as indicated above and have also found that 'repair' depends on the willingness to explore the process directly and non-defensively in the immediacy of the moment. A crucial factor in resolving supervisory alliance ruptures is to accept their interactional nature so that the supervisor is open and willing to explore his own contribution to the process. Successful resolution will be based on both participants in the supervision process taking responsibility for their shared communication and the constructions that may be placed on the material. Research into supervisor effectiveness suggests that the 'best' supervisors readily accept feedback about their own style of relating from their supervisees, whilst providing clear and direct feedback themselves to the supervisee (Allen, Szollos and Williams 1986, quoted by Leddick and Dye 1987: 144).

Research findings in developmental theory support our model

In the development of our model of supervision, we have drawn inspiration from developmental theories. In stressing the importance of the working alliance in particular, we have drawn on theories of attachment to underpin our hypothesis. Bowlby's research into infants and young children has shown how children develop internal working models of the mother/primary carer; this is an affective state that comes to be associated with a particular type of response. Such a working model will include a view of self and of the other coloured by an emotional tone. 'A securely attached child will store an internal working model of a responsive, loving, reliable care-giver, and of a self that is worthy of love and attention and will bring these assumptions to bear on all other relationships' (Holmes 1993: 79). The insecurely attached child develops a view of self as ineffective and unworthy of love and of the other as untrustworthy. In distinguishing, in his research, between secure and insecure attachment styles between children and their mothers, Bowlby has provided a concept by which to view bonding in adult relationships, the supervisory relationship being the one of particular relevance here. Secure attachment is marked by 'a relaxed state in which one can begin to "get on with things", pursue one's projects, to explore' (Holmes 1993). In such an atmosphere of safety and security, a person will be free to learn and experiment with new ways of doing things. Rutter (1981) found that the key to secure attachment lies in active, reciprocal interaction (quoted in Holmes 1993).

Research into adult attachment styles has evolved from Bowlby's work. Four such styles have been identified by researchers: secure, dismissing, pre-occupied, and fearful (Bartholomew and Horowitz, quoted in Feeney and Noller 1996). Based on their description of these adult attachment styles we have made the following hypotheses concerning the supervisory relationship. The supervisee who brings to the supervisory alliance a history of secure attachment will be ready to trust the supervisor to facilitate his growth as a psychotherapist; he will arrive with an attitude of curiosity and a readiness for exploration. If the supervisor is well grounded in her own secure attachment pattern, this will augur well for the success of the learning process.

The supervisee with a fearful attachment style will experience discomfort in getting close to others; ever sensitive to the possibility of rejection, he will be reluctant to raise his needs and vulnerabilities in supervision. For such a person, the warm and trustworthy supervisor may well provide a healing experience through the supervisory alliance, which will, however, take time and patience to establish.

The supervisee with a preoccupied attachment style will tend to be overly submissive to the supervisor, clinging to her every word and suggestion, scared of taking any initiative or expressing a difference of opinion. This person may feel undervalued by the other. Again patience and time will be required for the supervisor to develop a trusting alliance characterized by debate and a respect for differences of opinion in which true learning can take place.

The person with a dismissing attachment style is uncomfortable with intimate contact and does not desire it. This person values his independence and self-sufficiency and will not easily accept anything from the supervisor. It will take time and patience for the supervisor to reach into this person's world and gradually enable the person to benefit from what is available to him in supervision. The attachment status of the supervisor will contribute significantly to the processes outlined above. Realistically, we cannot assume that all supervisors have a secure attachment base; the co-creation of the supervisory relationship will be influenced by the 'working models' that both supervisor and supervisee bring to the relationship.

The focus on the intersubjective nature of secure attachment has been supported by the research of Stern (1985) in which he describes how the mother 'shares' the affective states of the infant by a complex process of attunement. The attunement behaviours of the mother do not merely mirror or reflect by rote the outward behaviour of the infant, but get to what lies behind the behaviour to the 'quality of feeling that is being shared' (Stern 1985: 142). These attunements share certain qualities: they suggest that a kind of imitation has occurred but they are not a faithful copy of the child's behaviour; the matching of the behaviour is cross-modal in that the mother, for example, matches the infant's movement with sound; the significant match appears to occur, not on the level of behaviour, but on the level of inner state (Stern op.cit.). It is the mother/primary caretaker who first attunes to the baby's responses and a delicate 'dance' between mother and child ensues. 'Affect attunement is the performance of behaviours that express the quality of feeling of a shared affect state without imitating the exact behavioural expression of the inner state' (Stern 1985: 142).

The mother attunes and responds to the child's rhythms, to the intensity of his expression, to the vibrancy of his activity so that the child feels met on an emotional level in this delicate dance. It is this intersubjective process that leads to a firm sense of self in the child. As an adult, the person will continue to respond positively to being attuned to accurately, and such attunement will support and strengthen the person's sense of self. This recent developmental research therefore suggests that the mother–child relationship may serve as a model for the psychotherapeutic and supervisory relationships, which are also based in accurate attunement to the recipient's needs. The need for attunement is not something that we outgrow; it remains as a basic relational need throughout life and surfaces as an important component of both the psychotherapeutic and the supervisory relationships.

The significant aspect of affect attunement as identified by Stern concerns the cross-modal nature of this process, so we will pick up from another person's voice tone or body language the confirmation of acceptance that is conveyed by words. The converse of course is also true. These are akin to the processes that were labelled congruence and incongruence by Rogers (1951). In the therapeutic relationship, the psychotherapist can provide such accurate affect attunement where someone may have been misattuned to as a child, and in this way provide a reparative experience in the present. Research into the supervisory relationship likewise suggests that it is the quality of the supervisory relationship that is related to effectiveness in supervision (Holloway 1987). In supervision, therefore, accurate attunement is equally relevant to a successful process and so we have chosen an integrative developmental approach focused on the centrality of the supervisory alliance as the core of our supervision model.

We consider that supervision frequently provides a reparative dimension for the supervisee in that the supervisory experience can compensate for misattunements that may have occurred in early childhood, or more commonly in subsequent educational experiences at school. Indeed, dealing with the results of academic traumata is one of the leading challenges for the supervisor who works in a training context. Without a sensitivity to the educational deficit that many people carry, the supervisor may unwittingly retraumatize an individual whose confidence in his own capacity for learning has been systematically undermined over many years. Any feedback may at first be experienced as critical and indeed 'devastating' until the supervisee gradually learns to trust the goodwill of the supervisor and is able to recognize this other person as genuinely interested in his welfare.

Holmes (1993) links Stern's concept of sensitive affect attunement to Bowlby's secure attachment and considers that insecure attachment results from mismatching in the maternal response. This might happen, for example, when the infant has to attune to the feeling state of the mother under threat of abandonment and in this process sacrifices his own feeling state or need. Insecure adults in supervision may well attune without question to the real or imagined needs of the supervisor, suppress their own feelings and end up fearful, insecure and above all not learning. This may result in a supervisee who ends up overadapting to the supervisor without due attention to his own perceptions and evaluations of the phenomena under observation and discussion. A person's sense of self is intimately related to his well-being and ability to be productive. How a person perceives himself and relates to himself will intimately affect the manner in which he relates to others. Attention to stages of self-development will be an inevitable focus in supervision where the supervisee's needs for recognition and confirmation will surface in the course of discussions of work with clients.

Coming out of his (and others') extensive observations of child development, Stern (1985) has constructed a theory of the development of the 'self' from childhood through into adulthood, which can be productively integrated into a supervision model. Stern (1985) considers the development of the sense of self a lifespan issue in that the self continues to develop and grow and require affective attunement from the environment for a person to function effectively. Stern originally outlined four 'senses of self', which emerge chronologically in the process of development and then continue to develop and co-exist concurrently. He later added a fifth (Zeanah *et al.* 1989; Stern 1999).

He speaks first of the infant's experience of the *'emergent sense of self'* from the time of birth onwards, which he links to the infant's apparent capacity to experience a world of perceptual unity. Infants would appear to manifest early on a capacity to organize the global qualities of their experience. We believe that Stern's concept of 'vitality affects', which he relates to the development of the emergent self, is pertinent to the relational essence of the supervision process. These vitality affects refer to the quality, intensity and vibrance of the mother's behaviour towards the child; vitality affects are embedded in her way of being, of moving, of touching and interacting with the infant. Expressiveness of this kind is a basic component of all human behaviour; the intensity, the rhythm, the variations in affective tone, changes in pacing, all contribute to the general quality of relating. 'There are a thousand smiles, a thousand getting-out-of-chairs, a thousand variations of performance of any and all behaviours, and each one presents a different vitality affect' (Stern 1985: 56). Such vitality affects may well relate to the personal chemistry that influences a person's choice of supervisor outside of conscious awareness.

From the age of 2–3 months, the child begins to develop a *'sense of the core self'*, which is related to an integrated sense of self as a distinct and coherent body. Stern describes several capacities that form part of the core self: self-agency (authorship of one's own actions), self-coherence (having a sense of being a whole person), self-affectivity (the capacity to experience coherent emotional states), self-history (having a sense of one's past that continues into the future) (Stern 1985: 71). We believe that the exercise of these capacities is essential for effective functioning in adulthood and can be related to the psychotherapy and supervision processes. For example, a well-developed sense of self-agency will lead to a person being ready to explore and reach out with curiosity and creativity. A person with a developmental deficit in this area may be scared to initiate any independent action and will be hampered in the process of effective learning by an overcautious approach to experimenting with new behaviours.

Between the seventh and the ninth month, the child begins to develop *'a sense of subjective self'*, which becomes apparent in the child's growing capacity for intersubjective relatedness and a need for greater intimacy, fostered by the mother's attunement to him. Stern's research with infants pointed to three dimensions that form the essence of affect attunement: intensity, timing and shape. Matching the other along these three dimensions conveys a sense of resonance, for example the loudness of voice matches the arm movements of the baby; or the mother picks up in her movements the rhythm of the child; or the mother nods her head to match the child's arm movements. This process does not involve an exact imitation, but rather 'a feature of behaviour that can be abstracted and rendered in a different act is matched' (Stern 1985: 146). The significance of these findings for adult communication has yet to be researched; however, we believe that there is much for us to learn here about the embedded aspects of effective relating.

During the second year the child develops *'a sense of verbal self'*, which links with the ability to create and share a joint meaning of our experience with others. But as Stern points out, the growth of language whilst facilitating interpersonal contact also 'drives a wedge between two simultaneous forms of interpersonal experience: as it is lived and as it is verbally represented' (Stern 1985: 162). For the client, the psychotherapist and the supervisor, this is an important component of the process between them. There will always be areas of experience for which we are struggling to find words, the 'unthought known' referred to by Bollas, which he describes as 'that which is known but has not yet been thought' (Bollas 1987: 128). We consider that the quality of contact between people may be one such domain, whether in psychotherapy, in supervision or in our daily contacts.

Finally, the child develops *'a sense of a narrative (consensually validatable) self'*, which refers to the evolution of a sense of the self that thinks over and shares the models for action and for relating to the world that form part of one's own internal schemata. This embodies the capacity to evaluate, think through and accept or reject the possible lines of action that a person is considering (Zeenah *et al.* 1989; Stern 1999). The narrative self is linked to the stories we tell ourselves about the actions we take and about the way we interface with the world at large. Stern (1999) makes the point that the child's narrative is built up in his interaction with his mother, even if she was not present at the actual events he is narrating. This narrative becomes the child's 'version' of events that becomes stored in memory, so the mother contributes intimately to the child's construction of his 'inner reality' (Stern 1999). Both the advantages and the dangers of this process are immediately evident because of the authority vested in the mother. Our memories of experience will inevitably be based on our own inner maps that have been constructed in this way. Our sense of a narrative self will include the capacity to evaluate the impact of our actions on others and assess the impact of their actions on us. In supervision this process is central to conceptualizing a treatment direction for a client, in assessing possible interventions and generally in developing, in our internal mental world, a 'map' of psychotherapy in practice. The supervisor is in a similar position to the mother, usually having no direct knowledge of the events being described and yet contributing to a version of the client's story. The power base in this warrants sensitive handling and humility.

The importance of contextual factors

As neither psychotherapy nor supervision are context-free, an appreciation of contextual factors that impinge on the relational process both globally or subtly must be an important consideration in any discussion of work with clients or supervisees. Supervision is always context-dependent and external circumstances will influence the quality and nature of the supervisory relationship and the choice of focus. By context we understand not only the immediate context of the supervisee's work (for example, an agency setting) but also the wider context (for example, in the United Kingdom as part of the European community) in which we all operate as psychotherapy supervisors. In addition, context refers to the present, to the past and to the future aspirations of the psychotherapist, of the client and of the supervisor, all of which will be influencing the processes of psychotherapy and supervision.

To enrich our understanding here we draw on field theory (Lewin 1952). He stressed the interrelatedness of a person with his environment, both his internal environment of sensations, feelings, thoughts, hopes and dreams as well as his external environment of people, plants, animals and the inanimate world. To understand human experience we need to understand the relevant factors in the total field or overall context in which the person is located. The field is a dynamic interrelated system in which every part influences every other part. Nothing is isolated and everything is connected to everything else in the field. In psychotherapy/supervision there is a co-created field of mutual, reciprocal influence between client and psychotherapist/ supervisee and supervisor. The current nature of the therapeutic relationship, together with the histories of both client and psychotherapist and psychotherapist/supervisee and supervisor impact the field. The present includes the past as remembered now and the future as anticipated now (Parlett 1991: 71).

Any change in the field affects the whole field such that an event is not caused by a single preceding event but there are multi-causal explanations (Zinker 1994). This is the principle of circular causality so well described by the family therapists who view all events as multi-causal, multi-determined and reciprocal in influence. In supervision this perspective on causality will prevent us from assuming a simple linear explanation and encourage the consideration of all the different aspects in the field: past, present and future!

Every situation and every person-situation-field is unique (Parlett 1991: 72) and it is the individual's need that organizes the field and influences what we attend to in our context. Meaning may be attributed very differently by two people in relationship and it is vital for the supervisor not to impose her meaning on the psychotherapist or the client but to engage in sensitive phenomenological exploration that may bring to the surface the embedded meanings in the client's world and in the supervisee's experience. A phenomenological approach seeks to develop awareness of the factors that are relevant to a particular client; it does not assume that certain factors will be relevant and impose the view of either the psychotherapist or the supervisor on the client's experience, whether intrapsychic, interpersonal or contextual and cultural.

From an existential perspective, the past is that which was as it appears to me now; and the future is that which will be as it comes to meet me now. The present is the living moment of my experience. Past events are relevant because of how the client configures (organizes his perceptions of) his field around himself in the present; what is significant is the narrative of events that the client lives within the present and how this is affecting his current functioning. Changes in the field change the figure (the aspect of his awareness) to which the person is attending. Any change in one part of the field affects every other part of the field so that a change in the field will affect an individual and a change in the individual will effect a change in the field. In supervision the field is significantly influenced by the presence of and by the interventions of the supervisor.

Watzlawick (1984) in another context refers to 'vicious' and 'virtuous' circles, which for our purpose could be usefully applied to the supervisory process. This means that the supervisee's way of being in a supervision session will impact the supervisor and the supervisor's way of being in supervision will affect the client, and the converse will also occur. In turn, this process will apply to the psychotherapist and to the client in their mutual interaction. These complex interlinked processes may become a destructive interactive cycle to the detriment of all the participants; trying to identify 'where the process started' may be less useful than looking at ways of interrupting the 'vicious' cycle since complex interactive phenomena cannot be adequately understood by analysing the separate component parts of such phenomena. The whole field or context or total 'Gestalt' needs to be taken into account in arriving at any explanations, which will be multi-causal rather than depending on linear causality.

The relationship between the supervisor and the supervisee is significant in that the manner in which each person experiences the past and present circumstances will be altered by the presence of another. The presence of the supervisor and the way in which the supervisor shows himself and accepts and confirms the supervisee may be one of the most influential factors in effective supervision. This links with the importance of affect attunement as described by Stern (1985) and the research into supervisory qualities that are linked with effectiveness.

A basic tenet of our position is that we consider all relationships as a co-construction between the two parties. We selectively perceive what is relevant to us in terms of our own frames of reference and construct meaning out of this material. Constructivism can be better understood by comparing it with essentialism. An essentialist way of thinking about the world and people assumes that there are essences of things and essences of people. A fundamental assumption is that all objects exist as objects distinct from the person who is perceiving them and that we are able to perceive them as 'essentially' for what they are. This version of essentialism is called realism in philosophy because objects are assumed to be 'real' in themselves and it is also assumed that we can perceive them as they 'really' are. It is further assumed that when the human mind gives a word-label to an object there is a complete or close correspondence between the word-label and the object which is thus labelled. In this essentialist way of thinking there seems to be a givenness about the world and a common sense response to the givenness of the world. Things are the way they are. Language and the world correspond (Wittgenstein 1921). Holding a belief that language and truth are intimately related gives language a power to define reality in a fairly final and unassailable way. As a consequence of this position words and the objects they are assumed to represent could result in reification in that word/object seem to constitute a thing in itself.

Wittgenstein's ideas profoundly influenced the development of logical positivism. Psychological theories still frequently make essentialist assumptions about the components of the human mind and the word-labels that are attached to these assumptions are given the weight of 'the truth'. This can lead to rigidity and an assumption that there is only one 'right' way of doing therapy, linked to a particular 'right' theoretical orientation. Despite the fact that Wittgenstein (1953) later changed his mind and said that language could not explain reality but could only describe it, psychological theories have not necessarily followed suit!

Another way of thinking about the world and word-labels we use to make sense of it is the constructivist position. The assumption here is that the human mind is not capable of directly contacting the world through any of the senses. Each of the senses transforms the external inputs through the neuro-biochemical system during the onward transmission to the brain where other biochemical processes are added. Furthermore, we then add the ways in which we have already learned to make sense of the unconscious data (schemata or organizing principles) so that what we see is the subjectively constructed result of the interaction of biochemical processes and schemata. There is always a gap between what is there in the external world and the constructive perceptions that we create. In other words, the mind externalizes internal perceptions of the world and then responds to these perceptions as if they were in the world and not as creations of the mind (Spinelli 1994). There is a significant difference between explanation and description, which adheres closely to the actual phenomena of our experience. There is an important connection between constructivist thinking and phenomenology in that phenomenology seeks only to describe and not explain.

Transferred to the psychotherapeutic or supervisory encounter a phenomenological stance seeks to help a client/supervisee to become aware and describe his subjective experience rather than take an analytically distant approach and interpret/explain the client's experience in terms of predetermined constructs. Wittgenstein coined the term 'language games' to emphasize that human knowledge is not a seamless robe but is disjointed. Language only appears seamless because of the similarity of the grammar we use to express language. Different forms of language allow different meanings to be ascribed to different situations. Just because sentences are constructed in the same grammatical way does not mean that they carry the same levels of meaning.

So, two sentences whilst grammatically similar, are hermeneutically different. That is, they convey different meanings. Grammar leads us to assume that words are being used in explanatory ways, that is, stating how things are, rather than merely establishing different forms of meaning. Language does not state facts, it creates meaning. Neimeyer and Neimeyer (1993: 2) write that a 'constructivist approach orientates towards assessing the viability (utility) as opposed to the validity (truth) of an individual's unique view of the world'. A socially constructed reality both creates and allows us to live in a social world in which words have a degree of similarity of meaning to permit some form of cohesion and convention, that is words 'by convention mean or represent or symbolize something beyond themselves' (Searles 1992: 60). It is because the socially constructed world is constructed that it can be deconstructed. It is porous, mutable and permeable. Rather than chasing the age-old ideal of objectivity 'we would do better to fully accept the notoriously different and more difficult situation of existing in a world where no one in particular can have a claim to better understanding in a universal sense' (Watzlawick 1984: 323). New ways of thinking can and do emerge from this starting point. However, it is important to be aware as is argued by Foucault and others (see Moss 1998) that the social world is premised on the power of powerful groups. Powerful groups define the social world in ways that meet their needs and suit their purposes as we shall explore further in our discussion of anti-oppressive practice in supervision.

Qualitative research (Reason 1994; Heron 1996; Cresswell 1998) is premised on a socially constructed reality where research can be usefully explored without making assumptions (hypotheses) about the 'final truth' of humanly experienced reality. Personal truth, culturally located and relationally constructed is foundational for human experience and meaning and does not need further validation by being credited with absolute or essential truth. There are several consequences of taking a constructivist position, which are summarized as follows. Language never captures the essence of objective or subjective reality; rather it allows us to create a world that we are constantly in danger of thinking is the only way in which the world can be conceptualized. All theories are constructions and not inviolate 'truths' and should be capable of being tested, not in order to prove them right or wrong but to provide evidence of their usefulness. A humanly constructed world of meaning has important moral dimensions in that it allows for emancipatory potential. The fixity of essentialism implies rigidity of opportunity and dogmatism. Finally, a constructed sense of our humanity, a constructed sense of self and identity is a model that allows for some personal choice, agency and diversity.

The constructivist theory of memory underpins our model

This approach to understanding the world and our experience, both present and past, relates very closely to the constructivist theory of memory. Bartlett (1932) proposed a constructivist paradigm for explaining the process of re-membering in terms of which humans constantly construct, deconstruct and reconstruct their memories in terms of the present context and what is of emotional relevance to them at a particular time. 'What you remember is driven to some extent by your emotional commitment and response to the event' (Baddeley 1993: 94).

Bartlett studied the normal processes of remembering meaningful stimuli in everyday life and concluded that social factors influenced remembering. We do not record every aspect of a situation in photographic detail as the trace theorists had once believed; rather human memory is selective. We choose to remember in terms of what is familiar and of interest to us at the particular time and dependent on context. In the process of reconstruct-ing our experiences, in order to make sense of them, we may emphasize certain features and ignore others influenced by the organizing principles we bring to the event. Barclay (1988, quoted in Baddeley 1993) distinguished between the 'truth' of a recollection and its 'accuracy'. Much of our auto-biographical recollection of the past is reasonably free of error in that we retain the essence of an experience, provided we are remembering the broad outline of events. It is when we try to fill in the details that errors may creep into our narrative. Baddeley sums up Barclay's conclusion as follows: 'A recollection is true if it represents the person's general experience of the situation and his attitudes to it, in short if it correctly conveys the gist of the experience. It would be accurate only if the detail were correctly reproduced' (Baddeley 1993).

In the process of living, people are constantly modifying, building on and reinforcing their personal narratives in the process of reconstructing their past in the light of present experience. This process enables us to create a narrative that explains for us our experience and enables us to construe the past in a way that is meaningful to us in our current lives. This is in line with Stern's research into the child's development of a 'narrative self' (Stern 1999). We regard this as part of a person's existential search for meaning; for a narrative that explains and supports who we are and gives a basis to our sense of self in the world.

Psychotherapy provides a safe context in which clients can embark on a re-evaluation of the meanings attached to their histories. Supervision pro-vides a reflective space where the supervisee can unfold his own narrative of his work with a client, reflect on this story with the supervisor as wit-ness and arrive at possible new meanings and insights that may further his work with a client. This process of construction relies on careful observa-tion, knowledge of the client's narrative, intuition, awareness of contextual factors, knowledge of psychotherapy theory and a myriad of other vari-ables too many to enumerate or even to identify in all their richness and complexity.

Questions for further reflection

1 Are you familiar with the findings of contemporary psychotherapy out-come research that support an integrative relational model of supervision?
2 What are the philosophical assumptions on which your model of super-vision is based and in what ways are these assumptions realized in your professional practice?
3 Increasingly supervisors are being sought who can provide supervision across a range of psychotherapy schools. What are the implications of this trend for your professional development?
4 'Supervisors are only required to be experienced psychotherapists and should not need further training in supervision.' Discuss.

7 Assessment, accreditation and evaluation in supervision practice

In this chapter we discuss the issues of evaluation and accreditation for both psychotherapists and supervisors. Since responsibility for the assessment of psychotherapist competencies is part of the supervisor's responsibilities, we give a list of competencies we consider important at the point of psychotherapist accreditation. This is followed with an overview of the evaluation of supervision and of supervisor competencies. The chapter concludes with a section on the importance of supervision for the supervisor as an essential component of good practice.

Evaluation as a crucial supervisory responsibility

Evaluation is a central feature of training supervision, both as an ongoing dimension of the training process and also in terms of the final accreditation process. Holloway (1995), in describing what she calls the 'Monitoring/ Evaluating' function of supervision, considers that this covers both formative and summative evaluation. She points out that in training supervision, assessment is usually formal and standardized, whereas in consultative supervision this aspect is more implicit, yet there too 'the supervisor's opinion and judgment, implicit or explicit, are important' (op.cit.: 34).

Carroll (1996) separates out the 'evaluating' from the 'monitoring' tasks of supervision. Evaluation in his view combines the formative, that is the provision of regular feedback during ongoing supervision, with the summative evaluation, or the overall evaluation of a supervisee's work, which takes place at specified points and particularly at the point of completing the requirements of a training course, usually the point of accreditation. Carroll (1996) states well the tension between the different roles of the supervisor as the provider of a safe, containing space for the supervisee to explore his work and simultaneously as the evaluator of his competence. 'In all the tasks of supervision this is the one where the power element is most clear' (Carroll 1996: 71).

Unless the supervisor has established a really sound working alliance with the supervisee in which there is mutual trust and respect, the task of evaluation may well be experienced by the supervisee as a critical and fault-finding procedure. Our own aim in this process is to discuss and develop with the supervisee the criteria by which the evaluation is undertaken. We take into account the learning outcomes specified by the course the trainee is attending and together with the supervisee put specific behavioural expectations to these criteria in line with the supervisee's theoretical orientation (in our experience very few courses are specific in this respect). Our focus here is on effectiveness, not on what is right and wrong, as we have expanded on elsewhere. This is a participative process in which the supervisee gradually internalizes the criteria for competent practice and their attendant behavioural markers into his own internal map of the psychotherapy so that he sharpens his own self-evaluative skills.

Criteria for evaluating competence at the point of accreditation

We summarize here some of the criteria we consider important in evaluating competence at the point of accreditation for the psychotherapist. These criteria can also be used as the basis for the formative assessment in the course of training supervision. From the criteria employed by various training institutes and from our own training and supervisory experience, we have come to consider the following evaluation criteria as central to a relationship-based training. We have put these in the form of questions we would put to supervisees both in the course of their training development to serve as evaluation guidelines and at the point of accreditation. Many of these questions are worded generally but are also intended to be used in the micro-analysis of audio- or video-tapes, or of case notes. Alternatively, they can guide the assessment of case study submissions.

1 Do you possess a coherent and integrated theoretical framework that informs your clinical practice?
2 Are you able to relate theory to practice and to talk about the theoretical concepts that underpin your clinical work?
3 Are you able to talk about a particular intervention in terms of your choice of this intervention with this client at this stage of the session and in terms of the overall stage of therapy?
4 Are you able to consider any alternative interventions that you may have used at this point and give a rationale for your choice?
5 Are you able to assess the effectiveness (or otherwise) of your interventions in terms of the outcome that you have achieved?
6 Are you aware when you 'miss' your client and when your intervention does not achieve the desired outcome?
7 Are you able to deal creatively with such empathic failures and repair the alliance with the client?
8 How do you conceptualize stages of treatment and future directions for the therapy?

9 Are you well-acquainted with the codes of ethics and professional practice of your organization?
10 Are you competent at thinking through ethical principles and drawing inferences from these when you meet an ethical dilemma?
11 Are you aware of the limits of your competence?
12 Are you aware of the principles that govern good professional practice?
13 What criteria would you use to judge that you have established a good working alliance with a client?
14 When do you consider that self-disclosure may be appropriate and when would you consider it an inappropriate intervention?
15 How do you think about transference? And how do you work with the transference as it emerges in your work with your clients?
16 What place do you give to dialogue in your therapeutic work?
17 How do you view the 'reparative' dimension of therapy?
18 How have you found a knowledge of child and adult development useful in your clinical practice?
19 How do you ensure anti-oppressive practice in your clinical work?
20 What place do you give to the transpersonal or spiritual dimension in your therapeutic work?
21 Describe the context of your practice, particularly in relation to your referral network, your liaison with other professionals and the support you can draw on in a crisis?
22 To what extent do you consider that the wider context should be considered in each therapeutic involvement?
23 What do you think about the developments in the field of psychotherapy both in the UK and more generally in Europe, and in a wider context?
24 Do you consider that psychotherapists have a wider social responsibility and what are your thoughts about your own prospective contribution in this arena?

Giving the 'good' and the 'bad' news

In the evaluation process it is particularly challenging to balance support and confrontation and we know that this balance is often precarious; clear feedback can lead to hurt and angry feelings. Here humility at our own limitations as supervisors and as human beings is relevant. We are likely to 'fail' our supervisees in this process and what is crucial is that we acknowledge the inevitability of this process. We consider it as part of the gradual process of disillusionment that Winnicott (1971) referred to in the course of the child's growing up. The process of matching our expectations with our ability has been a painful one for us personally and time and again we see our trainees facing a similar challenge either because they have underrated or because they have overrated their abilities. Sometimes no amount of hard work will give a person the result they desire and the process of acceptance of limitations is often a slow and painful one. We see this as an analogy of what often happens in the psychotherapeutic process as a client becomes more realistic about his own choices and about life's possibilities.

Nowhere has this been put as pithily as by Eric Berne: 'This is the most painful task which the script analyst has to perform: to tell his patients that there is no Santa Claus. But by careful preparation, the blow can be softened and the patient may, in the long run, forgive him' (Berne 1972: 153). This is the opposite of empowerment; the acceptance that we are neither entirely impotent nor are we magically omnipotent! The balance is achieved in realizing our own 'potency', a concept stressed in Transactional Analysis, which we have found useful to supervisors, clients and supervisees alike (Berne op.cit.).

Evaluation of supervision sessions and outcomes over time

The evaluation of supervision has been very well dealt with elsewhere (Clarkson and Gilbert 1991; Gilbert and Sills 1999). Clarkson and Gilbert (1991) look at the assessment criteria for an individual supervision session and focus on the importance of making and meeting a carefully considered contract. They also stress the process of focusing on priorities in supervision and the refining of the ability in the supervisor to identify the 'key' issues in supervision. Parallel process, that is the mirroring in the supervision session of the process between therapist and client forms an aspect of their focus. The supervisor needs to be alert to parallel process dimensions and take care not to step into these unwittingly and so compound the impasse for all parties concerned. A simple example of parallel process would be when the client is aggressive towards the therapist who feels paralysed in the situation; if the therapist in turn rounds on the supervisor who incapacitates as a result of this attack, the parallel process will render both supervisor and supervisee powerless to act. The supervisor needs to be ever alert to the possible parallel process and model for the supervisee an effective way of handling the impasse.

This capacity to model good effective practice forms an important criterion in evaluating supervisor competence. Gilbert and Sills (1999) have compiled a number of tools for evaluating not only intervention styles in supervision but also sessional outcomes and outcomes over time. They have drawn from the research literature, from their own experience and that of other writers and practitioners in the field to create a number of useful checklists for the practising supervisor. They also give a place to the self-assessment of the supervisor, suggesting such questions as: 'Did I as supervisor meet the supervisory contract? Does the supervisee feel "helped" by having a clearer idea of a way forward?' (Gilbert and Sills 1999). Rather than duplicate this useful work here, we wish to focus more specifically on the evaluation of the supervisor who espouses an integrative relational approach to supervision.

The effective psychotherapy supervisor

From our experience and based too on the work of Leddick and Dye (1987) we believe that competent relationship-focused supervisors will demonstrate the following capacities:

1 Flexibility; the capacity to move easily amongst theoretical concepts and not become tied to a particular explanation of events. Flexibility will also be seen, *inter alia*, in the choice of a variety of interventions to meet the individual learning needs of different supervisees.

2 The supervisor takes a multi-perspectival view of the issue; a meta-systemic perspective that enables him to appreciate the interactive nature of the field. In our model this would include the practice of inclusion (Buber 1965), acquiring the 'third-person' perspective (Wright 1991) and appreciating the 'reciprocal mutual influence' (Stolorow *et al.* 1994) operating between people.

3 The supervisor possesses a reasonable working map of the field of psychotherapy and an awareness of the three main streams of thought that constitute the history of this discipline in western thought. An integrative supervisor may well meet supervisees from different orientations who are seeking to extend their knowledge base or be requested to do cross-orientation supervision.

4 The supervisor needs an awareness of the philosophical values underlying the western practice of psychotherapy and the lack of relevance of these assumptions in many cultures, particularly in Africa and Asia. Some knowledge of helping traditions in other cultures would enrich her practice.

5 The capacity to manage anxiety, her own and that of the supervisee. 'Supervisors aim to manage, rather than eliminate tension in supervision to enable the trainee to reduce performance anxiety while stimulating motivation to learn' (Leddick and Dye 1987).

6 The supervisor needs to be open to learning from her supervisee who may possess expert knowledge she herself does not possess.

7 The integrative relational supervisor needs a sensitivity to contextual issues, to the wider world as this impacts the therapeutic process.

8 The supervisor needs to be schooled in the principles of anti-oppressive practice.

9 Humour, humility and patience are invaluable qualities in any supervisor.

An important place for supervised supervision

Supervised supervision forms an integral part of our model of practice. We generally do this in a group where several supervisors who are learning the craft come together to discuss their supervision practice; although individual supervised supervision is also a common and effective practice. For the sake of clarity we shall use the term 'consultant supervisor' or 'consultant' to designate the person who is approached by a supervisor for input about his or her supervisory practice. For the consultant supervisor, this is an interesting and challenging task. She is now at a further remove from the clients whose welfare is at stake and issues brought for consultation will as frequently involve the psychotherapist's performance as client material. In addition, members of such a group are all experienced practitioners in their own right and can contribute fully and effectively to the group. The consultant's role is as facilitator much of the time, and occasionally she will be called on for expert guidance and advice.

This type of supervision will more often focus on themes related to the general principles governing the practice of psychotherapy or to guidelines pertaining to ethical and professional matters. Some common issues at this level are:

1 ethical considerations, for example, a boundary problem involving the psychotherapist's relationship with a client;
2 professional matters, for example, how to feed back to a training pro-gramme concerns about the competence of some of its trainees who are in supervision with you;
3 a focus on the relationship between supervisor and psychotherapist where there is a strong transferential component, for example, where the psycho-therapist 'feels' that the supervisor is 'over-critical';
4 organizational issues where there is a three-cornered contract and the supervisor is supporting the psychotherapist to clarify the different strands of this contract, for example, where the organization asks for a detailed report of the work undertaken with clients;
5 professional issues in the life of the supervisor, for example, the question of further training in the theory and practice of supervision or in a specialist area such as post-traumatic stress disorder;
6 concerns about the level of competence or the limits of competence of the psychotherapist under supervision, for example, where the psycho-therapist is working in a voluntary organization and his first client ever is a person with a bipolar disorder;
7 issues pertaining to professional relationships with peers in the field of psy-chotherapy, for example, disputes that may have grown into complaints or court actions.

Below are three excerpts from three different supervisors' reports about their supervision practice, which demonstrate the incorporation of insights gained from the consultant supervisor and the supervised supervision group.

Excerpt 1

This involved the supervision of a trainee counsellor at the outset of seeing clients.

'I took my supervision of S's work to my supervision group and wasn't surprised that I was questioned about my contract with S. I realized that at the time of my "pre-supervision" and early supervision sessions with S, I hadn't spent enough time negotiating and clarifying the issues, which I now know to be so important, including the administrative contract, personal and professional information that might affect the tasks and process of supervision, ground rules (what we expected of each other in relation to how we do the work) and other items which could affect our working alliance. I feel that at the time I began to supervise S I was still uncomfortable with owning the power and authority inherent in being a supervisor and was paving the way for "being stitched up" by S – as one of my colleagues in the supervision group described the process – when S became aware of how lack of boundaries with his client B were leading to huge problems in his counselling work. My colleagues suggested that it was important to renegotiate the supervision contract with S over our next couple of sessions and to be prepared for "things to get worse before they get better".'

Excerpt 2

This involves the supervision of a practitioner involved in brief-term work with clients.

'In supervised supervision I reflected on my process with a new supervisee. She (supervisee) engaged swiftly with me, and I imagined that this was also her characteristic style with clients, in an appropriately modified form, and useful for time-limited contracts. She was quick to understand the role expectations of the supervisory relationship, and made it clear that she wanted above all to discuss the therapeutic process between herself and her clients. I formed the impression that, while clearly needing support, she was also open to challenge regarding her handling of clients, and would use this positively. I checked that she had a basic understanding of transferential issues and the parallel process, and noted that she had a fundamental sense of trust regarding the supervision process.'

Excerpt 3

This is an example of work with a senior trainee, which the supervisor brought to the consultant supervisor.

'I took to my supervised supervision the problem that I was experiencing with my supervisee, P, who recently approached me for supervision. P is very reluctant to give me any details of his work with clients and seems only to want to discuss "general issues". After several sessions of this kind I became concerned because I did not feel that I was getting any real information about his practice. My consultant supervisor asked me how I felt about the process and I soon became aware that I was actually rather scared that I was not going to live up to P's expectations (he had been referred by a colleague who highly recommended me to him). We reflected on the possibility of a parallel process, that P was perhaps feeling equally nervous of exposing his work to this new "super" supervisor. I then recalled that he had mentioned something in the first session about painful experiences at school. So I went into the next session more open to look at what was happening in our relationship . . . and this really opened up the process between us.'

'Supertransference': a challenge to supervisor narcissism

Teitelbaum has coined the term 'supertransference' to describe the supervisor's teaching problems and 'the effects of the supervisor's unresolved conflicts, blind spots, or inappropriate expectations' on the supervisee (Teitelbaum 1990: 244). He considers it crucial, for example, that the supervisor assess the impact of her own personality style and her own anxieties on her supervisees. The very nature of 'super-vision' lends itself to fostering grandiosity in the supervisor, to supporting the belief that the supervisor necessarily knows best by the very nature of her position. This countertransference weakness can easily lead to an abuse of the power base inherent in supervision. In his article Teitelbaum quotes the term 'disciple hunting' used by Benedek to describe a process in which the supervisor encourages supervisees to identify with her and her needs. 'The most deleterious influence in the supervisory situation is the manifestation of the supervisor's countertransference which causes him or her consciously or unconsciously to foster the candidate's identification with him or her, or the latter's dependence on him or her' (Teitelbaum 1990: 253).

In our experience we have seen this process work to the great detriment of the supervisee whose development is arrested and stunted by the narcissistic needs and demands of the supervisor. Supervisors who have subsequently had contact with people thus affected report that it takes a considerable time for these psychotherapists to recover a sense of their own self-worth, independent thinking and autonomy. The narcissistic process referred to here is extremely subtle; on the face of it the supervisee may be encouraged to develop himself and own his creativity but more covertly and unconsciously the message is 'you cannot manage on your own without my input' or even 'whatever you say or think is really my intellectual property; you are incapable of independent thinking'.

In our view the main challenge to the supervisor (and also to the trainer or teacher of psychotherapy) is to foster and nourish the growth and development of the supervisees in her care; to provide the fertile ground on which they can grow to 'adulthood' and take their place in the professional world as equals alongside the supervisor. To encourage this growth into 'adulthood' requires sensitivity and wisdom; budding supervisors and budding psychotherapists need a balance of support and encouragement to move out into the professional world in their own right. This process requires in the supervisor the humility and the wisdom 'to let go of' supervisees as they come into their own and develop skills that the supervisor may not even herself possess.

Quis custodiat ipsos custodes?

Who will take care of the carers themselves? As supervisors and trainers we continue to seek supervision from our professional peers who may possess an expertise different from our own. We support one another in the process of reviewing our work and our supervisory and training practices. One of the most helpful interventions we have found is to invite an outside trainer or supervisor to participate in some way in our own supervisory or training practice. Such a person will very quickly pick up on any 'blind spots' and omissions or grandiosities in the system and can give helpful professional input in this regard. This process of seeking feedback requires a belief and a willingness to accept that learning is a lifelong commitment and will also prevent us from sinking into a customary mould, which has worked in the past but may no longer be relevant to present-day circumstances. In the supervisory field, as much as in any other, constant updating is essential to stay abreast of a rapidly changing and evolving field.

Supervisor accreditation

As regards the accreditation of supervisors, there does not yet exist in the UK, a national register for psychotherapy supervisors, nor a national system of accreditation. The United Kingdom Council for Psychotherapy has so far confined its efforts to establishing a voluntary national register of psychotherapists; this organization is currently seeking statutory regulation for the profession of psychotherapy. Recently (1999), however, the Training Standards Committee of the United Kingdom Council for Psychotherapy was in the process of creating a discussion document about the possibility of creating a register of psychotherapy supervisors and trainers. In the Humanistic and Integrative Psychotherapy field, we know of two systems of accreditation for psychotherapy supervisors related to a specific orientation; that conducted by the Gestalt Psychotherapy Training Institute (GPTI) and the other by the International Transactional Analysis Association (ITAA), of which the Institute of Transactional Analysis is the UK branch.

Both these accreditation procedures require supervisors to possess a knowledge of supervision theory and to apply this to their practice of supervision. Both organizations assess actual sessions of supervision practice, the GPTI by means of an audio-taped submission, the ITAA by observation of a piece of 'live' supervision conducted before an examination board of four examiners. The focus in both these accreditation procedures is on the observation of the supervisor's actual practice and on his or her application of theory to practice; this provides a rigorous assessment of competence and can well serve as a model for future accreditation procedures in the supervision field. Besides these two components of the assessment procedure, supervisors are also required to have undergone some supervision training and supervised for a certain number of hours to ensure that they have gained practical experience linked with a theoretical understanding.

At best, formative and summative assessment procedures are combined in the training of supervisors and in accreditation processes. In the course of supervision training, the supervisor will usually gain much practical experience and ongoing feedback on the level of his skills and competence so that the final assessment takes on the character of a rite of passage rather than an examination. We are aware of an accreditation process for supervisors developed by the European Association for Supervision, which has gained some acceptance, but we do not have information of such accreditation schemes from other parts of the world. It seems that this type of accreditation is still in the process of gaining professional credibility.

Questions for further reflection

1 What qualities do you think may be important for the supervisor in giving effective feedback to supervisees?
2 What supervisor competencies are central and essential to good supervision?
3 'Supervision of supervision – what next? Does the cycle ever end?' Discuss.
4 What criteria would you use to evaluate the effectiveness of a supervision session?

8 ▷ Developing personal style as a supervisor

In this chapter we discuss a range of factors that contribute to the difference of 'style' among supervisors. Our personal experience and research suggest that supervisees prefer clear and direct feedback on their work from their supervisors. Several authors point out that effective supervisors are able to choose from a range of different 'tasks' in supervision according to the particular needs and individual levels of development of supervisees. A supervisor's style is also characterized by where she most frequently places emphasis in making choices in supervision. Other perhaps more controversial issues discussed include the judicious use of self-disclosure, the uses and abuses of the countertransference and the appropriateness of psychotherapeutic intervention in supervision.

Factors contributing to personal style

Supervisors will develop their own personal style of supervision as they integrate the new skills required of being a supervisor with their existing skills as a psychotherapist. In the course of our supervision training, we see supervisors retain some of the particulars of their own orientation to psychotherapy in their supervision style, but gradually add to this additional skills and practices that are related to the new role responsibilities, tasks and the authority required of the supervisor. Each supervisor will bring a particular configuration of relational skills to the supervisory task, which will derive from such factors as personality style, cultural background, orientation to psychotherapy, life experience and a developed expertise in communication that is the bedrock of the profession.

We have a high regard for the individual flavour that a person brings to the work of being a supervisor and seek to foster this uniqueness in our training of supervisors. The integrative relational model of supervision presented in this book provides a framework for individual supervisor development, which supports people to build up their own unique supervisory style. We aim at effectiveness in training rather than at producing a particular mould or style of supervisor. In this chapter we look at the personal style of the supervisor from a number of different perspectives, which have proved important to us in facilitating the development of supervisors, whether beginners or advanced practitioners in this field.

We start by looking at some of the broad parameters along which supervisors may differ. The first of these is the balancing of support and challenge. If you think of support and challenge along a continuum, then some supervisors will be closer to the supportive end of the continuum and some will be closer to the challenging end. The supervisor who is high on support and low on challenge will be warm and accepting sometimes at the expense of providing guidance and parameters for practice. The supervisor who is high in challenge may find that supervisees become scared and avoid openly discussing their difficulties. If the challenge is presented in a contemptuous or undermining manner, the result is most likely to be a supervisee who is plunged into a shameful place and does not learn from the encounter. Where the supervisor is authoritarian and shames the supervisee for diverging from her own theoretical orientation, trainee psychotherapists have registered their dissatisfaction.

Interestingly enough, trainees reported equal dissatisfaction with *laissez faire* supervisors who did not have a clear structure or did not set clear goals for supervision (Cherniss and Equatios 1977, quoted by Leddick and Dye 1987). Clearly support and flexibility is best combined with structure, mutually agreed goals and clear and direct feedback. A supervisee wants to know where he stands without being overcontrolled or simply left too much to his own devices. This means that a certain amount of tension is inevitable in effective supervision as the supervisee seeks to extend his learning and the supervisor guides and models good practice. If 'anything goes' and all is equally acceptable to the supervisor, the supervisee may enjoy the outing involved in supervision, but is unlikely to refine his knowledge or skills. Equally, if supervision is a shaming and frightening experience, the supervisee may simply learn to hide himself behind fabricated requests and never bring to supervision those issues in his work that are really troubling him.

Creating an open and honest supervisory alliance in which the supervisor can be as honest about her feedback as the supervisee can be about his client work remains the main challenge for the developing supervisor. We regularly ask of ourselves: 'How can I as supervisor balance support with challenge in an effective way so that the supervisee learns from the process of supervision?' This falls into the realm of the 'art' of supervision; people can learn the elements of the craft, but the development of the art involves an effective integration of support and challenge so that the supervisee is able to take in the new learning without defensiveness in an atmosphere of good will. To create and sustain such an atmosphere of good will forms the heart of an effective supervisory alliance.

The importance of clear, direct feedback

Both our personal experience and research into supervision suggests that supervisees prefer supervisors who give clear and direct feedback on their work (Leddick and Dye 1987). Giving accurate feedback will often be experienced by supervisees as confrontational since the supervisor may be focusing on areas of improvement in their practice. If this is balanced by a relationship in which the supervisee feels supported and respected, then the feedback is most likely to be heard and integrated by the person. Giving feedback to a supervisee is both an art and a skill that can be honed and refined by practice. Equally important is the process of encouraging supervisees to feed back to the supervisor what is proving effective in supervision and what elements are less helpful. Supervisors can encourage this by formal means, for example by using a questionnaire or checklist, or more informally by creating space from time to time for reviewing the supervision process. A natural time for evaluation in training supervision occurs at the end of each academic term when a review seems appropriate and well-timed.

Carifio and Hess (1987) report in some detail on a study on supervisor feedback conducted by Freeman (1985), which points to some important considerations for the supervisor delivering feedback. Effective feedback according to Freeman has the following characteristics:

1 It is systematic, objective and accurate. As far as possible feedback needs to be based on identifiable and observable examples of practice, and not be conveyed as vague impressions. In this regard we consider it vital that feedback be linked to specific examples of practice and/or aspects of therapist behaviour in response to a client, which are observable and can be identified by the supervisee as areas to focus growth and change. Generalized statements are usually unhelpful and relatively meaningless to a person attempting to learn new skills.

2 It is timely. It is important that feedback be given as close to the event as possible so that the supervisee can make the links with his own process before he loses touch with the experience. In this regard we have found the use of audio-tapes of sessions extremely useful to cue the supervisee's memory of a particular session so that he can recapture a sense of his own process at a particular point in time and reflect on his reasons for making particular interventions.

3 It is clearly understood. Both positive and negative feedback are best based on explicit performance criteria that are available to supervisor and supervisee alike. Such learning outcomes can be regularly reviewed in supervision and form the basis of self-assessment for the supervisee and serve as a guide for supervisor feedback. Feedback is best couched in unambiguous language that does not leave room for doubt. Supervisors are sometimes tempted to be evasive in order to spare the supervisee's feelings, which may leave the therapist with an unrealistic view of his own performance.

4 It is reciprocal. Feedback is best provided in two-way interactions in which suggestions are made, not as a prescription or as the only way to approach

a problem, but as only one of a number of potentially useful alternatives. This finding is very much in line with our approach, which focuses on the outcome and impact of interventions in order to assess their relative effectiveness, rather than producing inviolate rules or giving a 'blueprint' for practice (Freeman 1985).

The tasks of supervision as a method for measuring individual style

Individual differences in relational styles will mean that supervisors bring their own personal flavour to the supervision process. What contributes to this individual flavour? One of the helpful lenses through which personal style can be viewed comes from the work on the different 'tasks' in supervision (Holloway 1995; Carroll 1996). Both Holloway and Carroll point out that effective supervisors choose amongst a range of supervision tasks and combine these in different ways in the course of supervision delivery. Some supervisors move freely between tasks according to the particular needs and developmental levels of supervisees. But as Carroll (1996) remarks some supervisors 'lock into' certain tasks and restrict themselves to these to the exclusion of others. This accords with our experience and is in some cases related to the original orientation to psychotherapy practised by the supervisor which may privilege some of these tasks over others. Whether supervisors employ these tasks flexibly or restrict themselves to only a few will influence individual style and provide an unique supervisory profile.

A brief summary of these tasks based on Carroll's work, which incorporates the work of Holloway, is given below. Carroll (1996: 53) gives a map of the 'generic tasks of supervision', which he lists as: to consult, to counsel, to monitor professional ethical issues, to evaluate, to teach, to set up a learning relationship, and to manage administrative aspects.

Consultation forms the heart of the supervisory process; essentially supervision is a process of consulting with another who is valued as an expert in order to enhance our work with clients. Consultation involves discussion of information and reflection on the process of psychotherapy that is marked by mutuality and scholarly exchange. A supervisor whose style is discursive, who facilitates questioning of assumptions and who encourages exploration in a spirit of creative enquiry will rate high on the consultative task.

The counselling task involves attention to the feelings and responses of the supervisee in relation both to the client, to the supervisor and to the context in which the client work is being conducted. In our relational model, the counselling task will foster the development of inclusion as the supervisee is given support for owning his personal feelings and responses whilst appreciating the world of the client. Where, however, the counselling task is given predominance, supervision may begin to resemble psychotherapy.

The task of monitoring professional and ethical issues involves the supervisor in ensuring that the supervisee is practising in the best interests of the client and within the limits of his competence in accord with accepted ethical standards. In cases where the supervisor's anxiety may lead him to

constantly question every move that psychotherapist is making, the psychotherapist may end up being so cautious that he hardly intervenes at all in
the client's process. We are concerned that the gradually increasing emphasis
on litigation, whilst aimed at protecting clients, could also lead to an inhibi-
tion of creativity on the part of psychotherapists and so hamper effective
practice.

The evaluating task involves the assessment of the psychotherapist's effectiveness both on the level of individual interventions and also on the level
of overall outcomes for therapy. This task involves a judgement of the psychotherapist's skill and ability to meet goals and to produce effective outcomes with clients. Where evaluation is ongoing, as in training, this aspect
will naturally form a larger part of the supervisor's practice than in consultative supervision with qualified and experienced practitioners.

Supervisors will sometimes teach within the supervision context. The teaching task involves both the transmission of information and the teaching of
specific skills and strategies of intervention. This may form a larger or smaller
part of the supervisor's repertoire depending on how she views supervision:
is it primarily an exploratory space or does it also allow for teaching of
theory and the learning of specific skills?

The task of setting up a learning relationship involves the skills of establishing an effective supervisory alliance; this task is central to the model of
supervision that we are presenting here and we consider it the bedrock of
effective supervision. A supervisor who is low in relational skills is unlikely
in our opinion to deliver a good service to people. Finally, it also falls to the
supervisor to attend to the administrative tasks in supervision such as filling
in supervision reports, reading case reports, writing references, providing
information to accrediting bodies and many other related demands. Some
contexts are more demanding than others in this regard depending on the
organizational requirements.

Personal style is very much influenced by the particular combination of
tasks that the supervisor favours. The supervisor who prefers the counselling
task will focus very much on the supervisee's feelings and responses in relation to the client and runs the risk of turning supervision into psychotherapy and not meeting supervisory goals in the interests of the client's
welfare. Some supervisors focus heavily on the teaching task so that supervision becomes very much of a didactic exercise and may seem more like a
lecture than an exchange to the supervisee. Such supervisors may also 'teach'
the supervisee what they think is important rather than consulting the needs
of the supervisee. We can only too easily get 'hooked into' our pet subjects
and expound on these whether the supervisee is benefiting from this outpouring or not. It is always wise to check out carefully what will be helpful
to the supervisee and what is simply self-indulgence.

If a supervisor overplays the evaluating task, each supervision session may
take on the nature of a final assessment in which the supervisee is being
judged, rather than providing the very necessary help, teaching and consultation in an exploratory spirit that is required to facilitate the best interests of the client. Someone who is constantly expecting to be 'assessed' is
hardly likely to bring difficult problems and concerns to supervision. However,

if the supervisor is attending to the supervisory alliance to the exclusion of focusing on the actual work with clients, the supervisee may feel well received but may not learn anything. Supervision may then turn into a pally chatting session that has little or nothing to do with client work.

In contradistinction, if a supervisor is constantly called on to attend to ruptures and contractual irregularities in the supervisory alliance, a complete review of the supervision contract may be appropriate. Sometimes the supervision process is simply not working for a variety of complex reasons that will need to be unravelled before moving forward (or not as the case may be). The most creative resolution in some cases is to end the particular supervision relationship and refer the supervisee on to another supervisor.

An initial challenge for new supervisors often involves taking on the monitoring task as an essential aspect of supervision. This involves assuming the authority that is part of the supervisor's role and may initially conflict for the supervisor with providing warmth and unconditional acceptance in a professional relationship as they have been doing heretofore. A task analysis of supervisory styles will quickly throw up such struggles and raise interesting points for discussion and development. The administrative task may in some contexts absorb more and more of the supervisor's energy so that supervision ceases to be a creative learning space but instead becomes an exercise in filling in forms to keep the authorities happy.

The manner in which a particular supervisor combines these different tasks will ideally be influenced by the context of the supervision, by the specific issues that the supervisee is bringing for exploration and by the developmental level of the supervisees. However, our experience confirms that of Carroll's research findings that many supervisors lock into a few tasks and do not move across the range. This will then shape their individual style of supervision for better or for worse. Our suggestion to supervisors is to use these tasks as a checklist to assess where they tend to focus and which of these tasks they seldom or never use, and then to ask themselves what this means in terms of their personal style. Is this a conscious choice or simply an oversight or the result of habit? Or is their choice heavily influenced by their orientation to psychotherapy so that they use some tasks and never others? We believe that it can be an interesting challenge to the supervisor to experiment with extending her range and then to assess the impact of this change on supervisees. Such experimentation will alter the emphases in the person's style and lead to a new configuration of tasks.

The choice of focus as an indicator of individual style

A supervisor's individual style will also be characterized by where she more regularly lays her emphasis in terms of the choice of focus in supervision. In this regard a map of possible choices such as that provided by Hawkins and Shohet (2000) in the 'seven eyes' of supervision may provide a useful reference point. They map the following seven areas of focus for the supervisor/ supervisee: reflection on the content of the therapy session; exploration of strategies and interventions used by the therapist; exploration of therapy process and relationship; focus on the therapist's countertransference; focus on the immediate interaction between supervisor and supervisee as a mirror of parallel process; focus on the supervisor's countertransference; and finally a focus on the context (Hawkins and Shohet 2000).

In using this model as a basis for comparing different supervisory styles, we have found that a supervisor will focus on certain of these areas whilst avoiding others. This may be dictated by her theoretical orientation to psychotherapy, or simply by personal preference, or by reason of staying in her personal comfort zone. Some supervisors focus their supervision exclusively on client material (the first three choices) and never on the more embedded relationship dimensions, which are emphasized in the last four choices. In some of the cognitive therapies where more emphasis is placed on specific techniques or strategies that have been shown to be effective, the supervisor may confine her emphasis to client information and presenting problems and relevant interventions. This will result in a task-focused model of supervision where the primary goal is the learning of particular strategic manoeuvres. The unconscious processes of either psychotherapist, client or even of the supervisor will have little place in such a model.

With a Rogerian person-centred approach the primary emphasis may well be on the exploration of the psychotherapy process and relationship and the refinement of those skills that relate to the core conditions outlined by Rogers. A focus on the here-and-now aspects of the psychotherapist–client relationship and looking at this in terms of the immediate process between supervisor and supervisee characterizes a Gestalt or existential approach to supervision. In these approaches supervisor (and psychotherapist) self-disclosure are important aspects of process. Such an approach may in addition lead to a personal exploration of the psychotherapist's own issues as these are brought to the surface by his work with the client.

In contrast, we have found that the explicit emphasis on countertransference as a learning tool has come from psychoanalytic approaches to supervision, whether this relates to the psychotherapist or to the supervisor. In this sense then the particular orientation to psychotherapy will shape the supervisor's choices and so also his individual style of supervision. Some supervisors are particularly sensitive to context and will regularly explore organizational and contextual factors in supervision. In the integrative relational model of supervision that we are advocating all seven of these foci have a place and can be chosen by the supervisor dependent on the needs of the supervisee. The challenge for a supervisor in the process of extending her repertoire is to review her practice and identify where her favourite focus may be and to identify the one she visits seldom or never.

We wish to elaborate on three areas arising from our overview of the Hawkins Shohet model: the place of self-disclosure in psychotherapy and supervision; the use of countertransference in psychotherapy and supervision; and the place of psychotherapy with the supervisee in the supervision context. The relative emphasis that a supervisor places on each of these domains will shape her individual supervisory style in significant ways.

With the movement in contemporary psychoanalytic psychotherapy toward a more relational stance and the move within humanistically orientated psychotherapy to a recognition of the significance of the phenomena of transference and countertransference, together with a deeper understanding of the relevance of developmental themes, there is emerging a willingness to look beyond one's own approach to psychotherapy to see what may be learned from each other. We consider that intersubjectivity theory provides one such bridge between humanism and psychoanalysis.

Self-disclosure as an indicator of personal style

Ferenczi (1988) appears to have been the first advocate for psychotherapist's self-disclosure indicating that in the attempt to stay hidden the psychotherapist can repeat early injury and confuse the patient. The theory of reciprocal mutual influence (Stolorow and Atwood 1992) and field theory, with its focus on the indivisibility of the organism from the environment, both acknowledge that client and psychotherapist influence each other such that a client might intuitively know when something is being withheld that is of significance to the process.

The relevance and effectiveness of self-disclosure both on the part of the supervisor and of the psychotherapist warrants some detailed discussion. We look at the place of self-disclosure in psychotherapy and follow this with a discussion of its place and relevance to supervision. Any discussion of the efficacy of self-disclosure in psychotherapy and supervision should be set within the wider context of contemporary relational approaches to psychotherapy. Relational theory figures significantly across a diverse group of schools of psychotherapy but a trend towards convergence is apparent among those relational approaches that acknowledge the co-creation of meaning and experience as a central feature of relational therapy. Further areas of convergence are a stress on the interrelationship between the intrapsychic world and the interpersonal world, the 'intersubjective' space co-created by both psychotherapist and client, the recognition of the importance of affect, and an increasingly greater engagement of the psychotherapist in the ongoing process of therapy as dialogue.

Gestalt and other humanistic relational approaches to psychotherapy are focused more on contact rather than on transference such that the authentic person of the psychotherapist is brought directly into the therapeutic encounter. Contemporary psychoanalytic relational approaches have moved well beyond the original 'blank screen' and have challenged the notion of psychotherapist neutrality as exemplified by Mitchell's relational model (1988), which stresses the relational interactive aspects of the psychoanalytic endeavour.

Sandor Ferenczi early on in the history of psychoanalysis maintained that psychotherapist neutrality inhibited psychoanalytic treatment and that the client was healed through having a new experience in relationship (Ferenczi 1988). In the tradition of Ferenczi contemporary approaches to psychoanalysis, in particular intersubjectivity theorists within self-psychology, consider the appropriateness of the judicious use of self-disclosure by the psychotherapist. 'Neither disclosure nor withholding is neutral; each has a particular meaning in the context of a particular psychoanalytic treatment' (Orange *et al.* 1997). Specific decisions about self-disclosures need to be made on the basis of assessment as to whether their interactive meanings for client and psychotherapist are likely to facilitate treatment.

Greenberg (1995) writing within a humanistic tradition reflects that the issue of self-disclosure should be considered on the basis of the specific therapeutic situation; including variables such as the particular client, their character structure, the particular psychotherapist, the present situation and the particular moment in the therapeutic relationship. According to Greenberg such variables interact at any given moment to guide the psychotherapist into making a split second decision regarding the efficacy of self-disclosure. Greenberg acknowledges that such variables include both the psychotherapist's and patient's histories. Historically within the humanistic tradition self-disclosure has been a recognized part of the therapeutic dialogue and the presence of the authentic self of the psychotherapist is a given.

Unfortunately this has often been understood to mean that the authentic experience of the psychotherapist, whether it is relevant to the immediate situation or not, will always be healing for the client. This has often led to an indiscriminate use of self-disclosure, which has been unhelpful or even harmful to the client. Even if the experience of the psychotherapist is relevant in the immediate context of the therapy session it does not follow that the self-disclosure of the psychotherapist's experience will support the growth and development of the client. Indeed sometimes the client may simply experience a self-disclosure on the part of the psychotherapist as a competitive gesture impinging on the therapeutic space that the client regards as his province.

Such self-disclosure will not further contact or promote a genuine encounter between two people. Furthermore the over-indulgent use of self-disclosure can distract from the client's or the supervisee's focus of interest such that one can be left questioning whose needs are being dealt with in the process. Self-disclosure can reflect the psychotherapist's inability to tolerate and contain the psychic pain of the client and would in such a case be a profound failure of empathy.

The subject of self-disclosure has been focused on particularly within Gestalt therapy, where two types of self-disclosure have been identified: (1) where the psychotherapist shares an experience or problem from his own life, past or present, with the client; and (2) where the psychotherapist self-discloses his experience of the ongoing process in the immediate here and now of the therapeutic encounter. This latter type of self-disclosure can be particularly powerful in bringing to awareness underlying transferential processes. Laura Perls wrote 'I will describe some problems and experiences from my own life or from other cases, if I expect this to give support to the patient for a fuller realization of his own position and potentialities if it may help him to make the next step' (Perls 1992: 119). At best, this type of self-disclosure is a risky business and does carry the assumption or implication that the experience of the psychotherapist has a more than personal validity that carries some universal implications for others. This may not be consciously intended but it is likely to be what the client will take up. Polster and Polster (1973) rightly argue that it would be inappropriate for the psychotherapist to share each and every significant thought or feeling he has towards the client. They maintain that it is important for the psychotherapist to determine what to share and what to 'bracket off', and as a general guideline this decision is made by what seems most relevant to the therapeutic process in terms of leading to enhanced awareness and improved contact.

Supervision by its very nature lends itself more to self-disclosure than does psychotherapy. It is common in the supervisory context for the supervisor to share examples drawn from her own experience of work with clients to illustrate points of intervention or more general clinical thinking. This process fits well into the consultative task stressed by both Carroll (1996) and Holloway (1995) as a task that favours a sense of sharing among colleagues and a balance of power. Supervisors may also share with supervisees moments from their own professional development and the difficulties that they have experienced to provide a map for the supervisee who may expect to 'know everything now'! This type of self-disclosure may foster the 'twinship' selfobject need identified by Kohut. We have found that in their development as professionals supervisees value the sense that they are not alone in their struggles, that even those people whom they regard as authorities in the field have had and continue to have their own uncertainties and questions.

However, the use of self-disclosure in supervision needs to be used sparingly and with respect for the needs and sensitivities of the supervisee. Particularly in training supervision, there are usually strong elements of transference in the supervisory relationship, and the supervisor will need to be alert to these in sharing personal experiences of her clinical work as well as anecdotes about her own growth, development and ongoing challenges. Such information may be experienced by the supervisee in a shaming manner, as a possible indication that the supervisee is wanting in skills and somehow inferior as a clinician. As in the context of psychotherapy, self-disclosure in supervision is only likely to serve as an effective supervisory intervention in the context of a good working alliance.

Stephen Zahm (1998) has attempted to establish specific guidelines for the use of self-disclosure in psychotherapy and outlines factors that would inform his choice. He argues that it is important to encourage the client to trust his own experience for which the psychotherapist's self-disclosure serves as a model to further the dialogue and promote a positive longer-term relationship. He lists validation, communication, confrontation and challenging hierarchy as examples of the positive use of self-disclosure.

Similar general guidelines as those outlined by Zahm for psychotherapy can be employed in supervision. Self-disclosure can be used for validation as in the case where a supervisee was feeling overwhelmed and deeply upset by the revelations of a client's sexual abuse, it was a relief to her to know that the supervisor found revelations of this kind deeply unsettling as well. This communication validated the supervisee's responses and led to a reduction in her sense of isolation. At times when a supervisee is experiencing a moral dilemma concerning some aspect of a client's life, a knowledge that the supervisor has wrestled with similar problems can help to convey to the supervisee that the supervisor is not just an objective observer of his distress but actually knows the experience from the inside. We have found self-disclosure particularly effective in counteracting hierarchy and a sense of relational distance when the supervisee is faced with a challenging ethical choice point and is so scared of being judged that this scare interferes with the person's capacity to think about the problem. It is easy at a time like that to believe that one is the only person who has ever faced an ethical dilemma and had to make a difficult choice.

Finally, we do use self-disclosure as a confrontation to the supervisee. Here the supervisor may share his own subjective experience of some aspect of the supervisee's process or clinical work directly with him. One supervisor reported saying to a supervisee who was talking about a client in what the supervisor experienced as a very derogatory manner: 'I notice that you are talking about this client in a dismissive tone and I would like to explore with you what your feelings are towards her and what this may mean for your work with her.' This comment led to an exploration of the therapist's countertransference responses and to uncovering her fear of the particular client's perceived power over her.

In assessment situations, self-disclosure may also be used in a confrontation of some of the supervisee's assumptions. A particular challenge to the training supervisor is the supervisee who overrates his or her capacities. We have found this a challenge especially when dealing with the written presentation of case material for assessment purposes. Here again an honest statement from the supervisor may free up the process and allow the supervisee to move forward with the task: 'I am struggling to get your meaning in this section of your dissertation. I am not really getting the drift of your theoretical discussion. My concern is that if I who know you and your work well am experiencing this difficulty, then the external examiner will experience it even more strongly.' A personal statement of this kind is often acceptable to the supervisee as pointing a way forward whereas a general statement about the quality of a piece of work such as 'this is simply not up to standard' may be experienced as damning and inescapable.

A focus on countertransference as part of the supervisor's personal style

We now proceed with a discussion of the role of countertransference in supervision to show how an emphasis on this aspect of the relational process characterizes the supervisory style of certain people. However, our focus is both on countertransference as this relates to the psychotherapist's work with clients and to the supervisor's countertransference to the supervisee's process or to the clients being presented for supervision. When Freud first identified the countertransference of the analyst, he saw this as a hindrance to effective analysis and something that the analyst needed to identify in himself and overcome as 'no analyst goes further than his own complexes and internal resistances permit' (Freud 1910, quoted in Sandler *et al.* 1992). He regarded countertransference as an obstacle in the path of effective analysis and discouraged analysts from sharing any of their personal experience with their patients, hence the stress on remaining a blank screen in relation to patients. Apparently Freud never moved from this position to come to see countertransference in any way as facilitative to analytic work. Sandler *et al.* (1992), however, make the point very clearly that Freud did not regard the fact that the analyst had feelings towards his patient as in itself constituting countertransference; it was only when these feelings and conflicts stood in the way of his being 'a mirror in the analytic situation' that he considered it as problem in the analysis.

In this sense countertransference related to the analyst's unworked through issues and unconscious processes, to the analyst's own transference to the patient that required his attention in order for him to free himself to be effective with his patients. This view of the countertransference as an obstruction to effective analysis has persisted in the history of psychoanalysis until relatively recently when several authors have put forward a different view (Kohut 1984; Casement 1985; Bollas 1987; Langs 1994).

These authors share the view that the countertransference of the analyst is a valuable source of information about the analytic process. Stressing the interactional nature of the process between analyst and analysand, they consider that learning from the countertransference can be viewed as a vital and crucial part of analysis. Generally they hold the view that the client is constantly supervising the psychotherapist and letting him know what the client needs him to know through the nature of his communications. This is not simply related to a repetition of past relationship patterns but is intimately connected to this new relationship that exists between them and which offers the opportunity of a new and transformative experience in the present.

The client's transference is seen as having different facets, primarily that it can be seen as the person's attempt to communicate to the analyst in an indirect way about needs that have been suppressed, the operation of Winnicott's true self in action, or that it can be defensive in that it is motivated by the person's fear that these needs will once again meet with disapproval and so derive from the protective action of the false self. The intersubjectivity theorists within the field of self-psychology believe that both these aspects of the self-process will manifest regularly in analysis and that the analyst's job is to discern which is pre-eminent at any point in time and respond accordingly (Stolorow *et al.* 1994).

The common belief of these writers, who place an emphasis on the countertransference in psychotherapy and supervision, is that the psychotherapist's reactions to the client can serve a valuable function in providing information about the client's process. Bollas (1987) focuses on the analyst's 'countertransference readiness', his openness to his own experience so that he can welcome 'news from within himself that is reported through his own intuitions, feelings, passing images, phantasies and imagined interpretive interventions'. He points out that the analyst may frequently find himself in a state of 'not-knowing-yet-experiencing' and may well need to tolerate this 'not knowing' for quite some time as the process of analysis unfolds. Casement (1985) likewise in discussing forms of interactive communication speaks of 'communication by impact' to describe a process in which the patient stirs up feelings in the psychotherapist about something that he is unable to communicate as yet in words. If the psychotherapist can tolerate his own pain and confusion and persevere in a desire to understand, then a time may come 'when the unconscious purpose of these pressures becomes apparent' (Casement 1985: 73). Both these writers are talking of psychotherapist countertransference as a process of containment through which the psychotherapist is gaining valuable information about the client's process, which may take time to formulate in language.

Mann (1997) in his discussion of the erotic transference looks at the importance of the psychotherapist's awareness of his own erotic responses to the client and an integration of these into his thinking about the therapeutic process. He does not consider it either necessary or advisable to share these erotic feelings with the client on a conscious verbal level; rather that their acknowledgement by the psychotherapist as natural and acceptable will convey itself to the client on an unspoken level. His focus on the psychotherapist's level of openness to his or her own experience is of particular interest to us in our integrative model of supervision. We too consider it vital that the psychotherapist be aware of his own responses and feelings towards a client, so he can discern which of these responses are related to his own unresolved issues and which are more relevant to the client before him.

Speaking of erotic desires, alongside other feelings such as jealousy, rivalry, hate and compassion, Mann maintains that the central task for the psychotherapist is to contain his or her feelings and desires and reflect on these (Mann 1997). Once the psychotherapist has analysed and integrated his own feelings, their presence can have a positive effect on the psychotherapy. The client is likely to sense that such feelings are acceptable to the psychotherapist and begin to share them in the therapy. This has certainly been true both in our own clinical experience and in our experience of supervising others. In fact our trainees often laughingly comment that their clients seem to 'know' what issues they are currently working on themselves in their personal psychotherapy and then uncannily bring these to their own psychotherapy.

An interesting question arises concerning the use of the countertransference understanding in the therapeutic process itself. For Mann it is enough that the psychotherapist has understood, acknowledged and integrated his own eroticism; he does not consider it necessary for the psychotherapist to initiate the introduction of these feelings into the therapy room. Bollas considers that on rare occasions the direct use of his countertransference may indeed be helpful to the client, when the analyst in effect reports back in some way to the client his experience as the client's 'object'. He hastens to add that he is not advocating a 'thoughtless discharge of affect' on the part of the psychotherapist, rather a carefully considered intervention that forms part of a gradual use over time of the analyst's subjective experience. His clinical examples demonstrate how tactful and tentative he is in this respect, offering the interpretations so that they form a natural part of the therapeutic process (Bollas 1987). What is of interest to us is his acknowledgement that the impact that the client has on the analyst may be very much at a somatic level and that this somatic knowledge forms part of what he refers to as the 'unthought known' of the client's world, the knowledge the client possesses for which he does not as yet have language. Casement also advocates the careful use of the countertransference and distances himself from those psychotherapists who interpret too directly from their own feelings about the patient so that their countertransference intrudes on the analytic process (Casement 1985). Here again we consider the relevance of our earlier question: 'Whose need is being served here, the psychotherapist's or the client's?'

The countertransference of the supervisor can be a rich source of wisdom in the process of supervision. This could refer to the supervisor's response to the psychotherapist or to the psychotherapist's client as this manifests in supervision. The supervisor may become aware to repressed areas in the supervisee as he is presenting client material.

Here is an example from supervisory practice: the supervisee, a man in his early 30s was speaking of a female client with whom he was experiencing difficulty. The client would come regularly to sessions, sit back in her chair in a semi-reclining position and proceed to look steadily at the psychotherapist as though waiting for him to initiate the dialogue. When asked where she would like to start, she would invariably say that there was something important that she wanted to share with the psychotherapist but she was experiencing extreme difficulty in starting on the subject. She would then begin to writhe and slide down in her seat, covering her face with her hands. The psychotherapist was at a loss about how to proceed since a similar sequence was taking place in successive sessions. His observations that she was clearly struggling to find her words led nowhere! The supervisor became aware of a strong erotic sense in his manner of telling the story and asked how he responded to his client's sexuality. He was horrified at the question and said: 'I always leave my sexuality outside the room when I engage in therapy. That way I don't face any dangers. With so much therapist abuse of clients in the field, you cannot be too cautious.' The supervisor delicately suggested that the client might not be doing likewise and that he was perhaps meeting with the erotic transference in his client whose initial presenting problem had been to do with becoming comfortable with her sexuality and exploring this in her relationships with men.

The supervisee then recalled that she had indeed near the beginning of her psychotherapy with him mentioned that she found him attractive; but he had quickly moved on to the second part of her statement which referred to her difficulty in initiating conversation with people. The supervisor asked him to reflect on this process and the message his moving on may have conveyed to her. Once again, the supervisor tentatively asked him to reflect on his own feelings and responses to his client. He blushingly admitted that he was sexually attracted to her but believed that this was wrong and that the feeling should be suppressed. The supervisor was then able to help him own his own feelings, and begin to feel more comfortable with these whilst supporting his ethical stance about the matter of not acting these out in any way. As he realized that it was impossible to 'shut part of me down while I do therapy' he was gradually able to experience, tolerate and consciously contain his erotic feelings. Not altogether unsurprisingly, the client soon after this found her words and was able to talk about her erotic feelings and begin to explore their significance in her relationships. In this example, the supervisor acted on her own sense of the repressed material that was coming through to her in the manner in which he described his client.

The supervisor's countertransferential response to the client may be equally helpful and revealing. This may take the form of an image or a felt sense about some experience that may prove important in the subsequent therapy. On one occasion a supervisee was talking about a client who presented with social phobia; an extreme unease in the presence of others accompanied by a wish to 'sink into the ground'. At such times the client felt completely frozen and alone. The supervisor suddenly had an image of a small child alone at boarding school possibly being teased by other children, with no one to support her and nowhere to run to for comfort or safety. The supervisee said that the client had reported no such experience in her telling of her history. In a subsequent session when the client was again reporting on an occasion when she felt 'scared and frozen with terror and very small', the supervisee enquired about previous experiences of say, 'boarding school' or something similar. It turned out that the client had indeed been at boarding school when very young because her parents were working in another country and wanted her to be educated 'at home'. Soon afterwards they returned to their homeland and her ordeal was over – except for the memory of those days that she still carried in her bodily experience!

Supervisors are encouraged to be sensitive to their own responses and to share these with supervisees in a spirit of curiosity and enquiry. In a relational model of supervision and psychotherapy such interventions fit well into the overall frame and can be explored in a spirit of open enquiry to uncover whether there is any significance in such images or responses for the work with the client. This brings the supervisor's countertransference into the supervision process as a possibly enriching dimension. Again, the extent to which a supervisor will consider this relevant to supervision will shape her individual personal style of supervision.

Does psychotherapy have a place in supervision?

The final issue that we address in this section is the place of psychotherapy of the supervisee in supervision. This is a dimension along which supervisors differ vastly. Some supervisors would regularly contract to do pieces of personal work in supervision if they consider this relevant to the work with the client. Other supervisors would never do this, regarding such personal psychotherapeutic work as an intrusion on the supervisee's privacy. Yet others will very occasionally engage in personal psychotherapy with a supervisee in relation to a specific issue that has arisen in the countertransference with a particular client. Ekstein and Wallerstein (1972) make some interesting observations about the training of the early analysts. This originally consisted of a short analysis by Freud himself and certainly very little formal academic input about psychoanalysis. The assumption continued to be that the training analysis was the main source of learning.

In this model, most of a person's problems with a client were considered to be residual problems of the analyst's own. In some countries the 'controller' of the analyst's first case and his personal analyst were one and the same; in Vienna and elsewhere this 'controller' (supervisor) was a different person. The controller's role was mostly a didactic one. From these early beginnings, there have been powerful influences on all psychotherapy training. The Humanistic and Integrative Section of the United Kingdom Council for Psychotherapy requires that all trainees be in personal psychotherapy for the duration of their training. From the perspective of the present discussion there is also the influence of the underlying assumption that problems in the conduct of analytic work are related to unresolved issues of the analyst's own. This belief has permeated some forms of psychotherapy and social work supervision and affected the way the supervisor may regard the supervisee's presentation. Ekstein and Wallerstein ask the crucial question as to whether 'the supervisory process is not really a hidden form of psychotherapy?' (Ekstein and Wallerstein 1972: 251). We believe that for some supervisors today this still remains a relevant question since most of their emphasis may be placed on the supervisee's 'personal issues' to the exclusion of other possible hypotheses related to context, stage of learning, the relationship with the supervisor and their knowledge (or lack thereof) of a particular client group.

A different tradition in the growth of the practice of supervision emerged from counselling training in the United States where an educational model of supervision is apparent (Bernard 1993). These models of supervision focus on educational goals and the learning needs of supervisees. From this tradition has developed a wealth of material on developmental levels of supervisees, on individual learning styles and needs, and on the roles and tasks of the supervisor in an educational setting. Psychotherapy and counselling are viewed as crafts that can be directly taught and learnt. Bernard (1993) contrasts these educational models with what she calls the apprenticeship models in which the supervisor learnt his skills from having been supervised himself.

In such a model the supervisor is bound to draw on his psychotherapy skills in supervision with the consequence that they 'were inclined to focus on the supervisee's vulnerabilities as the centre of supervision' (Bernard op.cit.). Because educational models regard the supervisee as a learner interested in acquiring new skills, the focus is more likely to be on the person's individual learning needs and on the person as a learner. We consider that supervision in the UK has been very much influenced by these different traditions so that in developing individual styles of supervision, all supervisors will be deciding to what extent they regard supervision as an educational process and on what place they see for personal psychotherapeutic interventions in the course of a supervision session. Generally within the Humanistic training field in this country the place of personal psychotherapy as a separate aspect of the training process is accepted practice; but here we are looking at personal style. When would the supervisor do 'a piece of therapy' with a supervisee in the course of supervision, if ever at all?

Carroll and Holloway both identify the 'counselling task' in supervision, which describes those interventions when the supervisor facilitates the emotional experience of the supervisee in the interests of opening up the work with the client. We would accept this as a central aspect of a relational approach to supervision. However, we do not support turning the supervision session into a psychotherapy session. In situations where we feel tempted to label something as a supervisee's personal issue, we always ask ourselves what we need to do as supervisors that may help the person with this particular piece of learning. Saying 'I think you should take this issue to personal therapy', we consider to be intrusive, avoidant and poor educational practice. However, this still leaves us free to explore the supervisee's countertransference responses in pursuing an understanding of 'stuck points' in their psychotherapy with clients. Such explorations need to be clearly related back to the work with the client. We consider it important that an investigation of countertransference responses be conducted on an adult to adult basis (Berne 1961) to encourage the supervisee to reflect on what may be a familiar pattern of response for him that may be relatively unrelated to the client.

We accept that a response is never random and forms part of a co-created relational matrix, but we also accept that we only have one side of the relationship to work with in supervision. If the supervisee feels 'stuck' then we need to consider his current responses to the client from a number of different perspectives; for example, is it a matter of technique, has the problem been accurately understood on a diagnostic level, or are we dealing with a countertransference response on the part of the supervisee? If we decide to explore a countertransference response, this would be done after agreement with the supervisee that we explore his feelings in response to the client in order to further the work with the client.

There are certain guidelines that we consider crucial, the chief amongst these being that as supervisors we carefully avoid interventions that may induce regression in the supervisee by cathecting a child ego state; instead we encourage the supervisee to reflect from adult on his responses and identify the origins of these in order to understand their relevance or otherwise in his work with his clients. This process respects the capacity of the supervisee for self-reflection and does not infantilize him. We do not support the practice where the supervisor intrudes on the internal world of the supervisee gratuitously and without a contractual agreement. However, this does not mean that we would never engage on a personal exploration in the interests of opening up the work with clients. We are simply saying that both supervisor and supervisee are to agree to this process as indicated by the 'supervision problem'.

On one occasion, for example, the supervisor had attempted to deal with a specific issue from a number of different perspectives to no avail, the supervisee continued to bring this back to supervision as an impasse. The problem concerned the supervisee's sense of paralysis as a group therapist when there was any loud argument or even raised voices in the group. Different techniques, an understanding of her own fear of conflict from her family of origin, an analysis of the group process, none of these foci seemed to make a difference. The supervisor then suggested that the supervisee recreate the group in the supervision setting and imagine herself conducting a group session where the particular problem arose. As the supervisee did this, she reported feeling 'paralysed' and scared. The supervisor asked her to report further on her experience and she immediately answered 'I'm not in my group at all, I'm at home in my family terrified of being attacked if I say anything at all'. The supervisor asked: 'What is it that you needed to say then?' 'That I have a right to speak here!' The supervisor immediately related this back to her therapy group setting by saying: 'Now look at your therapy group as they are in the present.' This process freed the supervisee on a somatic level to react differently, whereas the other interventions had not really touched into the bodily basis of her fear *in context* and help her gain release from it. Thereafter, she was able to speak up as a group therapist and facilitate the resolution of conflict in the group.

The importance of humour as a supervisor's friend

In conclusion, we wish to mention the significance of humour as a means of facilitating learning. In our model, which views supervision as the co-creation of relationship in a spirit of the shared negotiation of meaning, the presence of humour can charterize supervision as a place where fun and laughter also have a place. Laughter in the service of learning allows for a humorous approach to our own struggles and can give a perspective on them that allows us to accept our stage of development and the goals that we still need to attain. The function that comedy has served through the ages is to give us a perspective on our human condition and its function in providing a realistic and balanced perspective in supervision can enrich the learning process for supervisor and supervisee alike.

Questions for further reflection

1 To what extent do you focus on the same general areas/themes in supervision?
2 Is your supervision task focused or process focused? Experiment with the alternative focus and reflect on the outcome.
3 Under what circumstances, if any, might you consider initiating a therapeutic intervention in supervision?
4 What factors do you consider in determining whether or not to make judicious use of self-disclosure in supervision? Do you make a distinction between disclosure of material from your personal life outside supervision and disclosure from within the process of supervision?

9 ▷ Ethical decision making in supervision

Our aim in this chapter is to establish a model of intentional decision making that adopts a comprehensive approach to ethical issues, which goes beyond mere codal interpretations, views it as an opportune learning experience, supports critical reflection of the outcomes and informs further development of ethical thinking and practice. Consistent with our approach throughout this book we believe that supervision of ethical issues, as with all other aspects of supervision, moves beyond individualism to mutuality of relationship, to include intersubjective theory, which challenges 'the myth of the isolated mind' and dialogical therapy that challenges the intrapsychic exclusivity of object relations theory. For us supervision of ethical issues embraces the interpersonal existentialism of Buber and, supported by field theory, is a co-created field of mutual reciprocal influence.

Ethics is the ground from which the figure of therapy emerges or, as Bond puts it, 'standards and ethics are the essential core of counselling and without these the relationship is not counselling' (Bond 1993: 209).

Novice supervisees are often intimidated by ethical issues, which is at least partly due to a lack of preparation during their initial training. Carroll writes that few therapy training courses spend substantial time training in the ethical/professional aspects of counselling and supervision, and fewer still on educating students in methods of ethical decision making (Carroll 1996: 148). Senior practitioners and supervisors can also feel intimidated by ethical issues and frequently experience frustration as a result of a natural inclination to desire clear guidelines by which to resolve ethical dilemmas. However, in our experience ethical dilemmas tend often to exhaust all attempts to achieve a confident resolution through reference to an ethical code. Indeed creating a foundation for ethical decision making on absolute ethical principles would simply be unrealizable. Quoting Hare (1971) Spinelli acknowledges that throughout life the many dilemmas we are confronted with are not principally concerned with questions of right versus wrong but about the choices we make between actions that, in themselves, contain elements of both 'right' and 'wrong' (Spinelli 1994: 124).

A not unfamiliar situation is that where a young person discloses that he or she has been inappropriately touched by an adult in authority, for example by a teacher. This particular dilemma is a case vignette (5) discussed in more detail later (see pp.138–9). If you break confidentiality you risk losing the trust of the young person. If you do not break confidentiality then a young person is left unprotected and so potentially are other youngsters. This dilemma is all the more urgent when the UK may only be a court case away from the situation in North America where supervisors appear to be liable to vicarious responsibility for the welfare of the client (Carroll 1996: 151).

Any application of absolute ethical principles clearly negates cultural differences. As Pederson writes, 'ethical principles generated in one cultural context cannot be applied to other substantially different cultural contexts without modification' (Pederson 1987: 224). Absolute standards of moral and ethical behaviour would also invariably result in further empowerment for the dominant culture at the expense of minority cultures, what Ivey calls a 'one size fits all' approach (Ivey 1987) and what Ridley asserts leads to consequences 'which are hurtful and profoundly dangerous' (Ridley 1995: 228). Ivey roundly criticizes the American Psychology Association and American Counselling Association for ethical guidelines that 'assume a dominant cultural perspective, and generally minimize or trivialize the role of culture in ethical decision-making' (Ivey 1987: 240). He goes on to condemn the bias toward individualistic perspectives that are not appropriate to collectivist cultures and an élitist bias that protects the profession.

Alternatively, adopting a purely relativist approach such that criteria are created within each cultural context and for every ethical situation would be equally unrealizable. 'Relativism makes moral discourse difficult and prohibits social accord toward intersubjective agreement' (Pederson 1987: 226). Pederson's solution to this dilemma is to maintain that it is possible to combine culture-specific manifestations of difference with a search for fundamental similarities that link each cultural context with every other context. He believes it is possible to find common 'ground psychological principles' that connect each group while at the same time allowing each group to manifest its own cultural identity and differences. In his view the alternative is to operate in the absence of principles and in a philosophical vacuum where practitioners are most likely to impose values that are most familiar (op.cit.).

In Chapter 10 we criticize the cultural encapsulation of mainstream psychotherapeutic theories with a consequent lack of awareness of multicultural issues and the unwitting perpetuation of oppressive practice. Cultural encapsulation is founded on the dominant western cultural norm of individualism where personal and professional maturity is synonymous with autonomy and self-sufficiency. The resulting alienation from self and other is accompanied by a profound loss of community. Writing from a Buddhist perspective on therapy Brazier argues that western ethical codes are designed primarily to curb and constrain the excesses of the individual and he portrays western morals as little more than a source of frustration to the individual 'necessary but irksome' (Brazier 1995: 36). Under the influence of Judaic-Christianity he argues that the western view of the human being is that we are sinful by nature and given to danger and destruction. 'The basic concept is that the natural person is sinful and that ethics exist to protect society' (op.cit.: 44). He concludes that codes of ethics exist to justify complaints. We have some sympathy with these views for codes of ethics often tend to reduce ethical values to written regulations which encourage codal interpretations that give maximum attention to the written word and minimal adherence to underlying values. Perhaps the increasing burgeoning of ethical regulations is in direct proportion to the apparent dwindling significance of moral values?

Whether one favours a more or less absolutist or relativist approach to ethical decision making the reality is that ethical codes are invariably developed through 'expert' committees deliberating on ethical principles (Lindsay and Colley 1995). This top-down approach is in relative isolation from the day to day encounters of clinical practice such that there is a lack of effective dialogue between those who devise ethical codes and the majority who aspire to implement them. It is therefore not surprising that 'we are better at identifying the ethical issues that face us than we are at thinking through how we should resolve them' (Pederson 1987: 224).

A pluralist society makes it extremely unlikely that common ground ethical principles can be sustained over time without at least some necessary modification to adapt to contemporary moral values and norms. Professional counselling and psychotherapy associations should commit to an evolving and open-ended attitude to the construction of ethical guidelines and be more responsive to the challenges faced by practitioners in the field. Indeed, we urge professional associations to establish mechanisms and procedures whereby experienced practitioners can be supported to periodically and, formally, reflect critically on contemporary ethical issues in ways that influence the review and revision of ethical guidelines. This would go some way to correct the top-down mentality that supports a dominant cultural perspective, which is largely unchallenged in the UK.

Psychotherapy implicitly transmits through its structural mechanisms and procedures values and attitudes about health, illness, human relating, and so on. It is essential therefore that the profession adopt a more positive and proactive approach both to the review and revision of its ethical and professional practice codes and the mechanisms and processes through which it does so. Too much time is spent 'on the back foot' interpreting ethical guidelines in reaction to complaints and too little time engaged in establishing guidelines that are responsive to the challenges in the field.

Figure 9.1 illustrates the various stages in our model of intentional ethical decision making, beginning with identification and clarification of the ethical issue/s through to planning, action, completion, and finally critical reflection and learning. The model demands far more than an uncritical application of a written code or regulation that may simply represent the typical knee jerk reaction or even an underlying process of avoidance.

We suggest that each stage of this cyclical process requires exploration and inquiry in five major areas: legal issues, moral values, ethical codes, multicultural factors and unconscious processes. All five areas will be present at all

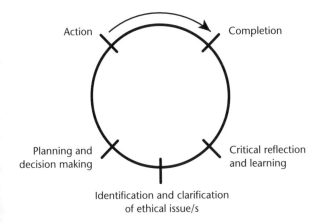

Action   Completion

Planning and   Critical reflection
decision making   and learning

Identification and clarification
of ethical issue/s

Figure 9.1   Stages in ethical decision making

stages of the cycle but certain areas will emerge as figural and therefore more significant at some stages than at others. For example, in the initial stage of identification and clarification of the issue/s it is likely that all five areas will need to be explored with obvious consideration of any legal issues that could, *in extremis*, overwhelm all other areas and completely dominate the field. Such a clear-cut situation is rare. At the planning and decision making stage unconscious processes might predominate as the level of anxiety rises as an ethical issue becomes an ethical dilemma. Such a situation is typical. The action stage might include the possibility of intentional non-action with the supervisor and supervisee accepting that there appears to be no way to progress the issue or that it is outside the domain of therapy. It can be an important point of growth for both supervisee and supervisor to acknowledge that a situation is outside their control. The completion stage of the cycle includes the possibility of living with an incomplete situation, a messy ending or a mistake. Whatever the outcome it is crucial that critical reflection on the content and process of ethical decision making is used to deepen awareness of the issues, inform future deliberations and contribute towards growing understanding and wisdom.

According to the *Concise Oxford Dictionary*, and the *Collins English Dictionary*, morality is concerned with the distinction between good and bad, right and wrong. Moral values are the moral principles or accepted standards of a person or group (*Collins English Dictionary*) and at a societal level are the 'learned preferences thought to be important and operationalized behaviourally' (*Websters New World Dictionary*). The law is the 'body of enacted or customary rules recognized by a community as binding' (*Concise Oxford Dictionary*) and a law is a rule instituted by Act of Parliament, custom or practice with the intent of punishing those who offend the conventions of society (*Collins English Dictionary*). Ethical codes are codes developed in accordance with the principles of conduct that are considered correct, especially those of a given profession or group (*Collins English Dictionary*).

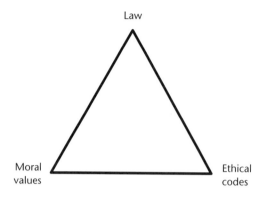

Figure 9.2   The basic triangle

Intentional ethical decision making will clearly need to include consideration of the law, moral values that may be relevant to a specific ethical issue and the ethical codes of a professional association (Figure 9.2). In an ideal world the moral values of a community would be enshrined in the laws governing behaviour within that community, which would in turn be compatible with the ethical codes of a particular profession. In reality there is usually a greater or lesser degree of compatibility between moral values, ethical codes and the law. In addition, each and all of these components will be influenced, to a greater or lesser extent, by unconscious processes (Figure 9.3).

The nature and efficacy of the relationship of supervisor and supervisee includes a focus on unconscious dynamics, for example parallel process, which may be the most significant factor influencing ethical decision making in specific instances.

Culture (Figure 9.4) may be described as the whole of the inherited beliefs, values and ideas, which together make up the shared basis of knowledge and social action of a community. If Figure 9.4 is rolled either to the left (Figure 9.5a), or right (Figure 9.5b), then it is clear that cultural issues impact on law, moral values, ethical codes and issues of process. As Ridley points out, 'In the process of making moral judgment it is essential to understand the moral reasoning within the cultural context where the behaviour being judged occurs' (Ridley 1995: 228).

We maintain that intentional ethical decision making will require of the supervisor the following major characteristics:

1 *Informed*: Intentional ethical decision making requires that supervisors are informed of relevant aspects of the law; that is, have a reasonable working knowledge of the law in relation to key areas of professional practice, for example confidentiality and dual relationships. In addition, supervisors should be committed to working towards the development of knowledge of multicultural issues. As Corey *et al.* assert, 'supervisors have an ethical responsibility to become aware of multicultural issues'

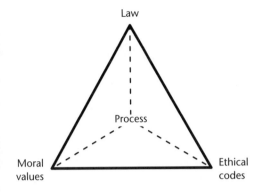

Figure 9.3 The basic triangle and process

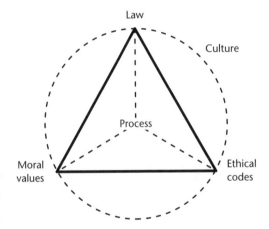

Figure 9.4 The basic triangle, process and culture

(Corey *et al.* 1993: 91). As suggested earlier we believe that this is an issue that requires investment not only from supervisors but also from training organizations and professional associations, if we are going to 'move toward pluralistic contextually sensitive ethical guidelines that accommodate different culturally learned assumptions for counsellors and their clients' (Pederson 1997: 268). Finally, and obviously, supervisors have a duty to maintain a familiarity with the current codes of ethics of their profession and be open to and develop their understanding of unconscious processes especially the countertransference and parallel process.

2 *Reflexive*: We believe that supervision requires of the supervisor the capacity/ ability to critically reflect on issues in relation to self and other. The following quotation from Pederson is applicable across the range of the

(a)

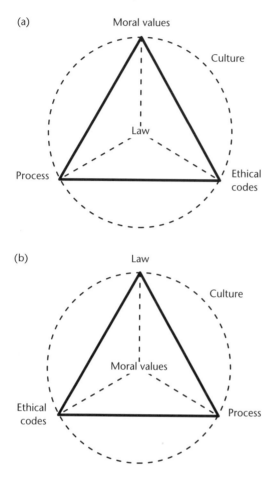

Figure 9.5   Universal impact of culture

domain of supervision, 'The best way to learn about ethical decisions in multi-cultural settings is to look at actual incidents where decisions were made and then evaluate whether or not the decisions were ethically appropriate' (Pederson 1997: 245). Farrel believes that intentionality is 'being self-concerned in being involved with the world' (Farrel 1994: 234) and reflexivity 'makes beliefs and intentions possible' (Farrel 1994: 238). Farrel maintains that it is through self-relating that one actualizes one's capacity to be self-determining and self-willing. We agree and would add that from a constructivist position the 'I' is a socially constructed experiential concept. One cannot stand outside one's culture so for any ethical standards to work the basic assumptions need to be identified and challenged in order for psychotherapists and supervisors to operate with intention in their ethical decision making.

Figure 9.6 The collaborative nature of the supervision process

3 *Collaborative*: The complexity of many ethical dilemmas requires consultation including supervision of supervision. Objection to this on grounds of seniority, experience and expertise suggests a resistance to consciousness raising that is potentially unethical. It seems to us that all practitioners, whatever their status or level of seniority, need the support of another person to reflect on process issues, especially the dynamics of power within a relationship. Figure 9.1 can be expanded (see Figure 9.6), to illustrate the collaborative nature of the supervision process. Inside the circle are the supervisor and supervisee but 'outside' in the environment are moral values, the law, ethical codes, multicultural factors and support for the supervisor in the form of supervision of supervision. Indeed it would not be possible to progress around the cycle without meaningful engagement with the environment.

4 *Emotional literacy*: The final characteristic of intentional ethical decision making we consider important is that of personal and professional maturity and, in particular, emotional literacy (Steiner 1984). We view maturity as a continuous process and not a fixed and static condition. Emotional fluency means to us, first, that the supervisor has a capacity to sustain vulnerability, second, a capacity to sustain ambiguity and, third, a capacity to live with the consequences of ethical decision making and action. This capacity to live with the consequences of one's decisions and actions touches on the personal and professional integrity of the supervisor, who may be in a position where their integrity requires stepping outside the law or going against established ethical and professional practice

to which people who have practised psychotherapy in oppressive regimes can amply testify.

In a recent article Lindsay and Clarkson published the results of a questionnaire sent to some 1000 psychotherapists on the United Kingdom Council for Psychotherapy (UKCP) Register. The psychotherapists were asked to respond describing some troubling ethical issues that they had encountered in their practice. The top four most troubling areas of ethical concern were confidentiality (31 per cent), dual relationships (12 per cent), conduct of colleagues (9 per cent) and sexual issues (8 per cent) (Lindsay and Clarkson 1999). Two further troublesome areas relate to issues of academia and training and professional competency. We now take each one in turn and discuss four related supervision vignettes (vignettes 5–8).

Vignette 5: Confidentiality

Earlier in this chapter reference is made to an ethical dilemma following disclosure to a counsellor by a 13-year-old girl of inappropriate touching by a school teacher. In supervision the emergent dilemma was whether to break confidentiality and risk premature termination of the therapeutic relationship or retain confidentiality and fail to protect the young girl and possibly others.

The young girl, whom we will call Caroline, was the eldest in a family of five children. Her parents were divorced and she lived at home with her mother and siblings and stepfather. Her relationship with her stepfather was characterized by conflict and with her mother was somewhat symbiotic. Caroline's mother was in poor health and Caroline undertook domestic responsibilities in excess of her years. Her friends were drawn from a peer group on her housing estate, which formed a subculture of delinquency bordering on criminal activity and with some of the older girls graduating to prostitution. Caroline was referred to the school counsellor because of her truancy and because of concern about her home situation. Initially morose and hostile Caroline had slowly and hesitatingly begun to form a fragile attachment to the counsellor and in a recent session had disclosed how a school teacher had grabbed her from behind and fondled her breasts. She had broken free and run off. When the counsellor expressed concern at this incident Caroline reacted anxiously and demanded that she tell no one because she did not trust any of the teachers and her mother would be upset. For the remainder of this session, during which the disclosure took place, the counsellor listened in a supportive and emphatic manner. There had been one more counselling session with Caroline prior to the supervision, during which neither Caroline nor the counsellor had referred to the disclosure in the previous session.

At the outset of the supervision session the supervisee established which clients she wished to review and did not present Caroline. It had been agreed at a previous supervision session that this session would be set aside for a caseload review. The supervisee had apparently 'forgotten' but responded positively to presenting an overview of her caseload. Some 15 minutes into the 60-minute supervision session the supervisee introduced Caroline describing her background, the reason for her referral and the slow and at times painstaking manner in which a degree of trust had now been established with the counsellor such that Caroline was able to share information about the inappropriate touching. The supervisee then began to move on and present another client. When the supervisor interrupted this process and raised the issue of protection for Caroline the counsellor looked startled, became anxious and emphasized the need to protect the still somewhat tentative therapeutic relationship. The supervisor also began to experience anxiety and became aware of a pull to collude by giving priority to protecting the therapeutic relationship rather than the child. Awareness of this change in the supervisor's perspective alerted the supervisor to the possibility of being drawn into a parallel process. Simultaneously the supervisee appeared to become less anxious and instead expressed surprise bordering on shock that she had not given sufficient attention to Caroline's protection. Further discussion revealed that the counsellor's concern for the welfare of Caroline and the need to protect the therapeutic alliance had temporarily blinded her to more immediate issues of safety and protection. The consequent dilemma for the counsellor was the knowledge that to break confidentiality would in all probability destroy the therapeutic alliance and confirm Caroline in her conviction that adults were not to be trusted. In this case the supervisor and supervisee agreed that there was a moral obligation to protect Caroline and also a legal duty. The law of confidentiality is somewhat ambiguous but in the case of children and young people, it does appear that a breach of confidence is defensible if it can be seen to be in the public interest, being enacted in accordance with a published code of ethics and professional practice and being restricted to people best able to act in the public interest, in this case the local social services department (Bond 1993).

Prior to making the disclosure the counsellor would first inform Caroline of what she was intending to do and the reasons for it. In this particular example there was a positive convergence of moral value, lawful conduct and ethical endeavour. In addition, the counsellor quickly became aware of the hitherto unconscious collusion to try and maintain the therapeutic alliance at the expense of the safety and protection of the client. She was also aware that the therapeutic relationship based on this degree of collusion could hardly be called an authentic alliance. The one major area of conflict was cultural in that Caroline belonged to a subculture which provided companionship and identity and would likely rebel against the counsellor's decision. Thus, after some initial difficulty, the ethical issue was clarified, decisions made, acted on and the likely adverse consequences for the therapeutic relationship accepted. Somewhat unusually the actual outcome was unexpected in that after some considerable protest from Caroline the quiet, persistent focus of protection and support from the counsellor was tearfully acknowledged by Caroline to be the only occasion she could remember in her life when someone other than her mother had shown any genuine concern for her. The therapeutic relationship survived this considerable threat to the working alliance.

Vignette 6: Conduct of colleagues

Samuel is a 32-year-old black social worker and graduate psychotherapist who works part-time for the local social services and part-time as a private psychotherapist. He has been a member of a supervision group for supervisees meeting monthly for four hours over a 12-month period. The supervisor requested supervision on her work with this supervisee and the group as the supervisee in question had remarked, in an offhand way, during the last supervision session, that he occasionally subsidized his supervision fees by selling an illegal recreational drug amongst his peer group. The supervisor had confronted the supervisee both for committing a criminal act and for potentially bringing the profession of psychotherapy into disrepute. Other members of the supervision group had supported her position, which the supervisee in question appeared ready to accept. However, in two subsequent supervision sessions the supervisee had, according to the supervisor, become withdrawn and defensive. The supervisor requested support to understand what unconscious processes might be at work and how she could move the supervision forward. The supervisor was invited to relate how she had approached the supervisee in their work at their last two meetings. The supervisor became quite animated and spoke at length of how she had addressed the supervisee. After a while it became apparent that she was asking the supervisee an inordinate number of questions and the more defensive he became, the more frequent the questions became. It was not difficult to appreciate that the supervisee might well be feeling intimidated by all these questions and it also became increasingly apparent that the supervisor was hiding her presence behind this plethora of questions, giving an initial appearance of working hard. In both sessions the supervisor only recalled one meaningful response from the supervisee and that was his struggle to build a psychotherapy practice. Currently he had three clients only. The supervisor's response was a further series of questions about what he might do to develop his practice. The consultant supervisor imagined that the supervisee might feel somewhat patronized by this.

While the supervisor had acted with moral integrity and complied with the law and professional code of ethics in confronting the supervisee, she was also missing the supervisee and unaware of the significance of unconscious processes or cultural factors in this case. The consultant supervisor was aware of the supervisor's personal and professional background and that she had first engaged in psychotherapy training as a single mother with two young children and shown considerable resilience and determination in successfully completing her training course and subsequently establishing a successful practice as a psychotherapist and supervisor. Working with the paradoxical theory of change (Beisser 1970) the consultant supervisor intentionally paralleled the process by repeatedly requesting information about the nature of her interchange with her supervisee and deliberately deflecting from being fully present. After several minutes she became more withdrawn and defensive, at which point he suggested that she consider providing additional supervision for this particular supervisee with the implication that she might do this free of charge? After a momentary experience of incredulity she rigorously protested, accused the consultant supervisor of not understanding how hard she worked and then 'the penny dropped'. She smiled, burst into laughter and then soberly acknowledged how patronizing she was being towards her supervisee. She further realized an underlying anxiety in being present with her supervisee, which she identified as concordant countertransference (Racker 1968) and understood to be feeling the feelings that the supervisee was resistant to bringing into awareness. She was then able to appreciate how her rapid fire questioning would be received with anxiety and fear, especially after the confrontation regarding criminal activity. During a further one-off follow-up session the supervisor shared her subsequent learning with her supervisee. In dropping the questioning and modelling presence the supervisee had also been more forthcoming and challenging. It emerged that his experience as a black therapist was that frequently white professionals expect him to do all the work for them. He correctly interpreted the questions as a lack of real presence and that white people have an unconscious expectation that it is the black person's task to educate them about issues of race and culture.

Vignette 7: Sexual abuse

The therapist brought to supervision a client who had been in therapy with him for one year, initially as part of the requirement of a psychotherapy training programme that she was attending. At the commencement of the second year of training she had disclosed to her training group that a former therapist had sexually abused her and she then immediately brought the issue to her individual therapy. The supervisee expressed considerable anger towards his client's former therapist coupled with concern that this person was still practising and possibly repeating the abuse with other clients. This former therapist of the client was indeed practising in the same city where the client's current therapist resides, was fairly well known and a long standing practitioner of an established therapy organization. The therapist also reported feeling somewhat anxious and a little fearful and unable to understand these emotions. On one level this was a straightforward ethical issue in that here was a clear and blatant abuse of power on the part of the therapist and the gross exploitation of the client. Prevailing moral values and cultural norms were also analogous. Indeed this was a situation where there was a clear discrepancy between ethical codes and prevailing moral values and the law in that sex between two adults is clearly not illegal. The law is deficient in its appreciation of transference phenomena. Had this been a minor then the situation would be different in law but an adult is considered consenting unless subjected to rape, which is in any case difficult to prove unless the perpetrator confesses. In our opinion sexual exploitation of clients within a professional relationship, whether it be psychotherapist–client, tutor–student, priest–parishioner, doctor–patient, should be considered a form of rape and so considered unlawful, not simply gross professional malpractice.

At the planning stage of ethical decision making unconscious processes became apparent when the psychotherapist wanted to write immediately to the former psychotherapist a letter of strong condemnation. It was at this stage that the psychotherapist's anxiety and fear began to surface and was connected with feelings of intimidation in making allegations against an established practitioner at a well known counselling organization. The supervisee was quick to appreciate that if he felt intimidated how much more strongly must his client feel so intimidated. With this came an appreciation that he was caught in a process of wanting to push the client along a path of his choosing and thereby unwittingly paralleling the process between the client and her former psychotherapist, albeit with more honourable intent. Supervision also revealed that the supervisee had an intellectual appreciation that she had been sexually abused but lacked conviction that the former psychotherapist was responsible. There were vestiges of guilt that she had allowed this to happen and concern that it would ruin his career. The supervisee was familiar with the victim's tendency to protect the abuser and was able to step back and allow the client to work at her own pace. After several months the client was able to experience and express her own sense of righteous indignation about the abuse and acknowledge that the responsibility lay with the psychotherapist. This awareness was in part precipitated by a chance meeting with the former psychotherapist who turned up at a public house that he knew the client frequented and propositioned her again. The client managed to have sufficient presence to confront him with abusing his power at which point he promptly withdrew and left the building. This actual confrontation of the abuser was an empowering experience for the client who then sought support from her psychotherapist to pursue the matter further. Subsequently both the psychotherapist and the client wrote letters to the director of the counselling organization that employed the former psychotherapist, broadly describing the allegations that his client was making, confirming her consent to write the letter and enclosing a letter from the client with a fairly detailed history of events. The organization acknowledged this correspondence within a matter of a few days and several days later wrote again to say they were pursuing the matter further with the person concerned. Eventually a letter from the Director confirmed that the psychotherapist had admitted that the allegations were true, had retired from practice and agreed to re-enter personal therapy. A brief letter of apology from the psychotherapist accompanied this letter. In our experience this is an unusually successful outcome in cases of this type.

A similar case produced a different result. Again the client was a new trainee on a psychotherapy training programme who had been sexually abused by a tutor acting in the role of student counsellor at a former college of higher education. Again the client worked on this issue in therapy for some considerable time and then requested support to confront the perpetrator. A letter was sent to both the tutor concerned and the college principal. After some three weeks when no response whatsoever was received the psychotherapist and client sent a further letter seeking a response. Several days later there was a cursory acknowledgement from the college principal, the contents of which were ambiguous in the extreme such that it was unclear whether the tutor concerned had been confronted and any outcome achieved. The client wrote a letter seeking clarification, which received no response.

Eventually, the college principal wrote a curt and dismissive letter to say that he was not pursuing the matter any further and again giving no indication as to what action, if any, had been taken. At this point the client drew a line under any further attempt to seek redress.

Whilst both clients were able to work through these issues to a considerable extent, the latter client reportedly was left with a certain melancholy or heaviness of the heart as her psychotherapist described her, such that hers was not quite the fullness of healing as the client who had had an acknowledgement that a wrong had been perpetrated on her. In this latter case clearly the situation was left incomplete and there was the frustration arising from this, together with an ongoing sense of injustice and a concern for the well-being of other students. In this case the supervisee experienced a degree of vicarious trauma for the duration of the client's personal psychotherapy.

Vignette 8: Dual relationships

This vignette highlights an ethical dilemma regarding a situation that was not illegal or immoral or problematic within the general culture – a situation where it is even unclear whether there was a breach of professional ethics. However, the situation resulted in a significant difficulty in terms of professional practice. The supervisee brought to supervision a couple who had initially come to him for couples counselling and after several seemingly constructive sessions each partner was able to identify significant issues that they might fruitfully work on in individual therapy. The psychotherapist offered to work with one of the partners and recommended a colleague to work with the other partner. Having seen the wife on two separate occasions she mentioned that her husband had been unsuccessful in securing psychotherapy with the recommended psychotherapist who was apparently now having to operate a waiting list. She also reported that he was quite anxious to proceed with his personal psychotherapy and suggested that the psychotherapist, who knew something about him, might consider working with him in the short term until the recommended psychotherapist had a vacancy. Several weeks later and the supervisee was still working with each partner and the husband was reluctant to transfer to another psychotherapist. The supervisee was now both concerned and intrigued about why he had got himself entangled in such a situation and felt pulled in both directions and reluctant to terminate therapy with either of the partners. He presented some fairly convincing reasons why it would be disruptive to either partner to transfer to another psychotherapist but he was beginning to experience some difficulty in working therapeutically in this situation. Specifically, it emerged that the husband had disclosed two extramarital affairs in the five years that the couple had been married, neither of which were known to his wife. The psychotherapist was now left compromised. He possessed confidential information from one client which if known to the other would clearly have a profound impact. On the other hand the husband seemed generally committed to working through issues to do with commitment and appeared desperate to resolve these issues.

The supervisee was challenged to reflect on whether the husband's history had any connections with his own? Immediately the scales fell from the psychotherapist's eyes and were replaced by tears as he recognized that he was identifying with the client and engaged in trying to rescue him. He went on to appreciate that the husband was repeating with his wife the same pattern that his father had with himself. The husband's father had apparently been a charming, persuasive and totally unreliable individual with a seductive personality. The client had seduced the psychotherapist into an unhealthy confluence replaying history in the present. An exploration of the unconscious processes at work identified the potential ethical issue to do with boundaries. The supervisee was aware that he had allowed himself to be seduced into confusing the boundaries and paralleling the process of the client's history rather than modelling good practice. It was apparent that there was only one appropriate course of action and that was to terminate the psychotherapy with the husband. Through the supervisee's subsequent therapy with the wife, she had reported that her husband had not liked the decision but had respected the reasons and secured an alternative psychotherapist, indicating perhaps a degree of internalization of appropriate modelling?

Reflection on the four vignettes

In critically reflecting on these four vignettes what impacts us most is the place of moral integrity in the work of supervision. In a pluralistic society and across a range of competing moral values it is apparent to us that the moral integrity of all supervisees and supervisors in these vignettes is the result of the internalization of the values inherent in the profession of counselling and psychotherapy: namely, honesty, critical self-reflection, altruism, commitment to competence, respect for clients and acknowledgement of their right to be different, willingness to confront structural and historical inequality, and to challenge abuses of power. Above all we are impressed by the supervisors' and the therapists' willingness in supervision to tolerate vulnerability and engage in the struggle for ethical and professional practice.

Complaints procedures: balance of probability or beyond all reasonable doubt?

It is universally acknowledged that a complaints procedure is established on the principles of justice and fairness for both the person making the complaint and the person/organization complained against. However, in the process of hearing complaints a problem frequently encountered by adjudication panels is the relative absence or paucity of 'external' supporting evidence. As a consequence of this there is an over-reliance on the 'evidence' of the two parties with their often differing perceptions of incidents, events and circumstances. On what basis should a decision be reached?

Balance of probability or beyond all reasonable doubt? The latter may unwittingly discriminate against the person bringing the complaint whilst the former may unwittingly discriminate against the person complained against. Conventional wisdom has tended to come down on the side of 'beyond all reasonable doubt'. Currently we favour this position because of the lack of adequate knowledge of legal issues and procedures within the profession rendering it difficult to arrive at confident and mature judgements on a balance of probabilities.

Complaints procedures are often inappropriately used to process complaints that may be better dealt with through alternative channels, for example a grievance procedure or disciplinary procedure. We are thinking especially of conflict that may arise as a result of a breakdown in the therapeutic alliance rather than any specific act of unethical or unprofessional behaviour. Transference acting out and projective identification can give rise to conflict with considerable personal distress for both client and psychotherapist. When such a therapeutic rupture occurs, it is unfortunately the case that the client has no alternative but to attempt redress through a complaints procedure. In such circumstances a complaints procedure is a totally inappropriate vehicle by which to attempt redress because inevitably the issues are polarized with the client having to concretize his distress by reference to specific instances, events, statements or behaviours and the psychotherapist having to defend herself. The situation is usually exacerbated when both sides are impelled to secure legal representation. Consequently, the focus is on establishing 'facts' and weighing so-called 'evidence' rather than on an exploration of the unconscious processes operating within the therapy. The psychotherapist is impelled to adopt a defensive posture because of the possible repercussions on his or her career.

Complaints procedures may also be used inappropriately to initiate a 'malicious' complaint whereby both the code of ethics and complaints procedures may be manipulated by one party against another and with a hidden agenda, for example, professional rivalry fuelled by envy, a wounded ego or financial gain. In this latter event, the complaints procedure is initiated solely as a transitory step to support a civil action with the aim of securing compensation. This reflects the shadow side of the profession.

We suggest there is a strong case for complaints to be taken up within the legal system where both parties should have access to legal support. There should be an extension of legal aid for clients and compulsory insurance cover for psychotherapists. The profession would retain initial responsibility for considering the appropriateness of any complaint. A panel of professional senior clinicians or some alternative group constellated for this purpose would first determine whether there are grounds to support an allegation of unethical behaviour and decide whether or not to direct the parties concerned to law. Should the legal proceedings find in favour of the complainant, then the professional body will rule on the psychotherapist's continuing status within the profession. Of course, just as psychotherapists are not educated in resolving legal issues neither are lawyers experienced in understanding unconscious process.

Alternatively we welcome the decision of the UKCP to create a grievance procedure and a disciplinary procedure in addition to, and separate from, the complaints procedure. This will permit many issues to be processed outside the formal complaints procedure. We also advocate greater use of mediation in the initial stages of grievance procedures and complaints procedures with a view to achieving reconciliation before positions become polarized and conflictual. In our view the quasi-legal basis inherent in any complaints procedure should be fully acknowledged and steps taken to establish within the profession a group of senior practitioners educated and trained in legal issues. Alternatively we advocate that lawyers involved in this type of work develop a speciality in the growing area of psychotherapy litigation to include an understanding and appreciation of the complexity of psychotherapy especially of unconscious process and its potential impact on the perspectives of *all* parties concerned.

Questions for further reflection

1 How well did your psychotherapy training equip you to deal with ethical dilemmas?
2 In what circumstances, if any, might you break client confidentiality and what support systems do you have to help you process any conflict between the law and the potential threat to the therapeutic alliance?
3 On what basis should the outcome of complaints be determined? Balance of probability or beyond all reasonable doubt?
4 Psychotherapists are not educated in resolving legal issues and lawyers are not trained to understand unconscious process. So who should hear complaints?

10 ▷ Multicultural aspects and anti-oppressive practice in supervision and in psychotherapy

In this chapter we argue that mainstream psychotherapy theories are culturally encapsulated and lack awareness of multicultural issues. Widespread ignorance, we maintain, is the single most significant factor perpetuating oppressive practice in psychotherapy. We further argue the overwhelming case for reform in psychotherapy training organizations together with an urgent need for greater attention to these issues by clinical supervisors. Action by both trainers and supervisors is necessary in order to combat the complacency that supports ignorance. We conclude with a brief example of some of the challenges that need to be addressed by training organizations when confronting their own oppressive practice and structures.

A definition of culture

In the concluding section of his book, *Counselling Supervision*, Carroll makes this statement concerning multicultural issues: 'there is no doubt the domain is fraught with difficulty' (Carroll 1996: 4). He cites the review of the literature on cultural issues by Leong and Wagner (1994), which concluded that little was known about cultural issues in supervision, alongside the research of Thompson (1991), which revealed that among four supervision training programmes canvassed there was little or no formal teaching on cultural issues. In the UK cross-cultural training in supervision is in its infancy and few supervisors have had in-depth training in multicultural counselling, so much the less in a multicultural framework for supervision.

Eleftheriadou (1994) defines culture as 'a way of creating shared ways of functioning in order to communicate effectively', including 'shared events, practices, roles, values, myths, rules, beliefs, habits, symbols, illusions and realities'. He points out that culture is dynamic, and ever-changing and 'exists inside people (psychologically) and outside (in the existing social institutions)'. It is not a closed and fixed system in that it changes with each generation as well as being influenced by exposure to new immigrants and therefore to other 'cultural constructions' (Eleftheriadou 1994: 2). The broad definition of culture suggested by Eleftheriadou is increasingly being accepted by authorities in the field (Bernard 1994; Ridley 1995; Pedersdon 1997) and extends culture beyond ethnicity and race. This broad definition goes further than the previous definitions that limited culture to multi-ethnic relationships and includes disability, age, religion, political affiliation, gender, sexual orientation, class and status. This accords with a field theory perspective that honours all the elements in a particular context as relevant to the supervisory process. It recognizes people in their overall complexity encompassing their racial and cultural identity and better equips therapists to deal with the complex differences within and between cultural groups in context.

Increasingly culture is seen as a social construction that is supported by, deconstructed and reconstructed through our social relationships. It 'cannot be accessed sufficiently through the narrow personal relationship between the psychotherapist and the individual client . . . especially not if the cultural background of therapist and client are markedly different' (Krause 1998: 4). Even where there are marked similarities derived from a 'shared cultural background' the supervisor is advised to be cautious about assuming a convergence of experience. One of the authors who left South Africa some 15 years ago, is keenly aware that people who are living in that country now have a widely differing social, political and cultural experience from her own under apartheid. Assumptions that may have had relevance then are often no longer applicable now. This position has implications for us as supervisors: we need to question our assumptions about the helping process as we know it and explore the relevance of our models of psychotherapy for people who come from different cultures, eras and contexts. Samuels supports this position 'depth psychology must face the problem that it is not possible to depict a person divorced from his or her cultural, social, gender, ethnic and, above all, economic and ecological contexts' (Samuels 1993: 201).

Recent developments in the United Kingdom

In the past five years we have noticed among psychotherapy trainees with a social science or psychology background a growing awareness of the significance of cultural pluralism in the West and a 'bottom-up' demand that training programmes attend to issues of oppression. There also appears to be a growing recognition of the importance of multiculturalism among the major professional organizations, for example: the Intercultural and Equal Opportunities Committee of the UKCP, the division of Race and Cultural Education (RACE) of the British Association for Counselling (BAC), the sub-section of race and culture of the British Psychological Society (BPS), the Transcultural Psychiatry Society, Nafsiyat – the intercultural therapy centre, and the creation of Psychotherapists and Counsellors for Social Responsibility. This, together with the increase in books and articles on multicultural issues has begun to impact on counselling and psychotherapy training programmes and may account for the fact that the number of participants from ethnic minority groups training in counselling and psychotherapy has shown a modest but definite increase in training institutes.

The perpetuation of anti-oppressive practice

However, these developments appear to us to be at the very leading edge and the influence of culture remains grossly underestimated both in society in general and within the mental health profession as a whole. Ethnic groups suffer educational, social and economic oppression giving rise to racial conflict in most nations in Western Europe and North America. Pilgrim (1997) highlights the disproportionate incidence in the compulsory detention of Afro-British persons for psychiatric treatment, their tendency to be diagnosed as schizophrenic and the severity of intervention with major tranquillizers and electro-convulsive therapy (ECT). According to Lowenstein (1987), there is a significantly higher drop-out rate from therapy among ethnic minority groups than the white population, with half not returning to therapy after the first session. We agree with Eleftheriadou that this is largely due to the ignorance, prejudice and racism of western mental health professionals (Eleftheriadou 1994). We consider it important that as practitioners and as supervisors we explore models of psychotherapy that are community based and sensitive to the needs of different groups in our country.

Indeed, we maintain that ignorance is the key factor in perpetuating oppressive practice in psychotherapy and that ignorance is supported by a complacency borne of the fact that the profession of psychotherapy occupies a privileged and powerful position and operates dominant normative models that are left largely unquestioned and unchallenged. Heath attributes this lethargy to 'the widespread tendency to elevate scientific methodology into an icon of theoretical confidence', which has influenced psychotherapy theory and practice, but there has not been 'the necessary testing of carefully articulated theories by equally rigorous research projects' (Heath 2000: 3). Monotheoretical based training programmes present the psychotherapies as rather self-contained bodies of knowledge often conveying the impression that a particular approach represents the 'truth' of psychotherapy. It is salutary to remind ourselves that Karuso (1984) identified over 480 different presumably universal and self-contained theories of counselling and psychotherapy (quoted in Dryden and Norcross 1990: 4).

Ridley (1995) makes the claim that many psychotherapists are unaware of the implications of their models in, for example, perpetuating racism and would confirm the view of Spinelli (1994) that psychotherapists are philosophically naïve. Psychotherapy should not avoid philosophical issues and their impact on the ways in which psychotherapeutic theories and concepts are put into practice. We believe that the epistemological assumptions of a psychotherapeutic theory should be stated as the 'assumptive foundation' of that theory, allowing these assumptions to be explicit and more accessible to critique. Writing from a feminist perspective Espin and Gawelek (1992: 88) make a similar point: 'Theories of . . . psychopathology have been notorious for their neglect of cultural variability as well as gender issues. Most psychological theory is literally Anglo-Saxon in its perspectives and conception of human nature'.

Models of mental health and oppression

In the psychotherapy profession normal and abnormal behaviour are represented by several different models of mental health. These are regarded as the professional standards by which psychotherapists can judge normality. Ridley (1995) identifies several models of mental health, beginning with the medical model, which is the dominant framework used by mental health professionals to understand and treat psychiatric problems shared also by classical psychoanalysis, which is 'unsurpassed in shaping the thinking and practice of mental health treatment' (Ridley 1995: 44).

The medical model focuses on illness, adopts the classical doctor–patient vertical relationship emphasizing professional expertise and knowledge and client dependency. The professional interprets meaning for the other, which we believe to be oppressive. According to Ridley the medical model leads to unintentional racism through the tendency to reduce all social problems to intrapsychic processes, the tendency to over-pathologize individuals and the consequent neglect of social, economic and political factors, for example, in assessment and treatment planning. The mental health services do not tend towards rehabilitation, instead focusing attention on reducing the effects of severe mental disturbance with limited attention to prevention and health promotion. It is hardly surprising that psychotherapy has been called the 'handmaiden of the status quo' (Halleck 1971, quoted in Ridley 1995).

The conformity model for evaluating normal behaviour evolving out of the scientific tradition of the social sciences assumes a normal distribution of characteristics and behaviours throughout a population. Interpretation of individual behaviour is referred to the normative or standardized sample such that norms provide an external standard permitting interpretation of individual behaviour. Ridley argues persuasively that this is another form of unintentional racism, which imposes majority group values on minority clients. The majority culture will determine what is regarded as 'normal' or 'abnormal'. In this way, what is regarded as deviance in another culture may be accepted as the norm in the prevailing one. How deviant does one have to be in order to be deviant? How often does one have to non-conform to be deviant? (Phares 1992, quoted by Ridley 1995).

The deficit model for evaluating normality views ethnic minorities as basically flawed. Minorities are regarded as possessing predetermined genetic deficiencies. These may be defined as an intellectual deficiency (born with an inferior brain) or a cultural deficiency (born into an inferior culture or having no culture at all). This is the most explicit racist model of mental health.

However, unintentional racism is implicit when supervisors either lower their expectations for certain supervisees or create unrealistically high expectations, thereby setting the supervisee up to fail.

The effects of oppression

Both oppressors and the oppressed have internalized certain assumptions about one another that shape their behaviours. In describing the nature of oppression Heath writes, 'Oppression results from deeply internalised, typically unconscious negative attitudes held by dominant groups in a society. . . . Domination is expressed through the asymmetry of power and through the imposition of dominant norms. Furthermore, negative attitudes, stereotypes and prejudicial perspectives do not merely reside in the minds of the dominant group but are deeply ingrained aspects of the structure of society' (Heath 1998: 2). A colleague reports that on securing a part-time appointment as a humanistic psychotherapist within a UK NHS community mental health centre, she was directed to supervision in an alternative approach to psychotherapy with a professional who worked from a different single school perspective and who had little or no knowledge of either the theoretical base or clinical practice of the new employee. Consequently, the new employee experienced oppression and marginalization. The organization maintained a rigid and inflexible stance accompanied by a derogatory attitude to her area of expertise. She 'resolved' the situation by arranging additional and parallel supervision about which she maintained secrecy.

The social structures, including our models of mental health create and perpetuate oppressive norms and what Smail (1998) calls 'The Tyranny of Normality'. The dominant knowledge of the western middle-class therapeutic professional, however benevolentized, inevitably devalues other forms of culturally constructed knowledge (Kareem and Littlewood 1992; Fulani 1998). Knowledge is power, said Francis Bacon in the early seventeenth century; knowledge is never neutral and the power of knowledge is powerful said Foucault in the twentieth century (Bertens 1995). Structural oppression gives power to those who have high and normative status, 'A Person Needs Power to Behave Like a Racist' Proposition 6 (Ridley 1995: 21). When oppression is structural conscious efforts to perpetuate oppression are not required because it seems unconsciously normal to the majority of people in the context.

Following the broader definition of culture, including issues beyond race, we give below an example of oppression in the UK in each of the following areas: gender, sexual orientation, education, politics and religion. A survey of Clergy reported in the *Observer* newspaper (5/4/98) uncovered emotional abuse of women priests who used the phrase 'glass ceiling' to describe blockages to promotion. This glass ceiling operates in professions and in the workplace where women and minority group workers can see the upper reaches of the hierarchy but effective barriers operate against getting there. Gay couples and lesbians cannot be legally married in Britain. Forty per cent of Oxbridge students are educated in private schools, which educate 7 per cent of UK children. Until 1999 hereditary peers formed part of the second chamber and were not elected, including Anglican bishops from the 'one' Church of England and only men!

Heath claims he can usually tell when a book is written by a male through the use of pseudo generic 'he' as if it applied to all people, cultures and sexes. 'Use of pseudo generic "he" hides a dominant form of discourse which assumes that male norms and perspectives are universally valid' (Heath 1998: 5). In Bronowski's *The Ascent of Man* there are 15 pages of index to the book but only two references to women; in Kenneth Clarke's *Civilisation* there are two references to women (Heath 1998: 5–6).

Philosophical support for a new perspective

Traditional psychotherapy and counselling theories are supported by philosophical assumptions that perpetuate oppressive practice. However, we believe that the postmodern paradigm is beginning to impact on the profession and will present the greatest challenge to psychotherapeutic theory and practice in the opening decades of this new millennium. Tarnas maintains that from the postmodern perspective reality and knowledge are constantly changing such that no single set of assumptions can be regarded as secure. 'Truth' is ambiguous, always a possibility, never a fact (Tarnas 1996). Fact is precisely what there is not, claimed Nietzsche in 1906. This is succinctly stated by Lyotard (1984) as follows: 'I define post modernism as incredulity to metanarratives'. Thus, what we know is what we construct as reality and is dependent on how we construct it. Culture creates knowledge and because cultures are different knowledge is different. In other words, people live in different realities dependent on their own individual and unique experience.

As discussed earlier, constructivism and field theory are the postmodern philosophical constructs that are the foundation of our approach to the theory and practice of psychotherapy and supervision. 'A constructivist approach orients toward assessing the viability (utility) as opposed to the validity (truth) of an individual's unique world view' (Neimeyer and Neimeyer 1993: 2). From the constructivist perspective human behaviour and knowledge are socially and culturally constructed. Consequently, as Krause argues much of the detail of human activity cannot be understood solely by examining internal bodily and mental processes and the psychotherapist is no longer able to be a separate and detached observer (Krause 1998: 66). In similar vein Samuels writes, 'The analyst is not an authority or teacher who has prior knowledge of the psychological implications of the patient's ethnic and cultural background. Rather he or she is a mediator who enables the patient to experience or express his or her own difference. When it comes to cultural differences, analysts should privilege individual experience over universal and abstract formations' (Samuels 1993: 328). We agree with Krause that constructivism is a revolutionary challenge to psychotherapy not least because it draws attention to the power asymmetry between psychotherapist and client. It challenges the paradigm where power and control are located with the psychotherapist (Krause 1998).

Whereas the classical science of Newtonian physics defines in terms of separation, for example, cause from effect, energy from mass, observer from observed, field theory recognizes the interconnectedness of phenomena such that meaning is achieved only through the relationship to the total field. From the field theoretical perspective a human being is conceptualized as existing in continuing interplay with the environment (the organism–environment field). Field theory embraces a holistic view of the person interacting with the environment, the social world, organizations and the cultural milieu. Everything exists in connection with everything else so that any change in any part affects all other parts of the field. Therefore an event is not caused by a single preceding event but phenomena are interrelated in a complex process. Consequently the client's dis-ease is not pathologized but viewed in context. 'The therapist cannot simply concern herself with an event but the whole physical, emotional, social and cultural context in which it took place' (Parlett 1991). Field theory and specifically multicausality mitigates against generalizing about causes and enables the psychotherapist to take account both of the client's total situation and how this is different from her own. Field theory, like constructivism, are potentially emancipatory concepts directing the therapist to focus 'awareness of those factors that are relevant to the particular client rather than assuming certain factors will be relevant' (Parlett 1993).

The field theoretical concept of figure and ground supports the psychotherapist to navigate through the 'confusion and complexity of their own and others' experience and understanding' (Heath 2000). The field is organized by needs so that some things will be more immediately important (figure) than others (ground). Of course the figure changes with changing needs so what was once figure recedes into the ground and a new figure emerges. Furthermore, because change in any part of the field affects the whole field, then changes in the ground (environment) changes the figure. The psychotherapist will thus impact the client and likewise the client will impact the psychotherapist in a field of mutual reciprocity. Support for the field theory perspective can be found in the fast developing field of consciousness studies. For example, Varela *et al.* (1993) explore what they call the enacted processes whereby human minds create consensually agreed constructions of reality. A person creates her world moment by moment but requires the existence of an other to do so, in co-dependent origination. The image offered by Varela and his co-authors is of the 'path created in walking'. Everything is co-created, including meaning. The philosophical underpinnings of our integrative approach to psychotherapy and supervision based in the dialogical approach originating with Martin Buber (1996) and in intersubjectivity theory is compatible with the biopsychosocial model advocated by Ridley (1995) as supporting a multicultural approach to counselling and psychotherapy with its emphasis on the whole person.

Our model is supported by, but elaborates on, the approach advocated by Eleftheriadou, who maintains that the therapy relationship should aspire towards equality. It is important for the psychotherapist to explore the client's feelings towards a psychotherapist of a different race and culture, 'including the ability to accept a client's distrust or anger toward the majority culture' (Eleftheriadou 1994: 34). Thus, the psychotherapist is not a detached observer giving 'expert' interpretations of the client's behaviour but works with an attitude of horizontalization or equalization, attempting to avoid hierarchies in description of behaviour. All phenomena are accepted as normal, as a person's subjective reality.

Eleftheriadou makes a helpful distinction, with which we agree, between a cross-cultural approach, which implies we 'use our own reference system to understand another person rather than going beyond our own world views' and a transcultural approach, which 'denotes that counsellors need to work beyond their cultural differences' (Eleftheriadou 1994: 31). Phenomenological analysis can transcend culture because it honours the unique world views of both client and psychotherapist, and requires the psychotherapist to examine his or her own world view and value system and how it may influence the therapeutic work. 'True dialogue requires the appreciation of difference' (Evans 1996). Ridley calls the tuning in to the client's world the 'ideographic' perspective wherein every client should be understood from their own frame of reference with the recognition that persons are more than their racial and cultural identity. By focusing on the individual and refusing to be constrained by a single psychotherapeutic orientation the ideographic perspective is clearly transtheoretical (Ridley 1995: 82–83).

Reform in psychotherapy training organizations

In view of the limited knowledge and awareness that exists within the psychotherapy profession with regard to multicultural issues there is an urgent need to raise awareness of these issues and of the anti-oppressive practice inherent in mainstream psychotherapeutic theories. These include pseudo-universalistic assumptions that are largely unexamined; normative male and western-dominated theories; exclusion from dominant forms of discourse; and resistance due to internalized typically unconscious negative attitudes to the challenge of multiculturalism. Psychotherapy training should include explicit work on cross-cultural studies, which deal with different psychological and existential constructions of meaning, behaviour and pathology. In addition, work towards a more transcultural approach can extend theoretical perspectives beyond the parameters of a particular model and so further develop and refine psychotherapeutic theory. We agree with Corey, Corey and Callahan (1993) that supervisors have an ethical responsibility to become aware of multicultural issues. However, the burden cannot fall to supervisors alone but requires a shared responsibility with professional training organizations.

We set out below a brief summary of key features in an organization's engagement with multicultural issues through the development of an effective equal opportunities policy between 1996 and 1999.

In 1995 this organization had an equal opportunities statement running to a couple of sentences. There was no formal training in multicultural issues in the supervision training programme or in any of the organization's three psychotherapy programmes, other than the employment of an outside trainer to facilitate a three-day workshop on race for final (4th) year trainees of one of the psychotherapy programmes. However, this workshop was so well received by the students that they demanded a deeper engagement with the issues across the organization as a whole. Subsequently an outside consultant was employed and immediately identified a fundamental problem, namely that the equal opportunities policy statement had been written by only one person within the organization. As a result, the statement could not be truly owned by the organization and the finely worded statement lacked any real credibility. On the recommendation of the consultant the governing body of the organization agreed the creation of an equal opportunities committee that would consist of representatives of teaching staff, therapists, trainees and administrative and secretarial staff.

The committee's first task was to write an equal opportunities policy and statement via a process of consultation with the membership of the organization. The resulting statement was thus more authentic and credible and the process generated increased consciousness of multicultural issues. The organization agreed that the equal opportunities committee should become a standing committee meeting every six weeks and that it would create its own terms of reference and membership criteria. Significantly, membership included key personnel from the governing body so that responsibility and power were not divided and the committee was able to exercise its responsibilities with authority.

The committee identified several problem areas that required attention:

- A dearth of up-to-date literature on multicultural aspects of counselling and psychotherapy.
- Little or no training in multicultural issues by the majority of teaching staff.
- No formal training input on multicultural issues within the three psychotherapy programmes or the supervision training programme other than that mentioned above. However, a serious and reasonably successful attempt had been made to incorporate these issues into the counselling programme.
- Serious deficiencies in the physical environment, which adversely impacted on a range of disabilities.
- Insufficient information concerning multicultural issues/equal opportunities in the prospectus, newsletter, and other literature circulated by the organization to the general public.
- Only three trainees in the counselling programme from ethnic minority groups; the three psychotherapy programmes had one trainee from ethnic minority groups.
- No members of staff from ethnic minorities, with the exception of the visiting trainer to the three-day workshop above.
- No procedure for monitoring applications for training places to establish whether or not discrimination had been experienced in the process of application.

This initial review was completed by the equal opportunities committee in 1996 and made dismal reading. We suspect that this situation is not untypical across training organizations in the UK. This particular organization took up the challenge and between 1997 and April 1999 the following action was taken:

- The organization agreed an annual budget to purchase books and articles on multicultural issues so that by April 1999 this section of the library had an extensive range of material including most of the major texts published up to and including 1998.

- The organization agreed a policy requiring all training staff to undertake education in multicultural issues within 12 months as a priority of their commitment to continued professional development.
- In addition the organization employed an outside trainer to run a series of study days on anti-oppressive practice.
- From the commencement of the training year 1998/99 teaching on anti-oppressive practice was introduced into the first year of all three training programmes so that the issues could permeate throughout the four-year programmes.
- A procedure was agreed whereby programme leaders from all training programmes met once each year with the equal opportunities committee to monitor and review the incorporation of teaching on multiculturalism and anti-oppressive practice.
- The organization agreed and instituted a monitoring form whereby applicants for training programmes and all clients of the organization can, anonymously, inform the organization of any discriminatory practice.
- Physical changes were made to one of the training sites to allow wheelchair access and a hearing loop system installed in a major training area.
- Additional computers were installed for the use of all trainees and with priority use for trainees with dyslexia.

The three-year experience thus far has proved extremely challenging for all categories of membership within the organization and with several unexpected spin-offs:

- A greater transparency of procedures and processes within and between the various levels of the organization.
- An increase in communication and co-operation among and between teaching staff of the counselling, psychotherapy and supervision training programmes within the organization.
- The working through of unconscious processes and resistance to embracing a situation where diversity is on the way to becoming the 'norm' rather than mono-cultural exclusivity.

The organization accepts this is an ongoing process that requires continuous review and critical reflection. Further development and plans for the immediate future include:

- Training workshops on multicultural issues for all the clinical supervisors within the organization as a part of their continued professional development.
- The inclusion of reference to anti-oppressive practice in the ethical codes of the organization for practitioners, trainers and supervisors.
- The creation of introductory educational workshops in psychotherapy for members of ethnic minorities with tutors drawn from ethnic minorities.

We conclude with a provocative statement by Heath, 'One of the typical symptoms of oppression is that there are no resources available to address the oppressed groups' concerns and dilemmas. Only selected and dominant "truths" can be met. No time. No resources . . . means no inclination and no commitment' (Heath 2000: 7).

Anti-oppression audit

We invite the reader to complete the simple audit of oppressive practice below by critically reflecting on the make-up of your organization in terms of ethnicity, gender, sexual orientation, religion, political affiliation, class, status, age and disability.

- Examine your recruitment of psychotherapists, supervisors and trainers from ethnic and other minorities.
- Examine patterns of interaction between your teaching staff.
- Examine your client groups.
- Examine your training curriculum.

We wish to acknowledge the students who were courageous enough to acknowledge they belong to minority groups and asserted their right to have their perspectives listened to.

11 ▷ Psychotherapy and supervision in the UK, in Europe and in the wider context

Psychotherapy and supervision in the United Kingdom

The context of psychotherapy and supervision in the UK is rich, varied and extremely complex to unravel, especially for the newcomer to the field. We look briefly at the organizational context of psychotherapy in this country and then relate this to the wider context of the field in Europe. This is followed with a review of the field from the point of view of the practitioner working in this domain.

There are several organizations in this country involved in the training and delivery of psychotherapy. The main protagonists are the United Kingdom Council for Psychotherapy (UKCP), the British Confederation of Psychotherapy (BCP), and the British Psychological Society (BPS).

The UKCP started some 15 years ago, first as the Rugby Conference, then as the United Kingdom Standing Conference for Psychotherapy and more recently as the United Kingdom Council for Psychotherapy. It produces a voluntary register annually of all the registered members of its member organizations. From its inception, the aim of this organization has been to regulate the profession of psychotherapy by standardizing training requirements, drawing up codes of ethics and professional practice, publishing a voluntary register and providing a forum for issues impacting on the profession of psychotherapy. The UKCP is now rapidly approaching its goal of achieving statutory regulation for the profession. The UKCP comprises eight sections: Analytical Psychology; Behavioural and Cognitive Psychotherapy; Experiential/Constructivist; Family, Couple, Sexual and Systemic; Humanistic and Integrative Psychotherapy; Hypno-Psychotherapy; Psychoanalytic and Psychodynamic Psychotherapy; and Psychoanalytically-based therapy with Children.

From the start there have also been institutional members and currently these include the Tavistock Clinic and the Universities Psychotherapy Association. The British Psychological Society and The Royal College of Psychiatrists are 'special' members. The British Association for Counselling, which called together the first Rugby Conference, have remained as 'friends of the council'. The Rugby Conference included in its membership the Institute of Psychoanalysis and other core psychoanalytic trainings so that the conference was indeed representative of the field. In the course of the evolution of the UKCP, differences of opinion and emphasis led to the withdrawal of the Institute of Psychoanalysis and some other core psychoanalytic trainings who constituted themselves as the British Confederation of Psychotherapy and have published their own register. Other psychoanalytic trainings remain within UKCP to constitute the Psychoanalytic and Psychodynamic Psychotherapy Section with its 30 or so member organizations. The UKCP remains the largest organization and covers the widest range of orientations, modalities and approaches to psychotherapy in the United Kingdom.

The British Psychological Society also has within its membership a large number of practising clinicians, many trained in a cognitive-behavioural, a psychodynamic or an integrative approach to client work. The BPS now has its own Psychotherapy Section, which is promoting the interests of psychotherapists in the society.

The accredited psychotherapist in the United Kingdom is faced with a complex situation. He may work either in the private or in the public sector or combine work in both of these in his practice. A private practice takes time to establish since there are many other practitioners in the field and since reputations and networks take time and effort to build up in any geographical area. Most clients will be paying for themselves, except where their health care cover contributes a certain amount, so clients are usually from a more affluent section of society. Some private practitioners have joint practices, which provide a range of options to prospective clients and also ensure that the private practitioner is not working in isolation. These practices may have links with GPs, with Social Services and with other referring bodies. Psychotherapists in private practice are well advised to take good care that they have a supportive framework in the form of consultative and/or peer supervision and regular input from events providing continuing professional development.

There is now a growing number of Employee Assistance Programmes (EAPs) in this country that provide counselling in the workplace. These EAPs contract directly with business and industry to provide a counselling service for employees and then recruit therapists in different areas of the country to be on their lists and to provide this service. The psychotherapist will be required to send some kind of report back to the EAP concerning the service that he has rendered. EAPs almost invariably provide brief-term interventions, between four and six sessions is the norm, so psychotherapists who undertake this type of work need to be skilled in brief-term therapy. Many psychotherapists in private practice may well be linked into one or two EAP providers. The growth of EAP provision in this country is an interesting development and is still in the process of being tested and researched for efficacy. It remains to be seen if in the long run the EAPs will improve productivity and the well-being of the work force. A conflict for the psychotherapist working for an EAP is the question of priorities: what the company desires may not necessarily constitute the client's priority. These complex three-cornered contracts are challenging to manage keeping in mind that our first priority as psychotherapists is the welfare of our clients.

Many psychotherapists are employed in the public sector in psychotherapy departments attached to hospitals or community centres. These psychotherapists who are in full-time posts will see a wide range of clients, often those who would not be in a position to afford private psychotherapy. We have trained integrative, Gestalt and transactional analysis psychotherapists who now work in health care settings in the public sector. Another area that has drawn heavily on the services of psychotherapy graduates is primary care; many psychotherapists are employed in GP surgeries to provide a service to patients from a particular catchment area. Many practitioners will work in a GP setting for one or two or even three days per week and spend the rest of their working time seeing clients in a private practice setting. In July 1999, a little over 50 per cent of GP practices in England and Wales employed a counsellor. With the demise of GP fundholding and the creation of primary care groups, the future development of counselling in primary care is uncertain. At the beginning of 1999, a steering committee was established to raise standards of training and clinical practice of counsellors and psychotherapists in primary care and to establish a self-regulatory body. Sponsoring organizations include the Primary Care Trust, the Association of Counsellors and Psychotherapists in Primary Care, the Counselling in Medical Settings Division of the British Association for Counselling, Relate, the United Kingdom Association for Therapeutic Counselling and the United Kingdom Council for Psychotherapy. In 1999, the work of the steering committee culminated in the first national conference looking at standards of training for counselling and psychotherapy in primary care.

Another source of employment is in the many charities that provide a therapy service to the public, usually in a particular area, for example HIV and AIDS, bereavement or couples work. These organizations employ counsellors and also have many volunteers who offer their services to these counselling services.

The complexity of this situation from the point of view of the supervisor must by now be self-evident. A supervisor of the qualified psychotherapist working in Britain today will need a wide range of skills, knowledge and an awareness of this complex context. It is highly likely that the supervisor will be called on to supervise clients from EAP provisions, from GP surgeries, from voluntary organizations, from NHS based psychotherapy services and from a private practice, all with their own particular demands and specialist requirements.

One response to this complex situation has been the move toward the creation of occupational standards for counselling, therapeutic counselling and psychotherapy to assist employers to identify the skills levels required for specific tasks. It is anticipated that National Vocational Qualification Level 4 counselling standards will be completed by December 1999. Further work is envisaged to complete the standards for therapeutic counselling and psychotherapy. A further and possibly alternative response is the aspiration to secure state registration of counselling, therapeutic counselling and psychotherapy.

There are at least three possible future routes to statutory registration including an act of parliament; a route via the Professions Supplementary to Medicine; and an Order in Council. Currently, the UKCP has established a working party on statutory regulation and in collaboration with Lord Alderdice is preparing a private members' bill for submission to the House of Lords.

Supervision training and development for psychotherapists has grown in strength in the UK over the past decade with the emerging awareness of the importance of supervision as a separate discipline, albeit intimately related to psychotherapy. There are now a range of supervision trainings available to the aspiring supervisor, a sample of which we list under our resources section (see pp.163–9). For the past eight years the British Association for Supervision, Practice and Research (BASPR) has organized an annual supervision conference, which draws together supervisors from different orientations to dialogue and reflect on the supervisory process. The demand for this conference speaks eloquently to the need for an open forum for discussion for supervisors. There are also many books and articles on supervision that have appeared in this time, showing interesting developments in the field and welcome contributions to the supervision literature from a wide range of helping professionals.

Psychotherapy and supervision in the European context

The European Association for Psychotherapy was established in 1991 and by mid-1999 had approximately 50,000 members from some 26 European nations. It has established training standards for its member organizations together with a code of ethics and professional practice. Only two member nations, Austria and the UK have national psychotherapy associations that can claim to represent a large cross-section of the psychotherapy population. Several other national associations are not yet truly representative of all sectors of psychotherapy in their countries. In some nations, certain established schools of psychotherapy are noticeable by their absence from membership of the 'national associations'. While the European Association of Psychotherapy seeks to embrace all psychotherapy orientations there is little likelihood of this being achieved in the near future. Division and rivalry within and between the schools of psychotherapy appear likely to continue to thwart attempts to unify the profession on the European mainland.

Developments in supervision training are an emerging phenomenon in Europe, where at least two different organizations, the Association of National Organizations for Supervision in Europe (ANSE) and the European Association for Supervision (EAS), have attempted to draw together supervisors from across Europe. The aims of these organizations is to establish standards for the training and practice of supervisors with a common register for psychotherapy supervisors across Europe. ANSE represents more than 5000 qualified supervisors and about 50 certified training institutions in eight European countries and aims at an increasing professionalization of supervision across Europe. We see these as important developments in establishing supervision as a discipline in its own right.

The World Council for Psychotherapy (WCP)

This body was founded in July 1996 as an initiative of the European Association for Psychotherapy. It hosted its first world congress in Vienna in July 1996, which was attended by some 4000 psychotherapists representing all continents. The keynote address was given by Victor Frankl. The second world congress held in Vienna in July 1999 also attracted some 4000 psychotherapists. Apart from organizing two successful congresses, the WCP has not developed much beyond this. It provides a welcome umbrella organization for psychotherapists from many nations world-wide and encourages discourse and exchange of ideas.

We are also aware of some of the developments in the field of supervision world-wide as will be reflected in our resources section and can see that drawing together supervisors could well be a fruitful extension to the work of the WCP. However, this is a project for the new millennium!

Resources for the supervisor

12

Supervision trainings in the UK are proliferating and there is now a wide choice open to the practitioner seeking a specific training in the theory and practice of supervision. Many of these courses are aimed more at counsellors than at psychotherapists and many, too, are orientation specific, for example most are person-centred or psychodynamic. Some courses are more generally based and teach supervision as a discipline in its own right, not linked to a specific orientation, and could therefore best be described as generic in their approach to the field. We have carried out a brief informal survey of some of the supervision trainings that are broadly aimed at psychotherapists, counsellors or others in the helping professions in order to give the reader a sample of what is available. There are a growing number of supervision trainings world-wide some of which we will be listing here to give the prospective supervisor an idea of the range that is on offer. This list by no means aims to be comprehensive; rather to convey some idea of the range that is available to the person seeking a supervision training.

Carlo Moiso in Italy runs a training in supervision that stresses the importance of dealing with personal aspects, as they show up mostly in how people supervise and in what they choose to supervise, and of technical aspects, as shown in what supervisors actually say to the trainee. He also stresses the importance of distinguishing between actual supervision (the focus is on the trainee as a therapist) and case discussion (the focus is on the client/patient). He emphasizes comparative reading and the critical evaluation of approaches. For further information contact Carlo Moiso, Via Delle Barozee 65-67, 0040 Rocca de Pappa, Roma, Italy. Tel: +39-06-9498741.

Centre for Staff Team Development has been running supervision courses for over 20 years both in the UK and in other countries. They provide four 3-day courses: core supervision; therapeutic supervision; group supervision and advanced supervision. The courses are designed by Peter Hawkins and Robin Shohet, authors of *Supervision in the Helping Professions*. Those who attend at least three of the programmes and successfully complete 10 hours supervision on their supervision, including two tutorials and a self- and peer assessment are awarded the Centre's certificate in Supervision. For further information contact the Centre for Staff Team Development, c/o Bath Consultancy Group, 24 Gay Street, Bath BA1 2PD. Tel: 01225-333737. Fax: 01225-333738.

Elizabeth Holloway is a Professor of Counseling Psychology at the University of Wisconsin-Madison, USA. She offers workshops in supervision, mentoring and coaching to psychotherapists, managers, organizational consultants, and educators throughout Europe, Asia and the United States. Her book, *Clinical Supervision: A Systems Approach* (1995), is the basis of her teaching and is available in English, German and Chinese. For further information contact Elizabeth Holloway, PhD Professor and Chair, Department of Counseling Psychology, 1000 Bascom Mall, 321 Education Bldg, University of Wisconsin-Madison, Madison, WI 53706-1398, USA.

The Gestalt Academy of Scandinavia offers a training programme in supervision for graduates of the academy. The programme requires critical reflection on case material, reflection on the supervision process and a review of the literature in the field. For further information contact Kerstin Wickberg Borgh, email:jonasborgh@tugg.se, or write to Gestalt Academy of Scandinavia, Vasterlanggtan, Stockholm, Sweden.

Gordon Hewitt in New Zealand offers courses on Clinical Supervision Training, at Wellington Transactional Training Institute. This training is intended for psychologists, counsellors, psychotherapists, social workers, psychiatrists and other health professionals who provide clinical supervision. The course is divided into one block of four days and another of three days about a month later. Participants are provided with a small number of well tested supervision models and then given close coaching in a series of practice sessions, which help participants integrate these models into their current skill base. As well as practical issues of the content of supervision and how to help supervisees present their client work in the sessions in dynamic ways, participants will consider issues of transference and countertransference, the effect of supervision on the therapeutic relationship and ethics as they relate to supervision. In between the two blocks of the course, participants are expected to practise with each other and (if possible) with supervisees and the second block focuses on solving any difficulties encountered, fine tuning applications and allowing the participants to submit a short piece of written material if they require credit from the Institute. For further information, contact Gordon Hewitt, PhD, 30 Totara Street, Eastbourne, New Zealand. Tel/Fax: +64 (4) 562 7101. Email: gordon@wn.planet.gen.nz. Website: *http://www.wn.planet.gen.nz/~gordon*

IAS International, the Netherlands, has been running a two-year programme on supervision since 1991, which is designed for experienced professionals in the field of training, consultancy and counselling. The programme is based on an integration of concepts from transactional analysis, Gestalt, systems theory and group relations theory. A central focus point in the training programme is learning to intervene in complex change processes in individuals, teams and organizations in a working environment. Awareness of oneself in role, cultural self-awareness, and intervening on a process level, are seen as important qualities and skills to develop during the training. The programme is organized in the Netherlands on an international basis, with trainees primarily from the Netherlands, Germany and Switzerland. The spoken language is English. IAS International has a multilevel training system:

Level 1: Basic programme (1.5 years) for starting trainers and advisors
Level 2: 'Working on the boundaries', (2 years) for experienced trainers, coaches and counsellors, recognized Coach EAS
Level 3: Advanced programme (1.5 years) for supervisors in organizational and counselling fields of application, recognized Supervisor EAS (EAS: The European Association for Supervision)

For further information contact: Karien van Lohuizen, Jansstraat 14, NL, 2011 RX Haarlem, Netherlands. Tel: +31 (0)23/5420979. Fax: +31 (0)23/5420942.

The Institute for Applied Social Sciences (IAS), Switzerland, offers a three-year programme in supervision, team development and coaching, covering 63 days and 60 hours of supervised supervision. In the first year, techniques and theory of individual supervision are taught and trained. The second year focuses on group and team supervision, and the third year teaches basics of organizational consulting as considered relevant for supervisors. The programme consists of six parts: seminars on theory and applications, skills training seminars, yearly working conference, supervised supervision, peer groups, and supervision given by the trainee. In the working conference a number of training groups together build a large temporal organization in which different tasks have to be fulfilled by different groups in a number of learning events. Large group meetings make it possible to explore the dynamics of the system as a whole. For further information contact Institute for the Application of the Social Sciences, Bahnhofstrasse 17,7304 Maienfeld, Switzerland. Tel: +41813027703. Email: info@iasag.ch. Website: www.iasag.ch

The Interdisciplinary Centre for Psychotherapy Training (Cifp), France, conducts a supervision training in multi-referential psychotherapy run by Phillipe Grauer and Genevive Rollin. The multi-referential approach of the Interdisciplinary Centre for Psychotherapy Training in Paris, is based on a model of cross-orientation supervision by a number of psychotherapists with theoretical and methodological expertise in many fields. These psychotherapists belong to different schools or conceptual currents, or else come from the integrative movement itself. Case studies in training come from the particular trainer's frame of reference, with additional cross-referencing and clarification from other theoretical and practical viewpoints. This enables both a comparative multi-referentiality and a real deepening of the examination of clinical material. The idea is not to offer a ready-made integrative therapy and supervision model, but to encourage the students to build their own multifaceted frame of reference, with its own epistemological coherence and its own critical self-awareness. Integrative supervision deals with several levels: that of the patients and of psychotherapy, that of the psychotherapist and that of the psychotherapy field as a whole. For further information contact Faculte Libre de Developpement et de Psychotherapie FLDP, 38 rue de Turenne, F-75003, Paris, France. Tel: +48-04-3235. Email: fldp@wanadoo.fr

The Iron Mill Centre, UK, offers a certificate and diploma in supervision with a Higher Education award from Bath Spa University College and the opportunity to apply for accreditation through the European Association for Supervision. The course is designed for people who have a supervisory or mentoring role from a range of professional backgrounds. The course has a theoretical component providing a meta perspective covering a range of models of supervision and providing input about issues of power, *inter alia*. The course incorporates a 'live' skills training component. Further information is available from The Iron Mill, Oakford, Tiverton, Devon, EX16 9EN. Tel: 01398-351379.

Margherita Spagnuolo Lobb in Italy offers training in supervision for licensed psychotherapists. The maximum intake is six trainees in any one year. Training requires a presentation of cases with critical reflection on theory and practice. This training is open to Gestalt psychotherapists and to psychotherapists from other orientations. Completion of the course requires the completion of the training hours; there is no written examination. For further information contact Margherita Spagnuolo Lobb, Istituto di Gestalt H.C.C., 96100 Siracusa, Via A. da Lentini, 2 Italy. Email: gestalt@made in sicily.it

Metanoia Institute, UK, offers a certificate in supervision covering one year of study; in the second year students can continue, if they so choose, to complete a diploma in supervision. This course addresses supervision as a discipline in its own right and is generic in its approach rather than orientation specific. For this reason the course attracts practitioners from different orientations and from a variety of the helping professions. The certificate course provides theoretical input about different models of supervision, individual learning styles, issues of race and culture in supervision, *inter alia*. The diploma year involves further practice, a dissertation and the submission of a tape and transcript of supervision practice. For further details contact: Metanoia Institute, 13 North Common Road, Ealing, London W5 2QB. Tel: 0208-579 2505. www.themet.demon.co.uk

The Minster Centre, UK, offers a supervision training for counselling and psychotherapy practitioners. This training uses a general schema with modifications of the Hawkins and Shohet two-system model and also draws on Clarkson's relationship model and others. The therapy system covers: (1) contents of the therapy session; (2) strategies and interventions used by the therapist; and (3) therapy process and relationship. The supervision system covers: (1) therapist countertransference; (2) parallel process; and (3) supervisor countertransference. The professional context covers: ethics, professional practice and the context of work, including theory and practice in the field. The general format of the training will be seven 15-hour workshops comprising three hours on a Friday and six hours each Saturday and Sunday. For further information contact The Minster Centre, 1 Drakes Courtyard, 291 Kilburn High Road, London NW6 7JR. Tel: 0207-372 4940.

The Northern Guild for Psychotherapy, UK, offers a diploma in clinical supervision. This course is designed for those whose work involves the supervision of others within the helping professions. The focus will be on enhancing and extending supervisory skills. Theoretical perspectives on the supervisory role are provided as the basis for skills development. The course structure places an emphasis on practice in order to maximize opportunities for developing supervisory skills hand in hand with theoretical constructs. The course syllabus includes: the supervisory relationship, developmental stages in supervision, systemic models of supervision, interpersonal process recall (IPR), transference and countertransference in the supervisory relationship, and values and ethics in supervision. The course is offered at two sites, in Stockton-on-Tees and Newcastle Upon Tyne. For further details contact: The Northern Guild for Psychotherapy, 77 Acklam Road, Stockton, Cleveland, TS17 7BD. Tel: 01642-649004.

PCT Professional Development, UK, offers a training course in person-centred counselling supervision. This course is designed for person-centred counsellors (trained to diploma level) who want to develop their skills and theoretical understanding of supervision in a way that is consistent with the practice of the person-centred approach. This is a 120-hour course, consisting of four non-residential weekends of 15 hours each, 10 hours of study group meetings and 50 hours of private study. Participants are required to have a (small) supervision practice during the course. The location: Glasgow for the weekends, the study groups are organized on a geographical basis to minimize travel. The course runs every year from November to June. For further information contact PCT Professional Development, 40 Kelvingrove Street, Glasgow, G3 7RZ. Tel: 0141-3540339.

The Personal Counselling Institute in Ireland runs a 15-day supervision course divided into three 5-day modules (introduction to supervision, models and frameworks for practice, and practising ethical supervision). This course leads to a Certificate in Advanced Professional Practice (Counselling Supervision) and is validated by Bath Spa University through the Iron Mill Centre in Devon. The training is a blend of input, experiential work, group discussion, case discussion and small group supervision. For further information contact the Personal Counselling Institute (Josephine Murphy), 34 Convent Court, Convent Road, Clondalkin, Dublin 22, Ireland.

Philip McConkey in New Zealand offers a supervision course entitled 'Supervisory Skills For Professional Helpers'. This module course (five sets of three days) is a skill-development programme designed for a range of helping disciplines. It can be used generically, or adapted to the helping context or to the needs of a particular professional group (for example, counselling, nursing). All central supervisory issues are covered, but substantial use is made of participants supervising each other on real case material, and on their supervision practice on the course. To receive a 'Certificate of

Competency' trainees are assessed on a piece of self-supervised taped work, and on an essay that demonstrates the integration of philosophy and practice. The presenter, Philip McConkey, is a highly experienced social worker, psychotherapist and trainer, who has been teaching the practice of supervision in a variety of contexts for the past ten years. For further information contact Philip McConkey, 38 Georgina Close, Palmerston North, New Zealand. Tel: 64-6-358 7442(h), 64-6-356 5839(w). Fax: 64-6-358 1892(h), 64-6-355 3348(w).

Sherwood Psychotherapy Training Institute, UK, offers a diploma in supervision which involves six 3-day modules. Final assessment includes a theoretical paper and taped transcript of a supervision session. The course is intended for professionals in counselling and psychotherapy in the voluntary, public or private sectors and across the range of theoretical orientations. The resulting diversity of personalities and professional backgrounds provides a valuable resource and considerably enhances the learning environment. The course covers the theory and practice of supervision and requires a commitment to experiential learning as well as didactic learning. Participants are encouraged to share experience, perspectives and concerns in a way that recognizes and values difference. For further details contact: Sherwood Psychotherapy Training Institute, Thiskney House, 2 St James Terrace, Nottingham, NG1 6FW. Tel: 0115-9243994. www.spti.dot.net

VDO institute for advanced training and consulting, Hogeschool van Arnhem en Nijmegen, Netherlands (university for applied social sciences). Louis van Kessel runs a supervision training programme that involves supervision and other methods of coaching professionals. In this part-time postgraduate training programme students obtain and enhance their competence to deliver supervision, coaching (for individuals and teams), and to train intervision groups in different professional and institutional fields. Duration is 15–21 months (27 two-day training conferences) and the study-load is 840 hours (including individual study, exclusive of the practical work as a precondition).

The main parts of the curriculum are given as follows. Concurrent with their participation on the training programme, students have to deliver at least two cycles of supervision (one individual and the other group, at least 15 sessions each) and some form of coaching. In groups of three they take part in 18 sessions supervision-of-supervision, each lasting 2.5 hours. They take part in the group training programme (a mix of practice, theory and training, and in interaction with their own professional experiences), covering methodological and interventional aspects of supervision and coaching; professional learning processes; (intercultural) communication; the meaning of language; supervision as a function in professional education, as a function of staff- and organizational development; handling themes supervisees could bring to supervision and teams in processes of team development. In addition the students write a special paper to demonstrate integration of knowledge and practice experiences, and the ability to elaborate supervisory themes and to reflect on their own supervisory behaviour.

Admission requirements are:

- a masters degree or a diploma of a school for higher professional education;
- at least four years of actively practising their own basic profession;
- participation in two cycles of supervision (15 sessions each) delivered by a certified supervisor;
- a relevant job during the training programme.

This training programme is certified by the national council for advanced professional studies and the Dutch supervisor organization LVSB. To get registered by LVSB the graduates of the described training programme have to take part in a second cycle of supervision-of-supervision. For further information contact Louis van Kessel, Postbus 9029, 6500 JK Nijmegen, Netherlands. Email: Louis.vanKessel@ls.han.nl

References

Albott, W.L. (1984) *Supervisory Characteristics and Other Sources of Supervision Variance. Clinical Training in Psychotherapy.* Haworth Press.

APA (American Psychiatric Association) (1994) *DSM IV.* Washington, DC: American Psychiatric Association.

Atwood, G.E. and Stolorow, R.D. (1984) *Structures of Subjectivity.* Hillsdale, NJ: The Analytic Press.

Baddeley, A. (1993) *Your Memory: A User's Guide.* London: Penguin Books.

Bartlett, F. (1932) *Remembering.* Cambridge: Cambridge University Press (reprinted 1972).

Basch, M.F. (1991) Are self objects the only objects? Implications for psychoanalytic technique, in A. Goldberg (ed.) *The Evolution of Self Psychology: Progress in Self Psychology,* Vol. 7, 3–29. Hillsdale, NJ: The Analytic Press.

Beisser, A.R. (1970) The paradoxical theory of change, in J. Sagan and I. Shepherd (eds) *Gestalt Therapy Now.* Palo Alto, CA: Science and Behaviour Books.

Beitman, B.D. (1992) Integration through fundamental similarities and differences among the schools, in J.C. Norcross and M.R. Goldfried (eds) *Psychotherapy Integration.* New York: Basic Books.

Bergin, A.E. and Garfield, S.L. (1994) *Handbook of Psychotherapy and Behaviour Change.* New York: Wiley and Sons.

Bernard, J.M. (1993) *Clinical Supervision: Impending Issues.* Fairfield, CT: Fairfield University.

Bernard, J.M. (1994) Ethical and legal dimensions of supervision, in L.D. Borders (ed.) *Supervision: Exploring the Effective Components.* ERIC/CUSS Digest Series. Greensboro, NC: University of North Carolina.

Berne, E. (1961) *Transactional Analysis in Psychotherapy.* New York: Ballantine Books.

Berne, E. (1964) *Games People Play.* New York: Grove Press.

Berne, E. (1966) *Principles of Group Treatment.* New York: Grove Press.

Berne, E. (1972) *What Do You Say After You Say Hello?* New York: Bantam Books.

Bertens, H. (1995) *The Idea of the Post modern: A History.* London: Routledge.

Beutler, L.E. (1983) *Eclectic Psychotherapy: A Systematic Approach.* New York: Pergamon.

Bollas, C. (1987) *The Shadow of the Object: Psychoanalysis of the Unthought Known.* London: Free Association Books.

Bond, T. (1993) *Standards and Ethics for Counselling in Action.* London: Sage.

Brazier, D. (1995) *Zen Therapy.* New York: John Wiley & Sons.

Buber, M. (1923, 1996) *I and Thou*. Translated by W. Kaufman. New York: Touchstone.
Buber, M. (1926, 1965) *Between Man and Man*. Translated by R.G. Smith. New York: Macmillan.
Carey, J.C., Williams, K.S. and Wells, M. (1988) Relationships between dimensions of supervisors' influence and counselor trainees performance, *Counselor Education and Supervision*, 28: 130–9.
Carifio, M.S. and Hess, A.K. (1987) Who is the ideal supervisor?, *Professional Psychology, Research and Practice*, 18(30): 244–50.
Carroll, M. (1996) *Counselling Supervision. Theory, Skills and Practice*. London: Cozily.
Casement, P. (1985) *On Learning From The Patient*. London: Routledge.
Cashdan, S. (1988) *Object Relations Therapy: Using the Relationship*. New York: W.W. Norton.
Clarkson, P. (1992) *Transactional Analysis: An Integrated Approach*. London: Routledge.
Clarkson, P. (1994) *The Achilles Syndrome*. Shaftesbury: Element.
Clarkson, P. and Gilbert, M. (1991) The training of counsellor trainers and supervisors, in W. Dryden and B. Throne (eds) *Training and Supervision for Counselling in Action*. London: Sage.
Consumer Reports (1995) Mental health: Does therapy help? November.
Corey, G., Corey, M.S. and Callahan, P. (1993) *Issues and Ethics in the Helping Professions*, 4th edn. Pacific Grove, CA: Brooks/Cole.
Cresswell, J.W.C. (1998) *Qualitative Inquiry and Research Design: Choosing Among the Five Traditions*. New York: Sage.
Doehrman, M.J. (1976) Parallel process in supervision and psychotherapy, *Bulletin of the Menninger Clinic*, 40(1): 1–104.
Dryden, W. and Norcross, J.C. (1990) *Eclecticism and Integration in Counselling and Psychotherapy*. Ipswich: Gale Centre Publications.
Ekstein, R. and Wallerstein, R.S. (1972) *The Teaching and Learning of Psychotherapy*. New York: International Universities Press.
Eleftheriadou, Z. (1994) *Transcultural Counselling*. London: Central Book Publishing.
English, F. (1975) The three-cornered contract, *Transactional Analysis Journal*, 5(4): 383–4.
Espin, O. and Gawelek, K. (1992) Women's diversity: ethnicity, race, class and gender theories of feminist psychology, in L.S. Brown and M. Ballot (eds) *Personality and Pathology*. New York: Guilford Press.
Evans, K. (1996) True dialogue requires the appreciation of difference, *International Journal of Psychotherapy*, 1(1): 91–3.
Evans, M. (1998) Supervision: A developmental-relational approach, *Transactional Analysis Journal*, 28(4): 288–98.
Farrell, F.B. (1994) *Subjectivity, Realism and Post-modernism: The Recovery of the World in Recent Philosophy*. Cambridge: Cambridge University Press.
Feeney, J. and Noller, P. (1996) *Adult Attachment*. London: Sage.
Ferenczi, S. (1988) *The Clinical Diary of Sandor Ferenczi* (ed. J. Dupont). Cambridge: Harvard University Press.
Fiedler, F.E. (1950) A comparison of therapeutic relationships in psychoanalytic, non directive, and Adlerian therapy, *Journal of Consulting Psychology*, 14: 239–45.
Freeman, E. (1985) The importance of feedback in clinical supervision: implications for direct practice, *The Clinical Supervisor*, 3(1): 5–26.
Friedman, M. (1992) *Dialogue and the Human Image*. Newbury Park, CA: Sage.
Fulani, L. (1998) *The Psychopathology of Everyday Racism and Sexism*. New York: Harrington Park Press.
Gilbert, M. and Sills, C. (1999) Training for supervision evaluation, in E. Holloway and M. Carroll (eds) *Training Counselling Supervisors*. London: Sage.
Goldfried, M.R. (1995) Towards a common language for case formulation, *Journal of Psychotherapy Integration*, 5(3): 221–44.

Goulding, M.M. and Goulding, R.L. (1979) *Changing Lives through Redecision Therapy.* New York: Brunner/Mazel.

Greenberg, J. (1995) Self disclosure: Is it psychoanalytic? *Contemporary Psychoanalysis,* 31(2): 193–205.

Hagman, G. (1997) Mature self object experience, in A. Goldberg (ed.) *Conversations in Self Psychology: Progress in Self Psychology* Vol.13. Hillsdale, NJ: The Analytic Press.

Hawkins, P. and Shohet, R. (2000) *Supervision in the Helping Professions,* 2nd edn. Buckingham: Open University Press.

Heath G.M. (1998) *Oppression By Normative Universalistic Assumptions In Psychotherapeutic Theories.* Nottingham: SPTI.

Heath, G.M. (2000) Philosophy and psychotherapy, Chapter 2 of book in process, *Psychotherapy Training.*

Heron, J. (1996) *Co-operative Inquiry.* London: Sage.

Hess, A.K. (ed.) (1980) *Psychotherapy Supervision.: Theory, research and Practice.* New York, Wiley.

Holloway, E.L. (1987) Developmental models of supervision: Is it development? *Professional Psychology: Research and Practice,* 18: 189–208.

Holloway, E.L. (1995) *Clinical Supervision: A Systems Approach.* Newbury Park, CA: Sage Publications.

Holloway, E.L. and Allstetter Neufeldt, S. (1995) Supervision: Its contributions to treatment efficacy, *Journal of Consulting and Clinical Psychology,* 63(2): 207–13.

Holloway, E. and Carroll, M. (eds) (1999) *Training Counselling Supervisors.* London: Sage.

Holmes, J. (1993) *John Bowlby and Attachment Theory.* New York: Routledge.

Horvath, A.O. and Greenberg, L.S. (1994) *The Working Alliance.* New York: Wiley and Sons.

Hycner, R.H. (1991) *Between Person and Person: Toward a dialogical psychotherapy.* Highland, NY: Centre for Gestalt Development.

Hycner, R. and Jacobs, L. (1995) *The Healing Relationship in Gestalt Therapy.* Highland, NY: The Gestalt Journal Press.

Ivey, A.E. (1987) The multicultural practice of therapy: ethics, empathy and dialectics, *Journal of Clinical Psychology,* 5: 195–204.

Kagan, N. (1980) Influencing human interaction – eighteen years with IPR, in A.K. Hess (ed.) *Psychotherapy Supervision.* New York: Wiley.

Kareem, J. and Littlewood, R. (1992) *Intercultural Therapy: Themes, Interpretations and Practice.* London: Blackwell.

Karpman, S. (1976) Fairy tales and script drama analysis, *Transactional Analysis Bulletin:* Selected articles from Volumes 1 through to 9. San Francisco, CA: TA Press, pp. 51–56.

Kaufman, G. (1992) *Shame: The Power of Crying.* Rochester, VT: Schenkman Books.

Kohut, H. (1971) *The Analysis of the Self.* Madison, CT: International Universities Press.

Kohut, H. (1984) *How does Analysis Cure?* Chicago, IL: University of Chicago Press.

Kolb, D.A., Rubin, I.M. and McIntyre, J.M. (1971) *Organizational Psychology: An experiential approach to organizational behaviour.* New Jersey: Prentice Hall.

Krause, I. (1998) *Therapy Across Culture.* London: Sage.

Langs, R. (1994) *Doing Supervision and Being Supervised.* London: Karnac Books.

Leddick, R.L. and Dye, H.A. (1987) Counselor supervision: Effective supervision as portrayed by trainee expectation and preferences, *Counselor Education and Supervision,* 27(2): 139–54.

Leong, F.T.L. and Wagner, N.S. (1994) Supervision: What do we know? What do we need to know?, *Counselor Education and Supervision,* 34: 117–31.

Lesser, R.M. (1983) Supervision: Illusions, anxieties and questions, in L. Caligor, P.M. Bromberg and J.D. Meltzer (eds) *Clinical Perspectives on the Supervision of Psychoanalysis and Psychotherapy.* New York: International Universities Press.

Lewin, K. (1952) *Field Theory and Social Science*. London: Tavistock.

Lindsay, G. and Colley, A. (1995) Ethical dilemmas of members of the Society, *The Psychologist*, 8: 448–51.

Lindsay, G. and Clarkson, P. (1999) Ethical dilemmas of psychotherapists, *The Psychologist*, 12(4): 182–5.

Linehan, M.M. (1993) *Cognitive-Behavioral Treatment of Borderline Personality Disorder*. New York: Guilford Press.

Lyotard, J. (1984) *The Post modern Condition. A Report on Knowledge*. Manchester: Manchester University Press.

Mann, D. (1997) *Psychotherapy: An Erotic Relationship*. London: Routledge.

Martindale, B., Morner, M., Rodriguez, M.E.C. and Vidit, J. (1997) *Supervision and Its Vicissitudes*. London: Karnac Books.

Masterson, J.F.M. (1985) *The Real Self*. New York: Brunner/Mazel.

McLeod, J. (1999) Counselling as a social process, *Counselling*, 10(3): 217–22.

Micholt, N. (1992) Psychological distance and group interventions, *Transactional Analysis Journal*, 22(4): 228–33.

Mitchell, S.A. (1988) *Relational Concepts in Psychoanalysis*. Cambridge MA.: Harvard University Press.

Moskowitz, S.A. and Rupert, P.A. (1983) Conflict resolution within the supervisory relationship, *Professional Psychology: Research and Practice*, 14: 632–41.

Moss, J. (ed.) (1998) *The Later Foucault*. London: Sage.

Moustakas, C. (1994) *Phenomenological Research Methods*. New York: Sage.

Nathanson, D.L. (1992) *Shame and Pride*. New York: W.W. Norton and Co.

Neimeyer, G.A. and Neimeyer, R.A. (1993) *Constructivist Assessment; A Casebook*. London: Sage.

Nietzsche, F. (1906, 1968) *The Will to Power*. Translated by W. Kaufman and R.J. Hollingdale. New York: Random House.

Norcross, J.C. and Goldfried, M.R. (1992) *Handbook of Psychotherapy Integration*. New York: Basic Books.

Orange, D., Atwood, G. and Stolorow, R. (1997) *Contextualism in Psychoanalytic Practice*. Hillsdale, NJ: The Analytic Press.

Parlett, M. (1991) Field theory, *British Gestalt Journal*, 1(2): 69–71.

Parlett, M. (1993) Towards a more Lewinian Gestalt therapy, *The British Gestalt Journal*, 2(2): 115–20.

Pederson, B.P. (ed.) (1987) *Handbook of Cross-Cultural Counselling and Therapy*. London: Praegger.

Pederson, B.P. (1997) *Culture-Centered Counselling Interventions*. London: Sage.

Perls, L. (1992) *Living at the Boundary*. Highland, NY: The Gestalt Journal Press.

Pilgrim, D. (1997) *Psychotherapy and Society*. London: Sage.

Polster, E. and Polster, M. (1973) *Gestalt Therapy Integrated*. New York: Vintage Books.

Proctor, B. (1986) Supervision: a co-operative exercise in accountability, in M. Marken and M. Payne (eds) *Enabling and Ensuring: Supervision in Practice*. Leicester: National Youth Bureau.

Racker, H. (1968) *Transference and Countertransference*. London: Karnac Books.

Reason, P. (1988) *Human Inquiry in Action: Developments in New Paradigm Research*. London: Sage.

Reason, P. (1994) *Participation in Human Inquiry*. London: Sage.

Rice, L.N. and Greenberg, L.S. (1984) *Patterns of Change*. New York: Guilford Press.

Ridley, C.R. (1995) *Overcoming Unintentional Racism in Counselling and Therapy: A Practitioner's Guide to Intentional Intervention*. London: Sage.

Rogers, C.R. (1951) *Client-Centered Therapy*. Boston MA: Houghton Mifflin.

Rogers, C.R. (1963) The concept of the fully functioning person, *Psychotherapy: Theory, Research and Practice*, 1: 17–26.

Roth, A. and Fonagy, P. (1996) *What Works For Whom?* London: Guilford Press.

Rycroft, C. (1979) *A Critical Dictionary of Psychoanalysis.* Harmondsworth: Penguin.

Ryle, A. (1990) *Cognitive-Analytic Therapy: Active participation in change.* Chichester: Wiley.

Safran, J. (1993) The therapeutic alliance rupture as a transtheoretical phenomenon: Definitional and conceptual issues, *Journal of Psychotherapy Integration,* 3(1): 33–49.

Safran, J.D. (1998) Workshop presentation, SEPI conference, Madrid, July.

Safran, J.D. and Greenberg, L.S. (eds) (1991) *Emotion, Psychotherapy and Change.* New York: Guilford Press.

Safran, J.D., Muran, J.C. and Samstag, L.W. (1994) Resolving therapeutic alliance ruptures: A task analysis investigation, in A.O. Horvath and L.S. Greenberg (eds) *The Working Alliance: Theory, Research and Practice.* New York: Wiley.

Samuels, A. (1993) *The Political Psyche.* London: Routledge.

Sandler, J., Dare, C. and Holder, A. (1992) *The Patient and the Analyst.* London: Karnac Books.

Smail, D. (1998) *How to Survive Without Psychotherapy.* London: Constable.

Spinelli, E. (1992) *The Interpreted World.* London: Sage.

Spinelli, E. (1994) *Demystifying Therapy.* London: Constable.

Steiner, C.M. (1984) Emotional literacy, *Transactional Analysis Journal,* 14(3): 162–3.

Stern, D.N. (1985) *The Interpersonal World of the Infant.* New York: Basic Books.

Stern, D.N. (1999) Keynote address at World Congress of Psychotherapy, Vienna, Austria, July.

Stolorow, R.D., Brandchaft, B. and Atwood, G.E. (1987) *Psychoanalytic Treatment: An Intersubjective Approach.* Hillsdale, NJ: The Analytic Press.

Stolorow, R.D. and Atwood, G.E. (1992) *Contexts of Being.* Hillsdale, NJ: The Analytic Press.

Stolorow, R.D., Atwood, E. and Brandchaft, B. (1994) *The Intersubjective Perspective.* Northvale, NJ: Jason Aronson.

Sullivan, H.S. (1953) *The Interpersonal Theory of Psychiatry.* New York: Norton.

Tarnas, R. (1996) *The Passion of the Western Mind.* London: Pimlico Press.

Teitelbaum, S.H. (1990) Supertransference: The role of the supervisor's blind spots, *Psychoanalytic Psychology,* 7(2): 243–58.

Thompson, J. (1991) Issues of race and culture in counselling supervision training courses. MSc thesis, Polytechnic of East London.

Tolpin, M. (1997) Compensatory structures: Paths to the restoration of the self, in A. Goldberg (ed.) *Conversations in Self Psychology: Progress in Self Psychology* Vol.13. Hillsdale, NJ: The Analytic Press.

Truax, C.B. and Carkhuff, R.R. (1967) *Toward Effective Counseling and Psychotherapy.* Chicago: Aldine.

van der Kolk, B.A., McFarlane, A.C. and Weisaeth, L. (eds) (1996) *Traumatic Stress.* New York: Guilford Press.

Varela, F.J., Thomson, E. and Rosch, E. (1993) *The Embodied Mind: Cognitive Science and Human Experience.* London: MIT Press.

Watzlawick, P. (1984) *The Invented Reality.* London: Norton.

Winnicott, D.W. (1971) *Playing and Reality.* London: Routledge.

Wittgenstein, L. (1921, 1961) *Tractatus Logico-Philosophicus.* Translated by D.F. Pears and B.P. McGuinness. London: Routledge and Kegan Paul.

Wittgenstein, L. (1953) *Philosophical Investigations.* Translated by G.E.M. Anscombe. London: Blackwell.

Wolf, E. (1988) *Treating the Self.* New York: Guilford Press.

Wright, K. (1991) *Vision and Separation: Between Mother and Baby.* London: Free Association Books.

Yontef, G. (1993) *Awareness, Dialogue and Process. Essays on Gestalt Therapy.* Highland, NY: Gestalt Journal Press.

Zahm, S. (1998) Therapist self-disclosure in the practice of Gestalt therapy, *The Gestalt Journal*, 21(2): 21–52.
Zeanah, C.H., Anders, T.F., Seifer, R. and Stern, D. (1989) Implications of research on infant development for psychodynamic theory and practice, *Journal of the American Academy of Child and Adolescent Psychiatry*, 5: 657–68.
Zinker, J. (1977) *Creative Process in Gestalt Therapy*. New York: Brunner/Mazel.
Zinker, J. (1994) *In Search of Good Form. Gestalt Therapy with Couples and Families*. San Francisco: The Gestalt Institute of Cleveland Press.

Index

IN SEARCH OF SUPERVISION
Michael Jacobs (ed.)

Following the success of *In Search of a Therapist*, this final book in the series provides a unique window into the supervisory process. It takes a session, with background information, from the editor's own work with a long-term client, Ruth, and presents the dilemmas faced by the therapist to five supervisors – each one from very different therapeutic traditions:

- communicative psychotherapy
- self-psychology
- person-centred psychotherapy
- cognitive-behavioural therapy
- family therapy

In Search of Supervision offers the first real insight into the process of supervision of an actual session and enables counsellors and therapists to see how different orientations or schools of therapy and counselling react to and understand the same client and therapist. This fascinating book ends with a final chapter in which the therapist and client comment on the impact of the five supervisors on the work of their therapy together.

In Search of Supervision will be of interest to a wide range of counsellors and therapists, not only those working as or training as supervisors, but all those who experience supervision.

Contents
Michael Jacobs: in search of a supervisor – Ruth and Michael Jacobs: the session for supervision – The reader's response – Alan Cartwright: psychoanalytic self psychology – Prue Conradi: person-centred therapy – Melanie Fennell: cognitive-behaviour therapy – David Livingston Smith: communicative psychotherapy – Sue Walrond-Skinner: family therapy – Michael Jacobs and Ruth: review and response.

Contributors
Alan Cartwright, Prue Conradi, Melanie Fennell, David Livingstone Smith, Sue Walrond-Skinner.

190pp   0 335 19258 0 (Paperback)

SUPERVISION OF PSYCHOTHERAPY AND COUNSELLING
MAKING A PLACE TO THINK

Geraldine Shipton (ed.)

- What do we really know about the supervision of therapy and counselling?
- What kind of things make it easier, and what gets in the way?
- How do therapy and supervision resemble one another, and in what ways do they differ?

In an effort to address these pressing questions, this volume brings together authors from a variety of different perspectives and orientations to comment on supervision. Although strongly influenced by psychoanalytic ideas, the book also offers humanistic insights into good supervision practices. It is recommended reading for all experienced therapists and counsellors, and will be particularly useful to those undertaking advanced courses on supervision.

Contents

176pp   0 335 19512 1 (Paperback)   0 335 19513 X (Hardback)

SUPERVISION IN THE HELPING PROFESSIONS
Second Edition

Peter Hawkins and Robin Shohet

Praise for the first edition of *Supervision in the Helping Professions*:

The authors of this book really do know their subject well and have organised the presentation in a clear, systematic, readable style, refreshingly devoid of trans-atlantic jargon. It deals with all aspects of supervision and most importantly provides a meaningful blueprint about how useful and effective supervision can be. Let me recommend this book to you without reservation.
Journal of the British Psychodrama Association

The one really powerful book in this area, a book that fundamentally changed the way in which people think about supervision and training.
Professor John McLeod, University of Abertay, Dundee, Scotland

A very readable book which is of immense help to anyone in a mentoring or supervisory relationship. It will appeal equally to educators, managers and students. All nurses will benefit from reading it. It is reasonably priced and well presented. Buy it.
Philip Burnard, *Nursing Times*

This timely book offers the reader a comprehensive and practical guide to the complex issues inherent in the supervision of health and social services personnel, from the student on field-work placement to the most experienced therapist.
British Journal of Occupational Therapy

If you are a supervisor in one of the helping professions, and particularly if you are responsible for training other supervisors, then this book is essential reading for you. It explores the purposes, models and different forms of supervision in counselling, psychotherapy, psychology, psychiatry, nursing, social work, community work, occupational and creative therapy, and the probation and prison services. Similarly, if you work in any of these professions and are interested in finding out more about how to obtain the support and supervision that you need, then this book will also be valuable reading for you.

The first edition was a 'ground-breaking book' in the development of supervision and supervisor training. This second edition retains the models for supervision in individual, group, team and organizational settings, but also contains new material including:

- an up to date review of the new literature, practice and training in the field
- a chapter on supervising across different cultures
- new models on supervising in groups
- ways of introducing better supervision into organizations.

Contents
Part One: The supervisee's perspective – 'Good enough' supervision – Why be a helper? – Getting the support and supervision you need – Part Two: Becoming a supervisor and the process of supervision – Becoming a supervisor – Maps and models of supervision – A process model of supervision – Working with difference: transcultural supervision – Supervisor training and development – Part Three: Supervising groups, teams and networks – Group, team and peer-group supervision – Exploring the dynamics of groups, teams and peer groups – Supervising networks – Part Four: The organizational context – Towards a learning culture – Developing supervision policy and practice in organizations – Conclusion: the wounded helper – Appendix 1 – Appendix 2 – Key terms – Resources – Bibliography – Index – Feedback request.

256pp   0 335 20117 2 (Paperback)   0 335 20118 0 (Hardback)